TWO STUDIES
IN THE GREEK ATOMISTS

TWO STUDIES IN THE GREEK ATOMISTS

STUDY I

Indivisible Magnitudes

STUDY II

Aristotle and Epicurus on Voluntary Action

DAVID J. FURLEY

PRINCETON UNIVERSITY PRESS
PRINCETON, NEW JERSEY
1967

COPYRIGHT © 1967 BY PRINCETON UNIVERSITY PRESS
ALL RIGHTS RESERVED

L.C. CARD: 66-11972

Publication of this book
has been supported by a grant
from the Henry Brown Fund of the University
of London Institute of Classical Studies
and from the Louis A. Robb Fund
of Princeton University Press

COMPOSED IN GREAT BRITAIN
BY R. & R. CLARK, LTD., EDINBURGH

PRINTED IN THE UNITED STATES OF AMERICA

PREFACE

THE world-picture of the ancient Greeks was not a matter of common agreement but was the subject of energetic controversy through several centuries. Many different cosmologies were defended and rejected. But in the course of time the hitherto scattered conflicts began to resolve themselves into a struggle between two parties, which we may label "Atomists" and "Aristotelians." As in the political struggle in modern democracies, the parties were able to accommodate some varieties of opinion, and could even borrow each other's doctrines when the occasion demanded it. The borrowings, however, were not so heavy that the essential differences were obscured.

Broadly speaking, the Atomists defended the atomic theory of matter, mechanical causation, the infinity of the universe, the plurality of worlds, and the transience of our world. The Aristotelians defended the continuous theory of matter, the supremacy of final causes, the finite universe, and the uniqueness and eternity of our world. The Atomist party, although in many ways it could claim descent from Empedocles and Anaxagoras, first attained its identity at the end of the fifth century, with Leucippus and Democritus; their cause was taken up at the end of the fourth century by Epicurus, and again in Roman times by Lucretius. The opposite party consisted of Plato, Aristotle and his pupils, and the Stoics. The crucial area of the struggle lay in Aristotle's attacks upon the Atomists and the Epicureans' attempts to rebut his critical arguments.

The echoes of this battle were heard from time to time in medieval Europe, and it flared up again with great intensity in the sixteenth and seventeenth centuries. It is one of the most important parts of the legacy of classical thought. Yet it may be doubted whether it has been satisfactorily treated by classical scholars, who

Preface

have rarely attempted to examine the conflict as a whole, and have often lost sight of it altogether, particularly in dealing with the Epicureans.

This book does not contain the comprehensive history of this struggle that should some day be written, but only two preliminary studies. They are on unrelated subjects, and the only excuse for combining them is that they are both connected with the same theme. Both aim to explain difficult features of Epicureanism by viewing them as attempts to rebut or accommodate some arguments of Aristotle. They will be successful if they provoke others to take up this theme until perhaps between us we make it clear.

MUCH of the work connected with this book has been done in the Institute of Classical Studies in the University of London, and I wish to express my gratitude to the staff for providing such a pleasant and convenient place to work. The University of Minnesota helped me when I was a Visiting Lecturer there by leaving me with a generous amount of leisure for my researches.

I have had generous help from friends. Parts of this book have been read by Mr. M. F. Burnyeat, Dr. A. R. Lacey, Mr. I. R. D. Mathewson, Professor Otto Skutsch, and Professor T. B. L. Webster; I am most grateful for their critical comments, which have enabled me to correct many deficiencies. Professor G. E. L. Owen has given me much help and stimulus, both by his invaluable publications and by his swift and unerring dialectic.

I am particularly grateful to Professor Gregory Vlastos for his constant encouragement and interest, and for his helpful criticisms of my manuscript. He has given much time to discussing it with me, and it has profited greatly from his comments.

I am entirely responsible, of course, for the thesis of these two essays and for all the mistakes which remain.

I wish to record my gratitude to the Princeton University Press, which has shown me great consideration, and particularly to Mrs. Dorothy Hollmann for the careful attention she has given to the production of this book.

CONTENTS

	PAGE
Preface	v

STUDY I. INDIVISIBLE MAGNITUDES

Introduction   3

PART I

CHAP.
1. Epicurus' *Letter to Herodotus* §§ 56.5–59   7
2. The Evidence of Lucretius on the Theory of Minimal Parts   28

PART II

3. Pythagorean "Atomism"   44
4. The Eleatic Concept of an Indivisible Being   57
5. Zeno   63
6. The Atomists' Reply to the Eleatics   79
7. Indivisible Magnitudes in the Academy   104
8. Aristotle's Criticisms and Epicurus' Answers   111
9. Epicurus and Diodorus Cronus   131
10. Epicurus and David Hume   136
11. Conclusion   148

STUDY II. ARISTOTLE AND EPICURUS ON VOLUNTARY ACTION

Introduction   161
1. Lucretius 2.251-293   169
2. The Voluntary and the Compulsive, in Aristotle's Ethics and Epicurus   184
3. Outline of Epicurean Psychology   196
4. Psychology of Action, Epicurean and Aristotelian   210
5. The Weight and the Swerve of Atoms   227

Contents

Bibliography

	PAGE
Ancient Authors, with editions cited	239
Modern Works: Study I	243
Modern Works: Study II	247

Indexes

Passages Cited	251
Names	255

Study I

INDIVISIBLE MAGNITUDES

INTRODUCTION

THIS essay has grown larger than I intended at first. My original intention was simply to write an explanatory commentary on Epicurus' exposition of the theory of the minimal parts of atoms, in his *Letter to Herodotus* §§56–59. The existing commentaries all seemed to me inadequate, in various ways. I gave a brief account of my first results in a paper read to the Classical Association meeting in Nottingham in 1958. Shortly *after* this, I came across the monograph published by Dr. Jürgen Mau in 1954, referred to in the Bibliography. I found that Dr. Mau had anticipated my results in most of the essential points, and I therefore did no further work on the subject for some time.

But this theory of *minimae partes* is a queer and fascinating theory. The reasoning with which Epicurus supports it is interesting, and the problem situation which made it appear necessary to him was still far from clear to me. So I resumed my investigations and tried to write a history of theoretical indivisibles from Parmenides to Epicurus. Of course this meant going over ground that had already been covered by Dr. Mau's monograph, and also by an important paper published in 1932 by S. Luria. However, I think there is no great need to apologize for publishing another essay on the subject, though I realize that its originality is small in comparison with Luria's paper. It happens that both of these earlier works have been neglected by scholars writing in English; books are still being written on Greek philosophy which ignore this important feature of Greek atomism altogether. It seems to me impossible to understand the development of atomism out of Eleatic metaphysics without considering theoretical indivisibles as well as physical atoms.

ONE of the main difficulties I have experienced in writing this essay and in discussing its theme with others has been to find English

Indivisible Magnitudes

words which will describe the views of the ancient atomists without committing them to more than they would have wanted to assert. We have to distinguish two kinds of division. I call the first kind *physical division*: that is, the division of something in such a way that formerly contiguous parts are separated from each other by a spatial interval. This is opposed to *theoretical division*: an object is theoretically divisible if parts can be distinguished within it by the mind, even if the parts can never be separated from each other by a spatial interval. Clearly the physical divisibility of an object entails its theoretical divisibility; but the converse is not true; Epicurean atoms were theoretically divisible, but not physically divisible. (It will be observed that I am using "theoretically divisible" in a specially restricted sense. To say that Epicurean atoms are theoretically divisible might be taken to mean that they might *in theory* be physically divided, though there is some *practical* difficulty. This is obviously not what I mean.)

I use the word *magnitude*, as the Greeks used "$\mu \acute{\epsilon} \gamma \epsilon \theta o s$," to mean spatial extension, or any object which has spatial extension.

The *minimae partes* of atoms in Epicurean theory were theoretically indivisible portions of matter; that is to say, they were such that no parts could be distinguished within them by the mind.

It will be as well to consider now some other terms which have been applied to the concepts of the Greek atomists.

Instead of "theoretical," some historians have used the adjective "mathematical" or "geometrical." (We are concerned all the time with objects which have extension, so that geometry is the relevant branch of mathematics and we need not consider any distinction between "mathematical" and "geometrical.") There has been some controversy about whether or not Democritus was a *mathematical* atomist. But expressions like this can be ambiguous. I think Democritus was a mathematical atomist, in the sense that he believed in units of matter which were theoretically indivisible; since mathematics is one kind of theory, these units can certainly be described as mathematically indivisible. But in another sense a mathematical atomist would be one who denied infinite divisibility altogether, for every extended magnitude, that is, one who substituted the principle of finite divisibility for the principle of infinite divisibility in his

Introduction

geometry. And I am not sure that Democritus was a mathematical atomist in this sense. It is not necessarily the case that all the implications of a theory are worked out at the same time as the theory. It would appear that the assertion of theoretically indivisible units of matter entails geometrical atomism—that is, a theory of indivisible units of extension as such. But it is possible that this entailment was not observed immediately.

It has been suggested to me that "geometrical atomism" is a contradiction in terms, since geometry is by definition a science which deals with an infinitely divisible continuum. But although most geometricians from the time of Euclid have in fact worked with the principle of infinite divisibility, mathematicians do not refuse to consider the possibility of a geometry of finite divisibility. It is not correct to say that we cannot even begin to consider geometrical atomism. For the most part, however, I have avoided the expressions "geometrical" and "mathematical" atomism. It is doubtful whether the theories of the Greek atomists were mathematical theories at all; and it is certain that they were not primarily mathematical theories.

There is another term which ought to be considered. In earlier versions of this essay (some of which have been read to various learned societies), I have used the expression "conceptual indivisibles" instead of "theoretical indivisibles." This suggests units in which no distinctions are conceivable at all. I was content with this for a time; but there is a snag. A unit which is theoretically indivisible (in the sense defined above) may still have extremities which can be *conceived* in distinction from the unit itself. This is really a point about the logic of "division" and of "part," rather than of the adjectives "theoretical" and "conceptual." For my purposes it will be necessary to distinguish between *parts* which may result from the division of an extended body, and other entities such as surfaces, edges, points, and so on. A solid may be divided into parts which are smaller solids, but never into planes or lines; so the planes and lines which may be found in it are not *parts* of it. It seems unreasonable to imply that the planes and lines contained in a solid are *inconceivable* in abstraction from the solid; we can make all kinds of true statements about them, such as that two of them are parallel

Indivisible Magnitudes

or that one is larger than another. Consequently I have stopped using the adjective "conceptual" and its cognates in this context.

But there was a reasonable excuse for using them in talking about the Epicurean theory, since Epicurus made a mistake about the extremities of bodies. He failed to distinguish between extremities and parts. Apparently he argued that the extremities of a body (its surfaces and edges and points) must be of the same order of being as the body itself. The surface of a sensible body can be *seen*; so it must be made of visible material. Vision is produced by atoms; so the surface must be made of atoms. Similarly with a body that is not visible but "intelligible"; its surface must be a part of it. So Epicurus concluded that extremities have dimensions: a surface is not something having length and breadth but *no* depth, but something having length and breadth and *minimal* depth. This is a mistake which led Epicurus into trouble: it meant that he was unable to give a satisfactory account of the *juxtaposition* of the *minimae partes*, as we shall see.

THIS essay is divided into two parts. In the first, I have set out the first-hand evidence about the Epicurean theory, from Epicurus and Lucretius. The two chapters of Part I are detailed studies of Greek and Latin texts, and their intention is simply to establish what Epicurus and Lucretius wrote and what they meant. I have therefore begun with the texts, and have added a translation and commentary.

The second part is a history of the origin and development of the theory of indivisibles. In these chapters I have tried to use English throughout, and to keep Greek and Latin intrusions to the minimum; I have translated the quotations used as evidence, printing the originals in footnotes. My hope is that Part II may be intelligible to historians of science and philosophy who do not read Greek and Latin.

I have tried to keep all my reasoning in the text, and to avoid long and frequent notes. For this reason, and others, it has been impossible to make constant acknowledgments to the books and articles I have consulted. I have listed them in a Bibliography at the end of the book.

PART I

CHAPTER I

EPICURUS' *LETTER TO HERODOTUS* §§56.5-59

In considering this passage we have to deal with three types of minimum quantity. There is first the atom, the minimum physical quantity; second, the theoretical minimum, the smallest quantity that can be conceived or thought about or imagined; and third, the minimum perceptible quantity. I claim that the passage to be discussed offers no argument at all for the existence of a physical minimum, but assumes it; the argument is entirely concerned with the existence of the theoretical minimum, and part of the argument is by analogy with the visible minimum. This relationship between the three types of minimum has escaped the notice of all previous commentators on this passage, so far as I can judge, except Mau (see his *Zum Problem des Infinitesimalen* . . ., 1957).

The *Letter to Herodotus* gives an epitome of Epicurus' natural philosophy, set out fairly systematically and with some attempt at a progressive order. There is first a note on semantics and the method of investigation (§§37-38), then some basic metaphysical propositions. Nothing comes into being out of nothing or passes away into nothing, and the universe is a closed system—it has no relations with anything outside it. The irreducible contents of the universe are bodies and space; everything else can be reduced to these. The bodies in question are "physically indivisible and unchangeable, if all things are not to be destroyed into non-being but are to remain durable in the dissolution of compounds—solid by nature, unable to be dissolved anywhere or anyhow. It follows that the first principles must be physically indivisible bodies."[a] The

---

[a] ἄτομα καὶ ἀμετάβλητα, εἴπερ μὴ μέλλει πάντα εἰς τὸ μὴ ὂν φθαρήσεσθαι, ἀλλὰ ἰσχύοντα ὑπομενεῖν ἐν ταῖς διαλύσεσι τῶν συγκρίσεων πλήρη τὴν φύσιν ὄντα κα' οὐκ ἔχοντα ὅπῃ ἢ ὅπως διαλυθήσεται. ὥστε τὰς ἀρχὰς ἀτόμους ἀναγκαῖον εἶναι σωμάτων φύσεις. *Letter to Herodotus* (§41).

Indivisible Magnitudes

expression is muddled, but I think the argument is unambiguous. Real things cannot be destroyed into "non-being"; but unless there were a limit to physical divisibility this is what would happen; therefore there is a limit to physical divisibility.

Having thus outlined the argument for the existence of two kinds of first principle, body and space, Epicurus goes on to consider their properties. Both are infinite (§§41-42); atoms have innumerable different shapes (§42), and move in various ways (§§ 43-44). Next follows a digression on the existence of infinite worlds (§45) and on sense perception (§§46-53). Then (§54) Epicurus takes up the subject of the atoms again. They have none of the properties of sensible things except shape, weight, and magnitude, and whatever necessarily goes with shape. Every quality is necessarily liable to change, but change is ruled out for atoms "since at the dissolution of compounds something must remain, solid and indissoluble, to bring about changes *not* into non-being or out of non-being, but by rearrangements and additions and subtractions."[b] So the only properties of atoms are shape, weight, and magnitude. Not every magnitude is possible for atoms, since if it were, some would be visible; but some differences of size are necessary to explain phenomena.

At this point we must study the text in detail. The object of summarizing the argument so far has been to show that the *existence* of physically indivisible bodies may now be taken as proved, and that the subject is now the properties of these bodies.

Epicurus' argument is difficult and the text is doubtful, so it may be useful to begin with a paraphrase of the argument as I understand it.

Paraphrase of §§56.5-59

(A) In a finite body such as the atom, there cannot be an infinite number of parts with magnitude, however small they may be.
This implies:
(B 1) the body cannot be divided into smaller and smaller parts to

---

[b] ἐπειδή περ δεῖ τι ὑπομένειν ἐν ταῖς διαλύσεσι τῶν συγκρίσεων στερεὸν καὶ ἀδιάλυτον, ὃ τὰς μεταβολὰς οὐκ εἰς τὸ μὴ ὂν ποιήσεται οὐδ' ἐκ τοῦ μὴ ὄντος, ἀλλὰ κατὰ μεταθέσεις ἐν πολλοῖς, τινῶν δὲ καὶ προσόδους καὶ ἀφόδους. Ibid. (§54.)

Epicurus' "Letter to Herodotus" §§56.5–59

infinity (if we admitted this, we should put the whole of the real world on an insecure foundation; when we tried to get a firm mental grasp on the atoms we should find it impossible, because our mental picture of them would crumble away until nothing was left); and (B 2) the process of traversing in the imagination from one side to the other of a finite body cannot consist of an infinite number of steps, not even progressively diminishing steps.

We establish (A) on the following grounds:

(C 1) If someone asserts that there is an infinite number of parts with magnitude in an object, then that object must be itself infinite in magnitude; this is true however small the parts may be. Moreover: (C 2) In the process of traversing an object in the imagination, one begins with the outermost distinguishable portion, and moves to the next; but this next must be similar to the first; hence it must be possible, in the view of one who asserts that there is an infinite number of such parts, to reach infinity in thought, when the object is totally grasped by the mind.

We establish C 2 by the following analogy:

(D 1) The minimum *perceptible* quantity is like larger perceptible quantities except that no parts can be perceived in it. (D 2) The fact that it is like larger perceptible quantities, in which parts *can* be perceived, may suggest that we can distinguish one part from another in the minimum, too. But this is false. If we perceive a second quantity, it must be at least equal to the first, since the first was a minimum. (D 3) We measure perceptible objects by studying these minima in succession, beginning from the first. They do not touch each other part to part (since they have no parts), nor do they coincide in one and the same place. They are arranged in succession, and they form the units of perceptible magnitude; more of them form a larger magnitude, fewer of them a smaller magnitude.

(E) Similarly with the minimum in the atom—though it is much smaller than the perceptible minimum. The similarity is to be expected, since we have already argued that the atom has magnitude by an analogy with perceptible things, thus in effect projecting the atom on the larger scale of perceptible things.

(F) Furthermore, these minimal, partless extremities furnish the primary, irreducible unit of measurement, in terms of which we "see"

Indivisible Magnitudes

the magnitude of atoms of different size when we study them in thought. So much can be inferred from the analogy with perceptible things (D 3); but the latter of course are liable to change, and we must not be led by our analogy to think that atoms too are liable to change, in the sense of being put together out of separable parts.

Text, Translation and Commentary*

(A) Πρὸς δὲ τούτοις οὐ δεῖ νομίζειν ἐν τῷ ὡρισμένῳ σώματι ἀπείρους ὄγκους εἶναι οὐδ' ὁπηλίκους οὖν. (§56)

(A) Moreover one must not suppose that in the limited body there are infinitely numerous parts, even parts of any size you like.

ἐν τῷ ὡρισμένῳ σώματι. Bignone and Arrighetti: "in un corpo limitato." Bailey: "'In any limited body'; [Epicurus] proceeds to apply the idea to a perceptible body in 58 and by analogy to the atom in 59." Mau: "in dem beschriebenen Körper."

The previous paragraph has shown that οὐδὲ δεῖ νομίζειν πᾶν μέγεθος ἐν ταῖς ἀτόμοις ὑπάρχειν. It is probable therefore that when he writes τὸ ὡρισμένον σῶμα Epicurus has in mind the atom. The proposition is, I believe, true for all magnitudes in the Epicurean system, but not all magnitudes are relevant here. Bailey's comment is misleading; what Epicurus does in fact is to state his proposition first, then give some arguments for it, including the argument from the analogy of the perceptible body, and finally expound his original proposition in more detail.

Mau asserts that ὡρισμένῳ does not mean "limited" but "defined," for the opposite of it is not ἄπειρον but ἀόριστον. He uses this argument to prove that τὸ ὡρισμένον σῶμα is the atom, for in the previous sections, he asserts, "wurde der Begriff 'Atom' bestimmt (ὥρισται)." But as a matter of fact, ὡρισμένον is of course frequently used as an opposite to ἄπειρον—as for instance in Aristotle's *Metaphysics* 1002 b 18 ἀρχαὶ ὡρισμέναι ἀριθμῷ, in many other instances listed in Bonitz's index, and in Epicurus *Letter to*

---

* In chapter 1 quotations of modern authors are from the editions of Epicurus listed in the Bibliography of Ancient Authors (p. 239), with the following additions, all listed in the Bibliography of Modern Works (p. 243): Arnim, H. von (1907); Giussani, C. (1896); Mau, J. (1954).

Epicurus' "Letter to Herodotus" §§56.5-59

Herodotus §42.2; moreover, as has been said, the kind of definition that has just been given to the concept "atom" is precisely that the atom is finite in size. Thus though Mau seems to be right in saying that this phrase refers to the atom, he is right for the wrong reason.

More is at issue here than the meaning of this single phrase. If the phrase refers to the atom, it is impossible that Epicurus should write in the next sentence that his first proposition rules out the possibility of the infinite *physical* division of things—i.e., that it entails the existence of atoms. If on the other hand the phrase refers to *any* limited body, then such a sequel might be less surprising. Most commentators have believed that this is in fact the sequel, and have therefore had a motive for taking the phrase in the more general sense. I believe (with Mau) that the sequel says nothing about physical atoms; to interpret τὸ ὡρισμένον σῶμα in the more restricted sense as referring to the atom raises no difficulties to this view.

οὐ δεῖ νομίζειν ἀπείρους ὄγκους εἶναι οὐδ' ὁπηλίκους οὖν. Does this οὐδέ mean "not even" or "and not"? That is to say, are we to rule out one proposition, or two? If we examine Epicurus' reasoning carefully, I think we are forced to the conclusion that only one proposition is meant here: "we must not believe that there are infinitely numerous parts, however small they may be." For the argument runs like this: Epicurus first asserts his main thesis, then deduces two consequences (in the ὥστε clauses below, B 1 and 2), and then gives the argument for his thesis (C 1ff.—note that the connection is "γάρ"); and from the nature of the argument we can deduce the nature of the thesis. But the argument, as we shall see, is entirely concerned with showing that there cannot be infinitely *numerous* parts in a finite magnitude, and not at all with showing that there cannot be "parts of any degree of smallness." There is indeed a statement (in C 2) about ἄκρα which might be taken for an independent argument to establish the impossibility of "parts of any degree of smallness"; but in the context even this is used in a proof that an infinite number of such parts adds up to infinity.

The establishment of the conclusion that "οὐδέ" means "not even" is important for the interpretation of the whole passage.

Indivisible Magnitudes

Giussani argues that there were two separate ideas, one of infinitely numerous parts and the other of infinitely small parts, and that the arguments against each of these alternated with each other throughout this section. This led him to some interpretations which add a touch of fantasy to Epicurus' already involved syntax. Bailey, following Giussani, made explicit what Giussani left obscure—namely, that the first of these arguments was supposed to be about *physical* divisibility, and the second about theoretical divisibility. Thus Bailey explains the next sentence as being composed of two sections: in the first, ἡ εἰς ἄπειρον τομή is "the physical process of infinite division which corresponds to the notion of ἄπειροι ὄγκοι"; in the second, μετάβασις is "a mental or ideal process of 'passing' in thought to ever smaller and smaller particles, which corresponds to the notion of ὄγκοι ὁπηλίκοι οὖν."

To Bailey's greater explicitness we owe our certainty that this interpretation is wrong. For it is abundantly clear that ἀπείρους ὄγκους οὐδ' ὁπηλίκους οὖν cannot mean "an infinite number of *physical* atoms nor *theoretical* parts of infinite smallness." Whatever they are, they must be ὄγκοι of the same type.

I take it then that οὐδέ means "not even," just as μηδέ means "not even" in the next sentence. (This is in fact the only natural way of interpreting οὐδέ ... οὖν, as Professor D. L. Page pointed out to me.) This raises a big problem about the phrase ἢ ὁπηλίκοι οὖν which occurs in the manuscripts below; I shall discuss that in its place.

ὄγκοι. Giussani (*Studi lucreziani* 78ff.) tried to make the word ὄγκος into an Epicurean technical term—but one with two meanings: (a) the *minimae partes* of the atom, (b) the minimum quantity of distinguishable substance (something like a molecule). I do not think he proved his point: ὄγκος seems to refer to anything having three dimensions. But this controversy is not relevant here. My translation "parts" imports an idea which is not necessarily implied by the word; one might use "quantities" or "quanta" instead, but both seem too clumsy.

(B 1) ὥστε οὐ μόνον τὴν εἰς ἄπειρον τομὴν ἐπὶ τοὔλαττον ἀναιρετέον, ἵνα μὴ πάντα ἀσθενῆ ποιῶμεν κἀν¹ ταῖς περιλήψεσι

Epicurus' "Letter to Herodotus" §§56.5–59

τῶν ἀθρόων² εἰς τὸ μὴ ὂν ἀναγκαζώμεθα τὰ ὄντα θλίβοντες καταναλίσκειν.

(B 2) ἀλλὰ καὶ τὴν μετάβασιν μὴ νομιστέον γίνεσθαι³ ἐν τοῖς ὡρισμένοις εἰς ἄπειρον μηδ' ἐ⟨πὶ⟩⁴ τοὔλαττον.   (§56)

[1] κἄν Usener: καὶ libri
[2] ἀθρόων B: ἀτόμων F
[3] γίνεσθαι Meibom: γενέσθαι libri
[4] μηδ' ἐπὶ Gassendi: μηδὲ aut μὴ δὲ libri: "dubito an μήτ' ἐπὶ τὸ μεῖζον μήτε Ep. scripserit" Usener

(B 1) Therefore we must not only do away with division into smaller and smaller parts to infinity, so that we may not make everything weak and in our conceptions of the totals be compelled to grind away things that exist and let them go to waste into the non-existent,

(B 2) but also we must not suppose that in finite bodies you continue to infinity in passing on from one part to another, even if the parts get smaller and smaller.

ἵνα μὴ ... καταναλίσκειν. We may now analyze the reason Epicurus gives for rejecting infinite divisibility, assuming that the arguments set out above are correct, and that the subject is *theoretical* divisibility. There are two parts to his reasoning, joined by καί; it is clear, I think, that the second is an expansion of the first. We must reject infinite divisibility, he says, for otherwise we should make everything weak—that is to say, when we tried to get a firm mental grasp (περίληψις) on the atoms, we should find them crumbling away into nothingness. Every time we thought we had arrived at the irreducible minima, we should have to admit that even these minima are divisible. And so our search for the reality of the atoms would be endlessly frustrated.

The rejection of infinite divisibility follows, says Epicurus, from the denial that there are infinitely numerous parts in the finite body (A). The ἵνα clause in B1 gives the reason for wanting to reject it, rather than the ground for rejecting it.

ἀλλὰ καὶ ... μηδ' ἐπὶ τοὔλαττον. This is the second consequence (B 2) of rejecting the idea of infinite parts in a finite whole. The difference between the first consequence and the second is not, as most commentators have said, that the first is physical and the second

Indivisible Magnitudes

is theoretical; both are theoretical. The difference is that in the first we consider the question of *what would be left* if an atom is divided an infinite number of times, and in the second we consider how an atom can be comprehended in the imagination, if such comprehension means taking note first of one part, then of another, to infinity. We shall see later that the difference between these two corresponds to the difference between two of Zeno's arguments (see ch. 5).

μετάβασιν. This is the process of traversing an object, i.e., of shifting one's attention from one part to another; so much is clear from the immediate context and from D 1-3 below. But I have not found other instances of the use of the word in this sense; it is not given in Liddell and Scott. It reminds one of Aristotle's use of the terms διέξοδος and διιέναι in his definition of the infinite (*Physics* Γ 204 a 3 ἕνα μὲν δὴ τρόπον τὸ ἀδύνατον διελθεῖν τῷ μὴ πεφυκέναι διιέναι, ὥσπερ ἡ φωνὴ ἀόρατος· ἄλλως δὲ τὸ διέξοδον ἔχον ἀτελεύτητον, ἢ ὃ μόγις, ἢ ὃ πεφυκὸς ἔχειν μὴ ἔχει διέξοδον ἢ πέρας).

(C 1) οὔτε γάρ,[1] ἐπειδὰν ἅπαξ τις εἴπῃ ὅτι ἄπειροι ὄγκοι ἔν τινι ὑπάρχουσι καὶ[2] ὁπηλίκοι οὖν, ἔστι νοῆσαι πῶς [τ'][3] ἂν ἔτι τοῦτο πεπερασμένον εἴη τὸ μέγεθος· πηλίκοι γάρ τινες δῆλον ὡς οἱ[4] ἄπειροί εἰσιν ὄγκοι, καὶ οὗτοι[5] ὁπηλίκοι[6] ἄν ποτε ὦσιν, ἄπειρον ἂν ἦν καὶ τὸ μέγεθος. (§57)

[1] γάρ F, Giussani: γὰρ ὅπως ceteri: γὰρ ὅλως Schneider: γὰρ ἁπλῶς Brieger
[2] ὑπάρχουσι καὶ Ernout: ὑπαρχουσιν ἢ libri: ὑπάρχουσιν οἱ Usener
[3] τ' om. Furley: ὅπως Brieger
[4] οἱ om. FP³Zf
[5] οὗτοι B: οὗτοι ἐξ ὧν ceteri
[6] ὁπηλίκοι] οἱ πηλίκοι F

(C 1) For when someone once says that there are infinite parts in something, however small they may be, it is impossible to see how this can still be finite in size; for obviously the infinite parts must be of *some* size, and whatever size they may happen to be, the size ⟨of the total⟩ would be infinite.

To criticize in detail every previous effort to make sense of this corrupt sentence would take up too much space. I offer my own

Epicurus' "Letter to Herodotus" §§56.5–59

conjecture. I do not think it does more violence to the text than other interpretations, and I think it makes better sense.

οὔτε. This is coordinate either with the "τε" following "πῶς" or with the "τε" following "ἄκρον" in C 2, or perhaps with the "τε" in D 1 (τό τε ἐλάχιστον κτλ.). I reject the first alternative because it leaves "νοῆσαι" without an object (see also my next note, on "ὅπως"), and the third because the two sentences thus linked would not be coordinate in sense. I take "οὔτε" to be coordinate with "ἄκρον τε . . .": the two coordinate sentences offer reasons for rejecting the hypothesis of an infinite number of ὄγκοι in a finite μέγεθος.

ὅπως, the reading of all the MSS except F, and all editors except Giussani, is impossibly difficult. Most editors take "ὅπως" to stand for "ὅπως τοῦτο δυνατόν ἐστι" or something similar, and to be governed by "νοῆσαι." The ellipse seems to me incredible, and the sense feeble. I guess that "ὅπως" is someone's correction of "πῶς" (just below), which has been wrongly incorporated in the text.

πῶς [τ']. This conjecture about "ὅπως" also explains the wrong inclusion of "τε" here. Once "ὅπως" has been included, "τε" is necessary to make sense of the passage.

καὶ ὁπηλίκοι οὖν. I have argued above that Epicurus is concerned with one hypothesis (an infinite number of ὄγκοι, however small), not with two (an infinite number of ὄγκοι, and infinitely small ὄγκοι). The reading of all the MSS (ἢ ὁπηλίκοι οὖν) strictly entails two hypotheses. The correction (NH into KAI) is a small one, and the mistake is entirely understandable: "οὐδέ" in the first sentence would suggest "ἤ" here to one who had not perfectly grasped the argument. (I reached this conclusion before observing that "καὶ" was proposed by Ernout, in *Lucrèce, Commentaire*, p. LXXII, n.1.)

καὶ οὗτοι. "ἐξ ὧν," which follows in all MSS except B, is omitted by the editors, as being an alternative to "καὶ οὗτοι."

Indivisible Magnitudes

The argument, with the text thus restored, is quite clear and should need no further elucidation.

(C 2) ἄκρον τε ἔχοντος[1] τοῦ πεπερασμένου[2] διαληπτόν, εἰ μὴ καὶ καθ' ἑαυτὸ θεωρητόν,[3] οὐκ ἔστι μὴ οὐ[4] καὶ τὸ ἑξῆς τούτου τοιοῦτον νοεῖν καὶ οὕτω[5] κατὰ τὸ ἑξῆς εἰς τοὔμπροσθεν βαδίζοντα[6] εἰς τὸ ἄπειρον ὑπάρχειν[7] κατὰ τοῦτον[8] ἀφικνεῖσθαι τῇ ἐννοίᾳ. (§57)

[1] ἔχοντος Gassendi: ἔχοντες libri
[2] τὸ ὑπὸ πεπερασμένου FP³: τὸ ὑποπεπερασμένον Zf
[3] θεωρητόν Co: θεωρητέον ceteri
[4] οὐ om. FP³Zf
[5] οὕτω P Co F²Zf: τοῦτο BF¹: οὐ τῷ Giussani
[6] βαδίζοντι Usener, Bailey: βαδίζοντες Co F²
[7] εἰς τὸ ἄπειρον ⟨εἰς τὸ "ἄπειρον⟩ ὑπάρχειν" Arnim, Mau
[8] κατὰ τοῦτον Furley: κατὰ τοιοῦτον libri: καὶ τὸ τοιοῦτον Muehll, Mau: κατὰ ⟨τὸ⟩ τοιοῦτον Schneider, Bailey, Arrighetti

(C 2) And if the finite body has an extremity which is distinguishable, even though it cannot be thought of in isolation, it must be that one thinks of the similar part next to this and that thus as one proceeds onward step by step it is possible, according to this opponent, to arrive at infinity in thought.

κατὰ τοῦτον. This small emendation was suggested to me by someone at a meeting of the Oxford Philological Association, but I cannot now remember who it was. I think the phrase refers back to the imaginary opponent mentioned in C 1 (ἐπειδὰν ἅπαξ τις κτλ....). If κατὰ τοιοῦτον is retained and it is taken to be neuter, then it would seem merely to repeat the force of οὕτω. Mau, reading "... βαδίζοντα εἰς τὸ ἄπειρον εἰς τὸ ἄπειρον ὑπάρχειν καὶ τὸ τοιοῦτο κτλ.," translates: "und so nacheinander von dem einen zum nächsten ins Unendliche fortschreitend gedanklich dahin zu gelangen, dass auch eben dies (das Begrenzte) unendlich ist." The ingenuity of this is more admirable than the result. Apart from the two alterations of the text, it destroys something of the force of Epicurus' argument: for there is a point, as we shall see, in the echo "νοεῖν ... τῇ ἐννοίᾳ" which is lost if "ἀφικνεῖσθαι τῇ ἐννοίᾳ" means simply "to conclude."

The argument is as follows. We are considering someone's suggestion that there are infinite ὄγκοι in a finite body. Starting

Epicurus' "Letter to Herodotus" §§56.5–59

from one edge of the body we imagine a minute part of it, "the extremity," inconceivable in isolation from the body. If we think of the part *next* to this extremity, we must necessarily think of another distinct part similar to the extremity itself. But according to our imaginary opponent, there are in our finite body an *infinite* number of such parts. So if we proceed in thought from one such part to another, it must be possible, when we traverse the whole object, to reach infinity in our thinking, which is absurd.

It will be seen that this argument needs support. It is not yet clear why the extremity is a minute *part*, nor why we can only think of the part *next* to the extremity as being similar to it. This support is provided in the next sentences, by an analogy with the visible minimum.

The absurdity of "arriving at infinity" is meant, I think, to be self-evident. The procedure is of taking successive "steps" forward. This procedure is of course the μετάβασις of the previous sentence; and again we think of Aristotle's remarks, quoted above on B 2.

(D 1) τό τε ἐλάχιστον τὸ ἐν τῇ αἰσθήσει δεῖ κατανοεῖν ὅτι οὔτε τοιοῦτόν ἐστιν οἷον τὸ τὰς μεταβάσεις ἔχον οὔτε πάντη πάντως[1] ἀνόμοιον, ἀλλ' ἔχον μέν τινα κοινότητα τῶν μεταβατῶν,[2] διάληψιν δὲ μερῶν οὐκ ἔχον.

(D 2) ἀλλ' ὅταν[3] διὰ τὴν τῆς κοινότητος προσεμφέρειαν οἰηθῶμεν διαλήψεσθαί τι[4] αὐτοῦ, τὸ μὲν ἐπιτάδε, τὸ δὲ ἐπέκεινα, τὸ ἴσον ἡμῖν δεῖ προσπίπτειν.

(D 3) ἑξῆς τε θεωροῦμεν ταῦτα ἀπὸ τοῦ πρώτου καταρχόμενοι καὶ οὐκ ἐν τῷ αὐτῷ, οὐδὲ μέρεσι μερῶν ἁπτόμενα,[5] ἀλλ' ἢ[6] ἐν τῇ ἰδιότητι τῇ ἑαυτῶν τὰ μεγέθη καταμετροῦντα, τὰ πλείω πλεῖον καὶ τὰ ἐλάττω ἔλαττον. (§58)

[1] πάντως om. F: παντὸς Zf
[2] μεταβατῶν Schneider: μεταβάντων libri
[3] ὅταν Cobet : ὅτε libri
[4] τι om. F
[5] ἅπτομεν B¹ (ex μενᵃ), Co: ἅπτομεν P
[6] ἢ om. Mau

(D 1) We must observe that the minimum in sensation, too, is neither quite the same as that which allows progression from one part to another, nor wholly unlike it; it has a certain similarity

to things which allow progression, but it has no distinction of parts.
(D 2) When because of the closeness of the resemblance we think we *can* make distinctions in it—one part to this side, one to that—what confronts us must be equal.
(D 3) And we study these parts in succession, beginning from the first, and not all within the same area nor as touching each other part to part, but, in their own proper nature, measuring out the sizes, more of them for a larger one, fewer for a smaller.

τό τε ἐλάχιστον τὸ ἐν τῇ αἰσθήσει. Mau is the only commentator to see that the minimum in sensation is not the same as the extremity mentioned above but is an analogy designed to explain it. Epicurus does his best to make this clear by emphasizing "νοεῖν" and "τῇ ἐννοίᾳ" above, by saying explicitly "ἐν τῇ αἰσθήσει" here, and by calling it an analogy in the next sentence.

οὔτε τοιοῦτον . . . οὔτε πάντῃ πάντως ἀνόμοιον. There are certainly some things, Epicurus assumes, which are too small to be perceived. It follows that there must be a minimum perceptible quantity. Any quantity larger than the minimum can be scanned or traversed by stages (τὸ τὰς μεταβάσεις ἔχον); the minimum cannot. Yet the minimum is not something of a different category from larger quantities: it is itself a quantity. Its only distinction is that it has no perceptible parts.

ἀλλ' ὅταν . . . προσπίπτειν. If we study such a minimum perceptible quantity, we may be tempted to suppose that since it *is* a perceptible quantity and since every other perceptible quantity has perceptible parts, it too must have perceptible parts. If we think we can distinguish two such parts of the minimum we deceive ourselves: it was after all a minimum, so that any perceptible quantity must be at least equal to it.

ἑξῆς τε θεωροῦμεν . . . ἁπτόμενα. Mau has pointed out that the phraseology can be understood fully only by comparing it with one of Aristotle's discussions of continuity. "ἐν τῷ αὐτῷ" corresponds to Aristotle's "ὅλον ὅλου ἅπτεσθαι" (cf. *Physics* 231 b 3): Aristotle argues that points cannot touch each other in a line, because they cannot touch part to part, since points have no parts, and if they touch whole to whole, they must coincide, and so cannot make

Epicurus' "Letter to Herodotus" §§56.5–59

a line. Epicurus denies this of his minimum perceptible quantities (and so, by analogy, of his minimum conceivable quantities). They *do* cohere, they do not coincide, and they have no parts. This is not, I think, just a stubborn denial of Aristotle's thesis; what happens in sensation is meant (as so often in Epicurean theory) to prove what happens in the realm of the imperceptible. In the minimum perceptible quantity we have something which has perceptible extension but no perceptible parts; why should there not also be a minimum *conceivable* quantity which has conceivable extension but no conceivable parts? Such a quantity would escape Aristotle's dilemmas. But this point must be discussed in its historical perspective (see ch. 8).

ἀλλ' ἢ ἐν τῇ ἰδιότητι . . . καταμετροῦντα. It may be that Mau is right to delete ἤ. ἀλλ' ἤ normally introduces an exception, not an antithesis. But I think it might be defended as parallel to some Aristotelian examples (for which see Denniston *Greek Particles* 2 p. 26), particularly the following: ὁ κόκκυξ . . . οὐδὲ τὰ περὶ τὴν κεφαλὴν ἔοικεν ἱέρακι . . . ἀλλ' ἢ κατὰ τὸ χρῶμα μόνον προσέοικεν ἱέρακι (Aristotle *Historia Animalium* 563 b 20 "nor is the cuckoo like the falcon in the head either: ⟨indeed there is no likeness⟩ except that it is like the falcon in colour only").

As to the meaning of the phrase, Mau observes gloomily that Epicurus himself probably could not give a clear explanation of it. I am not sure what it means, but the following seems to me the likeliest explanation. Three things must be borne in mind: (1) Epicurus is writing about the perceptible minimum, but always for the purpose of proving or explaining something about the theoretical minimum; (2) the phrase forms the positive half of an antithesis, of which the other half refers to and combats Aristotle's theory of continuity; and (3) it is about the function of the minimum as a unit of measure. These considerations suggest that we ought to look for a solution by studying the relation between the Aristotelian and the Epicurean theories of measurement.

A passage of Aristotle (*Metaphysics* I, 1) on the subject of units of measure will be examined in more detail later (see p. 48); here it will be sufficient to summarize it. Quantity, says Aristotle, is always measured in units. The unit of arithmetic is the model; other units

Indivisible Magnitudes

are formed by analogy with it. The difference between the model and the other units is this: the unit of arithmetic is in every respect indivisible, but other units, though treated as indivisible for the purpose of measuring, are themselves divisible into smaller units. The units of weight, distance, speed, etc. are to some extent a matter of convenience; they are not wholly arbitrary, though, but determined with reference to the facts of sense perception: "the first thing from which, as far as our perception goes, nothing can be subtracted, all men make the measure, whether of liquids or of solids, weight or size."

Now Epicurus certainly wished to remove any element of arbitrariness from the theory of measurement: it is contrary to his whole theory of knowledge to admit concepts which do not correspond to actual features of the real world. Perhaps, too, it is relevant to point to Lucretius' polemic against the doctrine of continuity (see p. 36), where it is argued that unless there is a fixed minimum quantity, there is no way of distinguishing between large and small things.

What Epicurus must insist on, therefore, in his argument against Aristotle, is that his minima furnish an *objective* standard of measurement, which is in no way arbitrary or a matter of convenience (we shall see in ch. 10, p. 140, that Hume argued against infinite divisibility in just the same way). I think, then, that "ἐν τῇ ἰδιότητι ... καταμετροῦντα" is contrasted with "ἐν τῷ αὐτῷ"; "μέρεσι μερῶν ἁπτόμενα" seems to be parenthetical—unless indeed Epicurus takes it to mean "overlapping," which is quite possible. We study these parts in succession, he says, beginning from the first. They do not all coincide in the same place (nor do they touch each other part to part, which Aristotle claims to be the only possible alternative). As we scan them one by one, they measure out the body whose parts they are; it is their own "proper nature" which forms the unit of measure.

Of course the picture is complicated because Epicurus is here talking about *perceptible* minima, and even Aristotle seems to say that the units of perceptible magnitude are *given* by the facts of perception. I doubt if this complication is important, however, since Epicurus is clearly thinking all the time of the general theory of continuity and magnitude.

Epicurus' "Letter to Herodotus" §§56.5-59

καταμετροῦντα. Professor Vlastos has argued (1965, pp. 135-137), that καταμετρεῖν here and καταμέτρημα in (F), below, have the technical sense which they are given in the opening definition in Euclid's Book V. In this sense A is a καταμέτρημα of B, if and only if B is an *integral multiple* of A. Starting from this proposition, Vlastos argues that in our passage Epicurus asserts only that there is a smallest atomic length (i.e., a length than which no atom is smaller) and that all atoms are integral multiples of it. That is to say, any atom is of one of the following sizes: q, $2q$, $3q$, . . ., nq. It is a matter of fact (according to this interpretation of Epicurus) that no atom is smaller than q, and that there is no atom of, say, $3q/2$ units. But there is nothing in the theory "to entail that q is the smallest possible lineal magnitude in geometry."

I leave aside for the moment the question of whether this is a geometrical theory (see Introduction and ch. 11). But I am not convinced that Vlastos's interpretation is sufficient. Of course, the *minimae partes* necessarily have also the properties which Vlastos gives them. They are καταμετρήματα of the atoms, in Euclid's specialized sense; and Epicurus uses them in his polemic against infinite variety of atomic size and shape. But that is not the whole, or the essential point, of the theory. The second part of this essay will show how Epicurus' doctrine evolved; it is a modification, adopted for the purpose of meeting Aristotle's criticisms, of a doctrine which the earlier atomists put together to meet and thwart the Eleatic attack on pluralism. Its provenance lies in the Eleatic puzzles about *divisibility*; and I do not think that Vlastos's interpretation does justice to this aspect of it. I agree with him that the theory asserts that all atoms contain an integral number of parts of uniform dimensions. These parts are distinguishable only theoretically. But he asserts that they are theoretically divisible, whereas I believe them to have been theoretically indivisible, since only on this assumption do they serve their purpose of circumventing the Eleatic divisibility puzzles. Apart from this argument from the historical context, there are two points of detail which may be mentioned in confirmation: first, Epicurus really does seem to deny infinite divisibility in a comprehensive way, in C 1-2; secondly, if the atom is theoretically divisible to infinity, the expressions τὸ ἐν τῇ ἀτόμῳ ἐλάχιστον and

Indivisible Magnitudes

minimae partes are distinctly misleading. For on Vlastos's interpretation, in an atom of volume (say) 8*q*, the *q*-sized unit is in no sense an ἐλάχιστον; it just happens to be equal to the smallest existing atom, but it has no special status in the atom of which it is a part.

(E) ταύτῃ τῇ ἀναλογίᾳ νομιστέον καὶ τὸ ἐν τῇ ἀτόμῳ ἐλάχιστον κεχρῆσθαι· μικρότητι γὰρ ἐκεῖνο δῆλον ὡς διαφέρει τοῦ κατὰ τὴν αἴσθησιν θεωρουμένου, ἀναλογίᾳ δὲ τῇ αὐτῇ κέχρηται.[1] ἐπεί περ καὶ ὅτι μέγεθος ἔχει ἡ ἄτομος, κατὰ τὴν ⟨τῶν[2]⟩ ἐνταῦθα ἀναλογίαν κατηγορήσαμεν, μικρόν τι μόνον μακρὰν[3] ἐκβάλλοντες.[4]   (§§58–59)

[1] κέχρηται Gassendi: κεχρῆσθαι libri
[2] τῶν om. libri, *supplevit* Usener
[3] μακρὰν Usener: μακρὸν libri
[4] ἐκβαλόντες Usener: ἐκλαβόντες Mau

(E) This analogy, we must believe, is followed by the minimum in the atom; for in its smallness, clearly, it differs from that which is perceptible, but it follows the same analogy. For we have already stated that the atom has magnitude, in virtue of its analogy with the things of this world, just projecting something small on a large scale.

κατὰ τὴν τῶν ἐνταῦθα ἀναλογίαν κατηγορήσαμεν. The τῶν here is an addition, first made by Usener and adopted by Giussani, Bailey, and (I think) Bignone. Hicks translates "on the analogy of things within our experience"; so probably his omission of τῶν from the text is a mistake, since this meaning can hardly be dragged from the words κατὰ τὴν ἐνταῦθα ἀναλογίαν. Mau retains the MS text but translates, consistently, "auf Grund dieser Analogie." There is thus a conflict between the view that we should read τῶν ἐνταῦθα, meaning "the things of this world," or ἐνταῦθα, meaning "the present," "this" (analogy)—i.e., that which we are talking about *here*. Probably we cannot decide between these two until we have studied the next phrase.

μικρόν τι μόνον μακρὰν ἐκβάλλοντες. The MS reading μακρὸν was emended by Usener, and his emendation is adopted by Giussani, Bailey, and Hicks. Mau retains the MS μακρὸν but emends ἐκβάλλοντες to ἐκλαβόντες, translating "indem wir nur etwas Kleines als Grosses veranschaulichten (hervorholten)." Mau's is such an unnecessary emendation that I have no hesitation in rejecting it. μακρόν does not often mean simply "large," and ἐκβάλλοντες seems to require an adverb; so I adopt Usener's correction.

But there is still much room for doubt about the meaning of the phrase. Bignone translates "non facendo altro che protrarre lontano un determinato grado di piccolezza." This finite degree of smallness is supposed to be that of the minimum perceptible quantity; we "extend" it (i.e., make it *smaller*, though still finite) for the minimum conceivable quantity. Bailey translates "only we placed it" (sc. the atom) "far below them" (sc. τὰ ἐνταῦθα) "in smallness." In defense of this very forced interpretation of μικρόν τι, he adds a note which I do not understand: "lit. only as a small thing casting it (the atom) far away." Hicks, who reads ἐκβαλόντες, translates "and this, small as it is, we have merely reproduced on a larger scale." Giussani has "solo che questa grandezza è di gran lunga più piccola (anche dei più piccoli corpi percettibili)."

One of the normal meanings of ἐκβάλλειν is "to produce" a line, in geometry (see LSJ, s.v. ix). I suppose it is possible that it *could* mean "to make smaller" something already small, as Bignone takes it; but this seems much less likely than that it has its normal meaning of "to make larger." So it seems to me that the μικρόν τι is the atom, or its magnitude. Epicurus is merely observing that in comparing the atom with something in our perceptible world we are in effect magnifying the atom.

We must now return to the problem of the analogy itself. The argument is this: we have to imagine that the theoretical minimum stands to the atom as the perceptible minimum stands to the perceptible whole, since clearly the theoretical minimum differs only in smallness from the perceptible minimum—"for that the atom has size we have already declared κατὰ τὴν ⟨τῶν⟩ (?) ἐνταῦθα ἀναλογίαν, merely greatly magnifying something small." The aorist "κατηγορήσαμεν" refers to something earlier in the exposition (the aorist "εἶπον" is similarly used in §64). It is not quite clear where Epicurus would say he first predicates size of the atoms. In §42, he argues that the atoms must have innumerable different shapes, "since it is not possible that so many varieties" (of observable

Indivisible Magnitudes

things) "should come into being out of the same limited number of shapes." In §54, he remarks that the atoms have no properties "except shape and weight and size and everything that necessarily goes along with shape," and continues with a defense of the proposition that atoms always retain their ὄγκους καὶ σχηματισμοὺς ἰδίους. In §55, he begins to discuss the question of size in more detail. He assumes that atoms *have* size, and now argues that they must have different sizes "since if this is the case a better explanation can be given of what happens with regard to our feelings and sensations." This last point seems to be essentially the same as that made in §42: he says there that the hypothesis of different *shapes* is necessary to explain the variety of perceptible things, and here that the hypothesis of different *sizes* enables us to explain our perceptions better. But variations in shape are not essentially different from variations in size in Epicurean theory, and are used similarly in explaining the properties of compounds (see the examples in Lucretius 2. 333*ff*.). I think it likely therefore that when he says "κατηγορήσαμεν" Epicurus is thinking of what he has said earlier in §42 and §55.

If this is so, then "⟨τῶν⟩ ἐνταῦθα" would appear to be the better reading. The atoms have been declared to have size "by analogy with the things of the visible world." And since we have used this analogy once, Epicurus says, we can use it again here in discussing *how* the atoms have size.

(F) ἔτι τε τὰ ἐλάχιστα καὶ ἀμερῆ[1] πέρατα δεῖ νομίζειν τῶν μηκῶν[2] τὸ καταμέτρημα ἐξ αὐτῶν[3] πρώτων[4] τοῖς μείζοσι καὶ ἐλάττοσι παρασκευάζοντα[5] τῇ διὰ λόγου θεωρίᾳ ἐπὶ τῶν ἀοράτων. ἡ γὰρ κοινότης ἡ ὑπάρχουσα αὐτοῖς πρὸς τὰ μετάβολα[6] ἱκανὴ τὸ μέχρι τούτου συντελέσαι· συμφόρησιν δὲ ἐκ τούτων[7] κίνησιν ἐχόντων[8] οὐχ οἷόν τε γενέσθαι. (§59)

[1] ἀμερῆ Arnim: ἀμιγῆ libri
[2] μηκῶν BP¹Co(?): μικρῶν F: μακρῶν P³Zf
[3] αὐτῶν Usener: αὐτῶν libri
[4] πρῶτον BFZf
[5] hiatum indicavit Usener
[6] μετάβολα Furley: ἀμετάβολα libri: ἀμετάβατα Usener: μεταβατὰ Arnim
[7] τού⟨των ὡς⟩ τῶν Bignone
[8] ⟨οὐκ⟩ ἐχόντων Brieger

Epicurus' "Letter to Herodotus" §§56.5–59

(F) Further, we must take these minimum partless limits as providing for larger and smaller things the standard of measurement of their lengths, being themselves the primary units, for our use in studying by means of thought these invisible bodies. For the similarity between them and changeable things is sufficient to establish so much; but it is impossible that there should ever be a process of composition out of these minima having motion.

The argument, I think, runs like this. In D 1-3 Epicurus proposes an analogy which will explain the nature of the minimum theoretical part of the atom. It is like the minimum perceptible unit: this is of the same nature as larger perceptible units, but it differs from them in having no perceptible parts itself. We measure the size of perceptible bodies by running over these perceptible minima and counting them. (E) The atom must be regarded as analogous to a perceptible body—though of course it is really much smaller (the analogy is justified because it was by such an analogy that we established in the first place that the atom has size). (F) And we must believe that the indivisible extremities (the ἄκρα of C 2) of atoms also serve as the unit of measurement in their case—not now for measurement by perception, but for study in thought, which is what we *have* to use in the case of invisible things. The analogy between invisible things and the changeable things of the perceptible world holds good to this extent, though of course it must not be pressed too far: an atom is not *put together* out of its minima as a perceptible body may be put together out of its *parts*.

The MSS have ἀμιγῆ and nearly all editors retain it. Bailey defends it by referring to "solida simplicitate" in Lucretius 1.609; but as that is an attribute of *atoma*, not of their minimum parts, it is irrelevant. The only possible meaning of "ἀμιγῆ" here is "simple," "uncompounded." But there was never any suggestion that the minima are composed of a varied lot of ingredients, which would be the natural implication of this adjective.

"ἀμερῆ" on the other hand is very much to the point. It looks back to the point established in D 1-2, that the minimum *perceptible* parts do not themselves contain parts.

Indivisible Magnitudes

πέρατα. Bailey takes πέρατα as the complement, to avoid making νομίζειν govern the participle παρασκευάζοντα: "one must consider these least indivisible points as boundary-marks." But this is unnecessary, and makes poor sense. It is unnecessary, because Epicurus is quite capable of using a participial construction with νομίζω, for instance in §74.3 "ἔτι δὲ τοὺς κόσμους οὔτε ἐξ ἀνάγκης δεῖ νομίζειν ἕνα σχηματισμὸν ἔχοντας." It makes poor sense, because we do not need at this stage to be *told* that the minima are limits or extremities; they have already been mentioned as such in C 2. What we do need to be told is that these indivisible minima, already identified as the limits or extremities of atoms, function as units of measurement in the atoms exactly as the perceptible extremities do in perceptible objects.

τῶν μηκῶν. I suppose this is the right reading. It might be possible to adopt the reading of F, "μικρῶν," meaning the atoms, and to construe it with πέρατα. But I think the words τῶν μηκῶν τὸ καταμέτρημα make reasonable sense: μῆκος can mean simply "distance," "interval" (for instance in §46.9 ἡ διὰ τοῦ κενοῦ φορὰ . . . πᾶν μῆκος περιληπτὸν ἐν ἀπερινοήτῳ χρόνῳ συντελεῖ).

τῇ διὰ λόγου θεωρίᾳ ἐπὶ τῶν ἀοράτων. This explains a point about the analogy. For visible things we use sight; for invisible we use λόγος.

ἡ γὰρ κοινότης . . . τὰ μετάβολα. What is this κοινότης? The last clause of the whole passage is a warning: the similarity is sufficient to establish the conclusions so far reached, but *not* the further conclusion that there is "a process of composition out of these having motion." It is inconceivable that this last bit should refer to anything but a physical process of composition of atoms out of minima; for this is just what should be denied at the end of a discussion of parts of atoms. But what could suggest that atoms *are* generated in this way? Obviously, the analogy between visible compound bodies and their parts, on the one hand, and atoms and their parts, on the other—the analogy which has just been drawn. κοινότης must therefore refer to this analogy. Now αὐτοῖς can only refer to τὰ . . . πέρατα (or possibly to τῶν ἀοράτων), so the MS reading τὰ ἀμετάβολα cannot be right, since it has to refer to visible things or their parts, and the whole point of the sentence is that atoms are *not* changeable in spite of their resemblance to visible things which are. The simplest correction seems to be τὰ μετάβολα (LSJ quotes examples of this adjective from Plutarch and Ptolemy). Usener's ἀμετάβατα will not do, because visible minima and theoretical minima are both ἀμετάβατα.

CHAPTER 2

THE EVIDENCE OF LUCRETIUS ON THE THEORY OF MINIMAL PARTS

OUR elucidation of Epicurus' theory has so far neglected Lucretius, and we can therefore use what Lucretius has to say on the subject as some sort of check on our interpretation.

The section of Lucretius' poem which explains this theory in detail is unfortunately controversial. It seems best to look first at two perfectly lucid passages in Book 1 which follow the main exposition, in the hope that they may guide us in interpreting the more difficult lines.

The first passage is part of Lucretius' attack on Empedocles (1.746–752). Those who believe in a plurality of identifiable substances as *principia*, he says, are at fault, first because they admit motion without void (but this has been shown to be impossible, in 1.333*ff.*); secondly because they admit soft and rarefied bodies without void (but we already know that void is required in the explanation of such things, 1.565–573):

> ... deinde quod omnino finem non esse secandis
> corporibus faciunt neque pausam stare fragori
> nec prorsum in rebus minimum consistere quicquam;
> cum videamus id extremum cuiusque cacumen
> esse quod ad sensus nostros minimum esse videtur,
> conicere ut possis ex hoc, quae cernere non quis
> extremum quod habent, minimum consistere ⟨menti⟩.
>
> (746–752)

> ... next, because they assume that there is no end to the cutting up of bodies, and that no stop is made in their breaking, and indeed that there is no minimum at all in things; though we see that there exists in everything that last extremity which is seen to be the minimum with respect to our senses, so that you may infer from this that of those things which you *cannot* see the last extremity is the minimum ⟨with respect to the mind⟩.

The Evidence of Lucretius on the Theory of Minimal Parts

The first two lines obviously refer to the physical division of things. Lucretius' charge is that the pluralists do not admit the existence of atoms; but atoms have been shown to be necessary, so he thinks, earlier in his exposition. "And indeed (they assume) that there is no minimum at all in things": the introductory words *nec prorsum* show that this is a more fundamental statement than what has preceded it; they do not merely reject physical atoms, but even say that there is no minimum at all. This line is therefore concerned with the theoretical minimum; and the reasoning which follows, too, is concerned with this.

In the last four lines, Lucretius evidently intends to summarize the argument which is to persuade us that there *is* an absolute minimum. Is this argument the same as the one we have studied in Epicurus' *Letter*? There, as the reader will remember, the point was made that there is a minimum visible quantity, which can be seen as the extremity of a visible thing, but within which no parts can be distinguished by sight. Lucretius says "we see that there exists in everything that last extremity which is seen to be the minimum with respect to our senses". Munro (in a comment on 1.600) remarks that in the visible thing the extremity *seems* to be a minimum, in the atom it *is* a minimum. But I do not think this is quite what Lucretius has in mind, since I do not see how one can deduce the existence of a genuine minimum from the fact that there seems to be a minimum. The point is rather that there *is* a minimum in visible things—a visible minimum—and from this we are to infer that there is a minimum in the things which are not visible but conceivable or imaginable. (The last foot of the last line is missing in the manuscripts. I think *menti* should perhaps be supplied, as an antithesis to *ad sensus nostros*. But Munro's *in illis* may well be right.)

The argument is, I think, the same as the one in Epicurus' *Letter*, though it is of course much less fully developed. It is indeed so compressed and allusive as to be barely intelligible by itself; and this is a reason for thinking that it may have been mentioned rather more fully in an earlier part of the poem. We shall return to this point in dealing with lines *599ff*.

It must be admitted in passing that Lucretius here combines and coordinates an argument about physical minima and an argument

Indivisible Magnitudes

about theoretical minima. This combination is precisely what I have dismissed as implausible in my interpretation of the passage of Epicurus. But the coexistence of the two arguments here does not persuade me to reopen the question there. Here, Lucretius is briefly summarizing objections to the pluralists' theory of matter, and he *must* mention their contradiction of his notion of atoms, as well as their denial of the existence of a theoretical minimum. Epicurus, as we saw, had no reason to recall the physical argument.

THE second passage can be quickly dismissed. It is part of Lucretius' attack on Anaxagoras (1.843*ff.*). After a brief exposition of Anaxagoras' theory of *homoeomeria*, he raises two objections: there is no void in his theory, and no end "to dissecting bodies"—and he is therefore liable to the same objections as have already been brought against Empedocles. He goes on to object (line 847) that Anaxagoras made his *primordia* too weak: and with this we wonder if we are to have a repetition of Epicurus' point that infinite divisibility would make everything weak (see above, p. 13). But Lucretius turns the argument in a different direction. These *primordia* are too weak because they are of the same nature as "things themselves" (he means the things of the sensible world, which the *primordia* should explain), and these things are manifestly perishable. Disappointingly, there is nothing in this passage that throws further light on the theory of minimal parts.

WE MAY now go back to the main exposition of the doctrine of *minimae partes* (1.599–634). The context is this: after showing that the two ultimate elements of the universe are *corpus* and *inane*, Lucretius proposes to demonstrate that there exist "ea quae solido atque aeterno corpore constent." There follows a series of "proofs," whose conclusions predicate various combinations of *soliditas*, *simplicitas*, and *aeternitas* of the atoms. The series has given rise to extensive controversy. To avoid becoming involved in this unnecessarily, let us observe merely that the passage we have to study forms part of the series, in the traditional text. It is itself divisible into three

The Evidence of Lucretius on the Theory of Minimal Parts

parts; the first concludes by mentioning all three of these properties, the second mentions *soliditas* and *aeternitas*, and the third has no explicit conclusion. We shall consider later how the parts are related to each other.

> Tum porro quoniam est extremum quodque cacumen
> corporis illius quod nostri cernere sensus
> iam nequeunt, id nimirum sine partibus exstat
> et minima constat natura . . .
>
> (599–602)

> Then further, since there exists in every case a last extremity of that body which our senses are no longer able to discern, that extremity is certainly without parts, and its nature is minimal . . .

This is how the traditional text reads. As it stands, *corporis illius* must be the antecedent of *quod*. So the antecedent of *quod* cannot be the complement (or the subject) of *est*, and *est* must therefore mean "exists." This makes *quodque* hard to understand. Ernout and Robin, who retain this reading in their edition, quote the parallel of *quaeque* in 1.578:

> tamen ex aeterno tempore quaeque
> nunc etiam superare necessest corpora rebus,

"où *quaeque* pourrait être remplacé par *quibusque*, 'des éléments pour chacune des choses.'"

If this is correct, then Lucretius is clearly taking for granted that the atom—"that body which our senses can no longer discern"—has a *cacumen*, and he is apparently *deducing* the partlessness of the *cacumen* from the mere fact of its existence. What are the missing steps in this deduction? Bailey, who follows Ernout and Robin in keeping the traditional reading, explains it as follows (*Epicurus* p. 704): "since every atom has an extreme point, that point, *seeing that the atom cannot be divided and so a fortiori it cannot itself be divided*, must be without parts" (the italics are mine).

This explanation of Bailey's is certainly wrong. The conclusion of the section is stated clearly enough by Lucretius:

> sunt igitur solida primordia simplicitate.
>
> (609)

The first principles, then, are solid and simple.

Indivisible Magnitudes

But this conclusion is surely identical with what Bailey takes to be the first premise of the argument—"the atom cannot be divided." Moreover, the opening moves of the argument, in Bailey's account, are utterly fantastic: the atom cannot be divided, hence (*a fortiori*) its extreme point cannot be divided, hence the latter must be without parts. But the atom *can* be divided, in the sense required here of theoretical division into parts; indeed the entity whose partlessness is supposed to be deduced *a fortiori* is itself part of the atom! Confusion can hardly go further.

We must therefore reject Bailey's explanation of the opening sentences. Can we, without tampering with the text, find a better one? Ernout, who is the only other *commentator* I can find who retains the traditional reading, does not explain how he thinks Lucretius arrives at the partlessness and minimal size of the *cacumen*. I presume his view is that Lucretius, if pressed, would defend these propositions by means of the argument employed by Epicurus (see above p. 17) and later on in the same book by himself (see above' p. 28)—the argument from analogy with the *sensible* minimum. Lucretius' causal connection *quoniam* would then not be genuinely causal, but would be equivalent to a coordinating conjunction "the atom has an extreme point, *and* this is without parts."

On this assumption, we are asked to believe that although Lucretius knew a good argument for the existence of minimal parts and used it later on (746ff.), at the first and most important mention of this doctrine he offered no argument at all. I find this very improbable.

I therefore agree with those (Munro, Giussani, and Bailey in his 1922 edition) who mark a lacuna between 599 and 600. To fill the lacuna we must follow the guidance of the two passages (Epicurus *Letter to Herodotus* §§56-58 and Lucretius 1.747-752) just mentioned. The clause beginning *quoniam* should contain some proposition about the extreme point of a visible body, such that the existence of a *theoretical* minimum in the atom can reasonably be inferred from it. Munro suggested the following, on the supposition that the two lines fell out by homoeoteleuton:

tum porro quoniam est extremum quodque cacumen
⟨corporibus, quod iam nobis minimum esse videtur,

The Evidence of Lucretius on the Theory of Minimal Parts

debet item ratione pari minimum esse cacumen⟩
corporis illius quod nostri cernere sensus
iam nequeunt: id nimirum . . . etc.

This seems to me on the right lines, though I should prefer something which stated explicitly that the first *corpora* are visible. Munro translates the lines as follows: "Then again since there is ever a bounding point ⟨to bodies, which appears to us to be a least, there ought in the same way to be a bounding point the least conceivable⟩ to that first body which already is beyond what our senses can perceive."

The first step in the argument, if this reconstruction of it is correct, is from perceptible bodies to theoretical bodies, as it is in Epicurus himself. We *see* that a visible body has an extremity which is the minimum perceptible quantity; so a theoretical body must have an extremity which is the minimum conceivable quantity. And to say that it is the minimum conceivable quantity is to say that it has no parts, since any part is smaller than the whole. The argument is, admittedly, very greatly compressed as compared with the passage of Epicurus; one wishes it were more explicit.

Having stated that the invisible atom has a *cacumen* which is without parts and is the smallest conceivable quantity, Lucretius goes on to show—or to assert—that the *cacumen* has no separate existence:

> . . . nec fuit umquam
> per se secretum neque posthac esse valebit,
> alterius quoniamst ipsum pars primaque et una
> inde aliae atque aliae similes ex ordine partes
> agmine condenso naturam corporis explent,
> quae quoniam per se nequeunt constare, necessest
> haerere unde queant nulla ratione revelli.
>
> (602-608)

nor was it ever segregated by itself, nor can it be so in the future, since it is itself part of something else, a single first part, and starting from it other similar parts, one after another in order, in a close-packed row, fill out the body's nature; and since they cannot exist by themselves, they must necessarily cohere so that they can never be torn apart.

There is no corresponding argument in Epicurus' *Letter*; he merely says: (F) "but it is impossible that there should ever be a process of

Indivisible Magnitudes

composition out of these minima having motion."

Lucretius' argument is not very clear: the difficulty lies mainly in the words *primaque et una*. Are they to be regarded as belonging to the next line (*inde aliae atque aliae*, etc.)? If so, they are not part of the proof that the minimum part cannot exist in independence: this proof would be limited to the words *alterius quoniamst ipsum pars*. The extremity can never exist in separation from the body whose extremity it is, because it is itself—i.e., in its very nature—part of something else.

As an argument for the inseparability of the extremity, this seems to beg the question. Perhaps the reader is supposed to supply another argument from the analogy of sensible objects: the visible minimum is something that can *only* be perceived as the extremity of something larger (Epicurus makes this point explicitly, in D 1)—hence the theoretical minimum also "is *essentially* part of something else."

Since the argument is, on this view, a very weak one, it is tempting to bring the words *primaque et una* into it, in the hope that they may strengthen it a little. This is Giussani's solution. "Non basta essere *pars* per essere inseparabile; bisogna essere una *pars* la cui essenza sia appunto di non essere altro che *pars*, quindi non composta, non risultante alla sua volta di *partes*, quindi *prima pars*; e *una* s'intende di *unita interiore*, appunto non risultando di parti."

This is attractive, but it has the weakness that it separates *prima* from *inde aliae atque aliae . . . partes*; for it takes *prima* in the sense of "primary" or "elementary," and all the *aliae partes* are of course primary in this sense. But the natural way of reading the Latin is to take *prima . . . inde aliae atque aliae* as stating successive steps in a series.

If we look at the *Letter to Herodotus* for guidance, we find some confirmation of each of these interpretations of *prima*. In D 3, speaking of visible minima, Epicurus says "we study these in order, beginning with the first." But he uses πρῶτον in the sense of "primary" a few lines further on: "further, we must take these minimum indivisible limits as providing, for larger and smaller things, the standard of measurement of their lengths, being themselves the primary units."

The Evidence of Lucretius on the Theory of Minimal Parts

I am unable to solve this problem, and can only say that *somehow* Lucretius believes it to be established that the minimum part cannot possibly exist in separation. From this he goes on to his conclusion:

> sunt igitur solida primordia simplicitate
> quae minimis stipata cohaerent partibus arte,
> non ex illarum conventu conciliata,
> sed magis aeterna pollentia simplicitate,
> unde neque avelli quicquam neque deminui iam
> concedit natura reservans semina rebus.
>
> (609-614)

The first principles, then, are solid and simple; they consist of least parts tightly compacted and compressed—not compounded by the coming together of these parts, but rather enduring in everlasting simplicity; from them nothing is permitted to be torn away or diminished, by nature which preserves the seeds of things.

This then is a "proof" of the *solida simplicitas* of the atom. Visible objects have an extremity which is the ultimate limit of visibility; similarly atoms, which are conceivable but invisible objects, have an extremity which is the ultimate limit of conceivability. But such extremities are in principle inseparable from the atoms whose extremities they are, and the atoms are made up of rows of parts exactly similar to these extremities. No part of an atom, therefore, can be separated from it; the atom has *solida simplicitas*.

If this is indeed the argument, then it is a poor one. The premise "the extremity cannot be separated" is apparently asserted without a proper argument, as we have observed; and the possibility that, even if the minimum part is inseparable, the atom might have *other* separable parts is not considered. Nevertheless it is less vicious in this form than the blatant *petitio principii* which Bailey found in it.

THE next section is easier to understand but no better grounded.

> praeterea nisi erit minimum, parvissima quaeque
> corpora constabunt ex partibus infinitis,
> quippe ubi dimidiae partis pars semper habebit
> dimidiam partem nec res praefiniet ulla.
> ergo rerum inter summam minimamque quid escit?

Indivisible Magnitudes

nil erit ut distet; nam quamvis funditus omnis
summa sit infinita, tamen, parvissima quae sunt
ex infinitis constabunt partibus aeque.
quod quoniam ratio reclamat vera negatque
credere posse animum, victus fateare necessest
esse ea quae nullis iam praedita partibus exstent
et minima constent natura. quae quoniam sunt,
illa quoque esse tibi solida atque aeterna fatendum.

(615-627)

Furthermore, unless there is to be a minimum, the smallest bodies will consist of infinite parts, since the half of a half will always have its half, and nothing will put an end to this. So what difference is there between the sum and the smallest of things? There will be nothing to distinguish them. For though the whole sum is certainly infinite, yet the things which are smallest will equally consist of infinite parts. Since true reason rejects this, and says the mind cannot believe it, you must yield and acknowledge that there are things which exist with no parts, whose nature is the minimum. Since *these* exist, those also exist, you must admit—the solid and eternal atoms.

The main part of this argument is devoted to proving the existence of *minimae partes*. The last line and a half contain the step which takes us from the conclusion of this argument to the further conclusion that there exist solid, eternal atoms. This step presupposes the assertion, made in the preceding "proof," that the *minimae partes* cannot exist independently.

The argument for the existence of *minimae partes* is worth a little attention, since it seems to be something not found in the Letter to Herodotus. The argument is simply this: if everything is infinitely divisible, then the smallest bodies as well as the largest will be composed of an infinite number of parts, and there will be no difference between them.

This has been said to be directed against the Stoics. Chrysippus, we are told, held "bodies" to be infinitely divisible, not in the sense that a body could be divided into an infinite number of parts, but in the sense that there was no limit to division.*[1] It followed from this, as he observed, that there was no sense in saying that the whole of any extended magnitude contained more parts than any one of

---

* Please see end of chapter for numbered references.

The Evidence of Lucretius on the Theory of Minimal Parts

its parts. "Man does not consist of more parts than his finger, nor the cosmos of more parts than a man; for division of bodies continues to infinity, and of infinities none is greater or smaller than others."[2] This Stoic doctrine is a more precise and deliberate formulation of a principle first announced by Anaxagoras: [3] "Of the small there is no smallest, but always a smaller, since what exists cannot cease to exist; also there is always a larger than the large. And it [sc. the large] is equal to the small in number . . . ." As Professor Sambursky points out, Anaxagoras' proposition occurs in the context of his theory of "seeds," and its significance in this context is not that *any* extended magnitude, however large or small, may be said to have an infinite number of parts, but that everything, however large or small, must have in it a portion of everything. That this is its significance can be seen from its second occurrence: [4] "And because there are equal portions of the large and the small, thus also everything must be in everything." It is worth noting, too, that Chrysippus appears to have avoided saying that two infinities are *equal*; he said that no infinity is *greater or smaller* than another. This is significant, in view of his use of the concept "neither equal nor unequal" in handling problems concerned with convergence on a limit.[5]

It is assumed by the editors that Lucretius has this Stoic doctrine in mind here, but I doubt if they are right. It can be shown that Lucretius attacks specifically Stoic doctrines much less often than is usually thought.[6] It is therefore worth pointing to two non-Stoic sources which may be connected with what Lucretius writes. In the *Physics*,[7] Aristotle argues that it is impossible that the infinite should exist as an actual being, for in that case any part of it you like to take will be infinite, and it is impossible for the same thing to be many infinities. In the pseudo-Aristotelian *On Indivisible Lines*, which we shall look at again in chapter 7, the first of the arguments (968 a 2 ff.) for the existence of indivisible lines is quite similar to Lucretius' argument. The main point in this, as in Lucretius, is that there will be no difference between the large and the small if both consist of infinitely numerous parts. If this treatise is concerned with the theory of Xenocrates, as is usually believed, it may well be that Lucretius took his argument from an Epicurean source which did not refer

Indivisible Magnitudes

to the Stoics at all, but to an earlier stage in the history of the divisibility problem.

However that may be, how does Lucretius answer his opponents? He shows that the doctrine of infinite divisibility entails that both the largest and the smallest body have infinite parts, and then merely exclaims that "the reason rejects this and says the mind can't believe it." This is not an argument at all. But it is possible to see why he finds the doctrine incredible. The idea of an infinite *potentiality* for division, never realizable, was repugnant to the Epicurean mind. To say that a body is infinitely divisible is (for an Epicurean, but not for a Stoic or an Aristotelian) to say that it consists of infinitely numerous parts; and it is hard to imagine that both the largest and the smallest body must contain the same number of *actual* parts.

THE third argument in this section is described by Bailey as "very much compressed and extremely obscure."

> denique si minimas in partis cuncta resolvi
> cogere consuesset rerum natura creatrix,
> iam nil ex illis eadem reparare valeret
> propterea quia, quae nullis sunt partibus aucta,
> non possunt ea quae debet genitalis habere
> materies, varios conexus pondera plagas
> concursus motus, per quae res quaeque geruntur.
>
> (628–634)

> Finally, if nature the creator of the world had been accustomed to allow all things to be dissolved into minimal parts, she would then be unable to remake anything out of those parts, because things which are not extended by possession of parts cannot have—what generative substance must have—those various connections, weights, collisions, unions, and motions through which all things are done.

In this passage, Bailey maintains, Lucretius replies to a suggestion that the atom may be *divisible* into its minimal parts, and so lack *soliditas*, *aeternitas*, and *simplicitas*. His reply is that this is impossible, since the *minimae partes*, having themselves no parts, could not move, meet, and unite so as to form things. The support for this assertion,

The Evidence of Lucretius on the Theory of Minimal Parts

unexpressed by Lucretius, is to be found, in Bailey's view, in the "general conception of existence implied in the theory of the atom and its *minimae partes*. Only that which has parts can have material or corporeal existence and therefore possess weight, which is the cause of movement, and so through movement undergo the collisions with other bodies, which are the cause of creation."

This interpretation raises several questions. If something must have parts if it is to have material or corporeal existence, then what sort of existence do the *minimae partes* have in Epicurean theory? According to Epicurus' "general conception of existence" (to use Bailey's phrase), they have inseparable existence; but this is precisely what is being doubted in the present argument, and it cannot therefore be used as a premise in it. Why, moreover, should the partlessness of the *minimae partes* entail that they lack *weight*? Apart from this passage, I can find only one other suggestion that they lack weight, in Alexander's commentary on Aristotle's *Metaphysics*;[8] but Alexander's testimony on this matter, as I shall show later (p. 98), is too confused to be helpful. If the Epicureans *did* say that the *minimae partes* lack weight, it would, I imagine, be in the sense that they have no tendency to move *independently*. But this, again, is the conclusion of our present passage, and therefore should not be one of its premises.

I wonder therefore if we are to place the emphasis on the adjective *varios*. It is not easy to see why the minimal parts, because they themselves have no parts, should lack "connections, weight, impacts, collisions, motions." But we can quite well see why they should for this reason lack the *various* connections, etc., which *genitalis materies* should have. For having no parts they cannot differ from each other in shape; and it was a well-established principle of ancient atomism that the variety of sensible qualities could only be explained by the assumption of different shapes and sizes in the elementary particles.

This idea receives immediate confirmation in the next section of the poem. For Lucretius continues with a refutation of the earlier monistic philosophers, on the ground that a *single* primary substance cannot produce a variety of things; and the transition from the subject of *minimae partes* to his refutation of the monists is marked by

Indivisible Magnitudes

the word *quapropter*. This word has caused the commentators much difficulty—so much, indeed, that Brieger, Susemihl, and Giussani all fell back on the usual last resort and announced that there is a lacuna between the two sections. Bailey rejects the idea of a lacuna, but thinks *quapropter* either refers back to the whole of the previous argument establishing the existence and character of the atoms, or else is "merely resumptive, as in l. 334." I think, on the contrary, that it refers back to the words *propterea quia*, four lines before it. Lucretius says nature would be unable to make things out of minimal parts, *for the reason that* they lack that variety in connections, weight, impacts, collisions, and motions, which is necessary for *genitalis materies*. He uses this idea then in his transition to a new subject: *for this reason* (i.e., lack of the necessary variety) Heraclitus' fire cannot be the *materies* of things,

> nam cur tam variae res possent esse requiro,
> ex uno si sunt igni puroque creatae.
>
> (645-646)

For how, I ask, could such *various* things exist, if they are made of nothing but pure fire.

WE can now consider the relation between these three sections and also the place of the whole passage in Lucretius' argument. Bailey, in his commentary, divides up the portion from 503 to 634 into eleven "proofs"—i.e., "proofs" of the *aeternitas*, *soliditas*, and *simplicitas* of the atoms. Without discussing the problems raised by the first eight, we can observe that our three do not seem to be independent of each other and therefore hardly qualify as three separate "proofs." The first section argues for the existence of theoretical minima from the observed fact of perceptible minima, and asserts that the atom consists of rows of such minima, which are essentially inseparable. The second takes a new starting point, in pure theory, and argues that since infinite divisibility leads to a contradiction, there must be a partless minimum; it then adds, startlingly, that since these minima exist, we must admit the existence of eternal and solid atoms. The idea that atoms are made up of rows of such minima, which are *inseparable*, is taken entirely for granted. But the third

The Evidence of Lucretius on the Theory of Minimal Parts

section contains nothing but a demonstration that things cannot be resolved into these minima, instead of into their component atoms. This seems designed to fill in the gaps in the preceding sections, rather than to stand in its own right as an independent argument; for it reinforces the proposition that the minima cannot exist in separation, which, as we saw, was greatly in need of support.

In fact, we cannot help concluding that the whole section is messily put together. We have neither a set of coordinate, independent arguments nor a single articulated unit of reasoning. It looks very much as if Lucretius took his arguments from a variety of sources and failed to impose his own order on them. And this, of course, is entirely consistent with an obvious point which we have so far ignored—that the theory of minima was not originally part of the argument for the *existence* of physical atoms. It was mentioned in quite a different context by Epicurus, as we have seen, and it was not intended to solve the same kind of problem as physical atomism. If anything, one would have expected it to be a stumbling-block to a theory of physical atoms. We can easily imagine an objection on the lines of Lucretius' third section: if atoms have parts, why should they not be physically divisible into their parts? Lucretius seems to have tried to make of this theory not a stumbling-block but a positive support for his physical atomism—but with very dubious success.

There is nothing in all this to make us modify our interpretation of Epicurus. We have merely to note two arguments from Lucretius, of which we have found little or no trace in Epicurus. The first is the argument that the partless minima themselves cannot be the ultimate constituents of the physical world because they lack the necessary variety (if my interpretation is correct). The second is that infinite divisibility is impossible because it would entail that both a whole and each of its parts would equally consist of infinite parts, and hence would not differ.

AT 2.478–499, Lucretius uses the theory of *minimae partes* of the atom in an argument designed to prove that there is only a finite number of different shapes to be found among atoms. An infinite

Indivisible Magnitudes

variety of shapes could only be accounted for on the supposition that atoms might be infinitely large, since any given number of *minimae partes*, can account for only a *finite* number of shapes.

This passage may be considered as offering a serious objection to the interpretation of the theory of minimal parts defended by Professor Vlastos (1965). (I have briefly discussed this interpretation in chapter 1, p. 21.) Imagine one atom of four minimal parts in the same plane, thus:

and a second atom thus:

In the second atom we may regard the two lower parts as having been shifted, so to speak, one place to the right. But what is to prevent a shift of half a place to the right, thus?

It would seem that there must be an infinite number of such intermediate positions, and therefore an infinite variety of atomic shapes which can be produced by four minimal parts, *unless some special provision rules this out*. This third atom, which is certainly an impossibility in Epicurean theory, appears to satisfy both the "laws of nature" which Vlastos finds in the Epicurean theory (p. 138, and n. 87):

L(I) "Atoms are so constituted that variations in atomic lengths occur only in integral multiples of the smallest atomic length."

L(II) "Atoms are so constituted that variations in their shapes

The Evidence of Lucretius on the Theory of Minimal Parts

occur only in permutations of a modular unit of invariant size and shape."

Vlastos recognizes, indeed, that more is required (n. 114): "It is certainly assumed in Lucretius' reasoning that the shape of the minima remains invariant *and that their geometrical conjunctions are restricted* (e.g., contiguous edges and surfaces must be congruent)." (The italics are mine.)

Thus Lucretius' argument, according to Vlastos, needs an extra assumption to explain it—an assumption which is quite arbitrary and is not mentioned by Lucretius or any other source. But if the account of the Epicurean theory put forward in chapter 1 is correct, then Lucretius' argument is almost self-explanatory. The third atomic figure in the diagram above is ruled out because it involves the concept of *half* of a minimum.

Notes to Chapter 2

1. Stobaeus *Eclogae* 1, 142.2 = SVF 2.482.
2. Plutarch *De Communibus Notitiis* 1079 a = SVF 2.484.
3. Anaxagoras B 3.
4. Anaxagoras B 6.
5. Plutarch *De Communibus Notitiis* 1079 f = SVF 2.489.
6. See now D. J. Furley, "Lucretius and the Stoics," *Bulletin of the Institute of Classical Studies*, 13, 1966.
7. *Physics* Γ 5, 204 a 20*ff.*
8. Alexander *Metaphysics* 36.25–27.

PART II

CHAPTER 3

PYTHAGOREAN "ATOMISM"

I F the early Pythagoreans were atomists, then they were the first in the field. We should have to examine their atoms and the use they made of them, and turn a critical eye on the claims to originality which have been made for Leucippus and Democritus. We could not help regarding the growth of atomism as something begun by the Pythagoreans.

But I do not believe that the early Pythagoreans were atomists, in any but a trivial sense. There were certain important differences between their ideas and those of Leucippus and Democritus, which make it thoroughly misleading to apply the same name to both. Much of the demolition work on the hypothesis of Pythagorean atomism has already been done by others (particularly W. A. Heidel, Gregory Vlastos, and G. E. L. Owen) to whom I am greatly indebted.*[1] In this chapter and in chapter 5 I shall go over the most important evidence and try to strengthen the case they have made.

It seems certain that the Pythagoreans up to the time of Aristotle held the view that all things are made of number. Aristotle says[2] they thought that number is the first principle or cause of what exists, in the sense that number constituted both its matter and its properties and dispositions. That is to say, they did not distinguish, as Aristotle did, between material and formal elements; they said that number is the cause of things, and so, in Aristotle's opinion, wished to explain both material and formal properties by deriving them from number.

There are many senses in which this fundamental Pythagorean proposition may be taken. Aristotle himself complains, in a series of objections to those who assert that numbers are the first of things, that

> it has never been determined in which of two senses numbers are the causes of substances and of being—whether as boundaries, as

* Please see end of chapter for numbered references.

Pythagorean "Atomism"

points are of magnitudes . . . . or that harmony is a proportion of numbers and so is man and everything else.[a]

What are the alternatives offered by this ungrammatical sentence? Aristotle explains the first one:[3]

> . . . as Eurytus used to determine what was the number of what (e.g., *this* is the number of man, *that* of horse) by representing the shapes of living things by means of pebbles, like the people who bring numbers into the shapes of triangle and square.[b]

It is clear that Eurytus' procedure involved finding the number of pebbles with which one could make a sketch of the object in question in such a way as to distinguish it from other objects. In a comment on this passage, the writer called Pseudo-Alexander explains it in these words:

> For the sake of argument, suppose the number 250 is the definition of Man, and the number 360 that of Plant; having laid this down, he [sc. Eurytus] used to take two hundred and fifty pebbles, some green, some black, some red, and of all kinds of color in fact. Then he would smear the wall with pitch and make a shaded drawing of a man or a plant; he fixed some of the pebbles in the drawing of the face, some in the hands, and so on, and thus completed the representation of the man with pebbles equal in number to the monads which he said defined man.[c]

It is obvious, I think, that if Pseudo-Alexander is anywhere near right about Eurytus' procedure, there is really no question of this being "atomism." If 250 were the number of atoms in a man, it would follow that each atom weighed half a pound or more, and

---

[a] οὐθὲν δὲ διώρισται οὐδὲ ὁποτέρως οἱ ἀριθμοὶ αἴτιοι τῶν οὐσιῶν καὶ τοῦ εἶναι, πότερον ὡς ὅροι (οἷον αἱ στιγμαὶ τῶν μεγεθῶν) . . . ἢ ὅτι [ὁ] λόγος ἡ συμφωνία ἀριθμῶν, ὁμοίως δὲ καὶ ἄνθρωπος καὶ τῶν ἄλλων ἕκαστον; (Metaphysics N 5, 1092 b 8-15.)

[b] ὡς Εὔρυτος ἔταττε τίς ἀριθμὸς τίνος, οἷον ὁδὶ μὲν ἀνθρώπου ὁδὶ δὲ ἵππου ὥσπερ οἱ τοὺς ἀριθμοὺς ἄγοντες εἰς τὰ σχήματα τρίγωνον καὶ τετράγωνον, οὕτως ἀφομοιῶν ταῖς ψήφοις τὰς μορφὰς τῶν φυτῶν. (Ibid. 1092 b 10-12.)

[c] κείσθω λόγου χάριν ὅρος τοῦ ἀνθρώπου ὁ σν ἀριθμός, ὁ δὲ τξ τοῦ φυτοῦ. τοῦτο θεὶς ἐλάμβανε ψηφῖδας διακοσίας πεντήκοντα τὰς μὲν πρασίνας τὰς δὲ μελαίνας, ἄλλας ⟨δὲ⟩ ἐρυθρὰς καὶ ὅλως παντοδαποῖς χρώμασι κεχρωσμένας· εἶτα περιχρίων τὸν τοῖχον ἀσβέστῳ καὶ σκιαγραφῶν ἄνθρωπον καὶ φυτὸν οὕτως ἐπήγνυ τάσδε μὲν τὰς ψηφῖδας ἐν τῇ τοῦ προσώπου σκιαγραφίᾳ, τὰς δὲ ἐν τῇ τῶν χειρῶν, ἄλλας δὲ ἐν ἄλλοις, καὶ ἀπετέλει τὴν τοῦ μιμουμένου ἀνθρώπου διὰ ψηφίδων ἰσαρίθμων ταῖς μονάσιν, ἃς ὁρίζειν ἔφασκε τὸν ἄνθρωπον. (Pseudo-Alexander Metaphysics 827. 9ff.)

Indivisible Magnitudes

was correspondingly voluminous. This is fantastically implausible. Pseudo-Alexander may of course have invented the number 250 "for the sake of argument," as he says, but the fact still remains that nothing in his description supports the idea that Eurytus was trying to count a man's component atoms. Moreover, this commentator seems to know something about the subject, since he is able to report in a confident tone several details which do not appear elsewhere. There is perhaps no need to labor this point further; the arguments against reading atoms into the story here have been well put by J. E. Raven in his *Pythagoreans and Eleatics*, chapter 8.

What of Aristotle's second alternative—"that harmony is a proportion of numbers, and so is man and everything else"? Tradition credits Pythagoras himself with the discovery that the important musical intervals are expressible as simple numerical ratios. Aristotle means that as the ratio 2:1 defines the octave, so perhaps some other ratio defines man. The octave is a ratio between lengths of string (or some other material); Aristotle indicates later (1092 b 18) that the only way in which he could understand the ratio that defines man is as a ratio between constituent parts or tissues or perhaps of elementary bodies ("e.g., the essence of flesh or bone is number only in this way, three parts of fire and two of earth").

Aristotle hesitates, then, between two interpretations of the theory that number is the cause of all things: either both forms of the theory were advanced and no decision was taken between them or, more likely, his complaint is that the theory as proposed left it ambiguous which interpretation was to be preferred. Both interpretations are incompatible with atomism. The first asserts that the number of a thing is the number of points which can represent its shape; the second, that the defining "number" is a proportion. The first of these is clearly distinguished from atomism; atomism counts the particles right *through* a body, not just the bounding points. How the proportion theory contrasts with atomism will soon be explained further. Obviously, then, Aristotle had never heard of a theory asserting that the "number" of man is to be obtained by counting the indivisible particles in a man. If he knew of this interpretation, he would not have hesitated between two others.

Eurytus belongs to the late fifth or early fourth century B.C.;

Pythagorean "Atomism"

there is a century of Pythagoreanism to be accounted for before he arrived on the scene. It may be argued that Aristotle's evidence, as we have considered it so far, does not touch the earliest stages of development, though if this is so, Aristotle is strangely silent about this chronological reservation.

J. E. Raven asserts that the generation of Philolaüs and Eurytus undertook a "post-Zenonian revision" of Pythagorean theory. Before this revision, the Pythagorean theory of matter was quite different: it was based on the proposition that "all is number," in the sense that everything is defined by the number of "unit-point-atoms" it contains. "When . . . Aristotle speaks of number as . . . 'functioning as the material element in things,' or when as he often does he asserts that the Pythagoreans regarded the universe as consisting of numbers, he means that concrete objects were literally composed of aggregations of unit-point-atoms." [4] What is the evidence for this early Pythagoreanism?

Paul Tannéry was, I think, the first to attribute a kind of atomism to the Pythagoreans; and he did so in order to provide a target for Zeno's criticisms. "Pour les pythagoriciens, le point est l'unité ayant une position, ou autrement l'unité considérée dans l'espace. Il suit immédiatement de cette définition que le corps géométrique est une pluralité, somme de points. . . . D'ailleurs, à cette époque, aucune distinction ne pouvait encore exister entre un corps géométrique et un corps physique; les pythagoriciens se représentaient donc les corps de la nature comme formés par l'assemblage de points physiques."[5] Apart from the added bite which this hypothesis gives, so he thought, to Zeno's criticisms, Tannéry produced no more evidence for Pythagorean atomism.

Tannéry's evidence quite failed to support his conclusion, as many scholars have shown—particularly Gregory Vlastos (1953). The definition of a point as a "monad with position" is often mentioned by Aristotle, without being ascribed peculiarly to the Pythagoreans. As a matter of fact, Aristotle regards it as acceptable himself; at least, in his own definition, in *Metaphysics* Δ 6, he makes the point exactly analogous to the monad:

In general, the one is indivisible, either in quantity or in form. Now as to the indivisible in quantity, if it is totally indivisible and

Indivisible Magnitudes

without position, it is called a *monad*, but if it is totally indivisible and *has* position, it is called a *point*.[d]

If the mere consenting use of the "monad with position" for a point were enough to make an atomist, then Aristotle might be called an atomist.

However, Aristotle does differ from the Pythagoreans, by his own account. The exact nature of this difference has often been mistaken, I think, because Aristotle's analogy between the monad and the point is not exact, and it seems that he was not fully aware of the discrepancy. The monad, he says, is totally indivisible *and is also the unit of measure*; the point, on the other hand, is not a unit of measure. He explains this in a discussion of the meaning of "unity" which is of the greatest importance for our present problem.

> To be one is to be indivisible, . . . or to be whole and indivisible, but especially to be the first measure of each kind and above all of quantity. . . . Measure is that by which quantity is known, and quantity as such is known by means of a unit or by means of number; but all number is known by means of a unit, so that all quantity as such is known by the unit, and that by which ultimately quantities are known is *ipso facto* a unit; so the unit is the starting point of number as such. Hence in other cases too "measure" means that by which each thing is ultimately known, and the measure of each thing is a unit—in length, breadth, depth, weight, speed. . . . In all these cases, then, the measure and the starting point is one and indivisible, since even in lines they treat one foot as atomic.[e]

The unit of measure for number is called a monad; this, he adds, is the most exact of all such units, because the monad is *in every way indivisible*, whereas other units are used by analogy with it. It could

---

[d] πανταχοῦ δὲ τὸ ἓν ἢ τῷ ποσῷ ἢ τῷ εἴδει ἀδιαίρετον. τὸ μὲν οὖν κατὰ τὸ ποσὸν ἀδιαίρετον, τὸ μὲν πάντῃ καὶ ἄθετον λέγεται μονάς, τὸ δὲ πάντῃ καὶ θέσιν ἔχον στιγμή. (*Metaphysics* Δ 6, 1016 b 23-26.)

[e] τὸ ἑνὶ εἶναι τὸ ἀδιαιρέτῳ ἐστὶν εἶναι, . . . ἢ καὶ τὸ ὅλῳ καὶ ἀδιαιρέτῳ, μάλιστα δὲ τὸ μέτρῳ εἶναι πρώτῳ ἑκάστου γένους καὶ κυριώτατα τοῦ ποσοῦ . . . μέτρον γάρ ἐστιν ᾧ τὸ ποσὸν γιγνώσκεται· γιγνώσκεται δὲ ἢ ἑνὶ ἢ ἀριθμῷ τὸ ποσὸν ᾗ ποσόν, ὁ δὲ ἀριθμὸς ἅπας ἑνί, ὥστε πᾶν τὸ ποσὸν γιγνώσκεται ᾗ ποσὸν τῷ ἑνί, καὶ ᾧ πρώτῳ ποσὰ γιγνώσκεται, τοῦτο αὐτὸ ἕν· διὸ τὸ ἓν ἀριθμοῦ ἀρχὴ ᾗ ἀριθμός. ἐντεῦθεν δὲ καὶ ἐν τοῖς ἄλλοις λέγεται μέτρον ᾧ πρώτῳ ἕκαστον γιγνώσκεται, καὶ τὸ μέτρον ἑκάστου ἕν, ἐν μήκει, ἐν πλάτει, ἐν βάθει, ἐν βάρει, ἐν τάχει . . . ἐν πᾶσι δὴ τούτοις μέτρον καὶ ἀρχὴ ἕν τι καὶ ἀδιαίρετον, ἐπεὶ καὶ ἐν ταῖς γραμμαῖς χρῶνται ὡς ἀτόμῳ τῇ ποδιαίᾳ. (*Ibid.* I 1, 1052 b 16-33.)

Pythagorean "Atomism"

hardly be clearer: whereas the monad is the unit of measure for counting number, the *foot* (not the point) is the unit of measure for measuring lines. Aristotle adds that of course the foot is indivisible in a different sense (the text says "with respect to our sense perception") from the monad, because the foot is a continuous magnitude and everything continuous is divisible.

So the analogy between the point and the monad breaks down. But Aristotle continues to use it, and so it cannot be merely the use of the analogy that he objects to in the Pythagoreans. What he does object to is that they identify the abstract monad, which is the unit of measure in number, with the unit of measure in magnitude:

> The Pythagoreans say there is just one kind of number, namely the mathematical kind, only it is not separate but they say sensible substances are made out of it. They make the whole universe out of numbers, but not numbers composed of monads [i.e., monads in the Aristotelian sense, the altogether indivisible units of number] but they lay it down that their monads [i.e., the units of which *their* number is composed] have magnitude.[f]

The monad—that is, the abstract unit which is the "starting-point" of number—is altogether indivisible, in Aristotle's view. So when the Pythagoreans identified the monad with the unit of spatial magnitude, he took it to mean that the unit of spatial magnitude was also altogether indivisible; and this for him constitutes a great objection to their theory:[6]

> The Pythagorean way in one sense has fewer difficulties than those I have previously mentioned [sc. some theories of the Platonic school], but in another sense it has others peculiar to itself. Not making number *separate* removes many of the impossibilities; but that bodies are composed of numbers, and that this number is the number of mathematics—this is impossible. For (a) it is not true to say that there are indivisible magnitudes. And (b) even if this were the way of it, *monads* at least do not have magnitude, and how can there be a magnitude composed of indivisibles? Yet the number of arithmetic *is* made of monads, and they say that real

---

[f] καὶ οἱ Πυθαγόρειοι δ' ἕνα [φασὶν εἶναι ἀριθμόν], τὸν μαθηματικόν, πλὴν οὐ κεχωρισμένον ἀλλ' ἐκ τούτου τὰς αἰσθητὰς οὐσίας συνεστάναι φασίν· τὸν γὰρ ὅλον οὐρανὸν κατασκευάζουσιν ἐξ ἀριθμῶν, πλὴν οὐ μοναδικῶν, ἀλλὰ τὰς μονάδας ὑπολαμβάνουσιν ἔχειν μέγεθος. (*Ibid.* M 6, 1080 b 16-20.)

Indivisible Magnitudes

things *are* number—at least, they apply their theories to bodies on the supposition that bodies are made of those numbers.[g]

In this passage, what Aristotle attributes to the Pythagoreans themselves must be carefully distinguished from what he regards as the objectionable consequences of their view.[7] He certainly saddles them with the proposition that bodies are composed of numbers; and he says in the last clause that they treat the numbers of which bodies are composed as if they were the numbers of arithmetic. His last sentence states, as an afterthought, the explicit grounds on which his objections were made. Pythagorean number was just the ordinary arithmetical number. But (as all his readers know) the units of ordinary arithmetical numbers are the altogether indivisible monads. So the Pythagoreans were trying to compose their bodies out of indivisibles. But (a) there cannot be indivisible *magnitudes*—Aristotle has proved this elsewhere. And (b) *monads* have no magnitude anyway, being totally indivisible; and it is impossible to compose a magnitude from units that are totally indivisible and without magnitude.[8]

This analysis of Aristotle's argument shows, I think, that it was Aristotle himself who brought together the two properties "with magnitude" and "altogether indivisible." He did so because the *Pythagoreans* said that magnitudes are composed of monads, and *he* knew that monads are altogether indivisible units. I can see no ground here for attributing the almost technical phrase "atomic magnitudes" to the Pythagoreans. J. E. Raven (in *Pythagoreans and Eleatics*, p. 56) disagrees with this view, and adds: "In any case—and this is the important point—whether or not the Pythagoreans had actually spoken of ἄτομα μεγέθη, a belief in their existence does follow, as a logically inevitable consequence, from other propositions which they had undoubtedly accepted. If (i) bodies are composed of

---

[g] ὁ δὲ τῶν Πυθαγορείων τρόπος τῇ μὲν ἐλάττους ἔχει δυσχερείας τῶν πρότερον εἰρημένων, τῇ δὲ ἰδίας ἑτέρας. τὸ μὲν γὰρ μὴ χωριστὸν ποιεῖν τὸν ἀριθμὸν ἀφαιρεῖται πολλὰ τῶν ἀδυνάτων· τὸ δὲ τὰ σώματα ἐξ ἀριθμῶν εἶναι συγκείμενα, καὶ τὸν ἀριθμὸν τοῦτον εἶναι μαθηματικόν, ἀδύνατόν ἐστιν. οὔτε γὰρ ἄτομα μεγέθη λέγειν ἀληθές· εἴ θ' ὅτι μάλιστα τοῦτον ἔχει τὸν τρόπον, οὐχ αἵ γε μονάδες μέγεθος ἔχουσιν, μέγεθος δὲ ἐξ ἀδιαιρέτων συγκεῖσθαι πῶς δυνατόν; ἀλλὰ μὴν ὅ γ' ἀριθμητικὸς ἀριθμὸς μοναδικός ἐστιν· ἐκεῖνοι δὲ τὸν ἀριθμὸν τὰ ὄντα λέγουσιν· τὰ γοῦν θεωρήματα προσάπτουσι τοῖς σώμασιν ὡς ἐξ ἐκείνων ὄντων τῶν ἀριθμῶν. (Ibid. M 8, 1083 b 8-19.)

Pythagorean "Atomism"

units, (ii) the unit is indivisible (an axiom common to all Greek mathematics), and (iii) units have size, it is impossible to evade the two conclusions that Aristotle voices, that indivisible magnitudes exist and that units have weight." After the preceding discussion, it will perhaps be clear what has gone astray in this argument. It all depends on the sense of "unit" and the sense of "indivisible." As a matter of fact, Aristotle, or indeed any other Greek, could assent to these propositions, if the unit is the cubic foot, and "indivisible" is taken only in the weak sense in which Aristotle speaks of the foot as indivisible in the passage I have quoted from *Metaphysics* I 1. The assertion of these three propositions does *not* commit anyone to a belief in "atomic magnitudes" in the strong, technical sense —that is, altogether indivisible magnitudes. The thesis of "atomic magnitudes" follows only if the unit in question is altogether indivisible. Aristotle appears to attribute the thesis to the Pythagoreans (in an offhand sort of way, which would be hard to explain if they had asserted it explicitly) *only* because they identified the unit of arithmetic which he regarded as altogether indivisible with the unit of spatial measurement.

If my analysis of Aristotle's evidence is correct, it attributes atomism to the Pythagoreans *only* if their monads were altogether indivisible—that is, only if they used the term "monad" in the strict and precise sense in which it was used by Aristotle. I can see no reason to attribute such precision to them, and I am therefore not convinced that Aristotle's evidence has any tendency to make atomists out of them. On the contrary, I think there are good reasons for saying that they were *not* atomists, and we must now turn to this side of the argument.

It is well known that the Pythagoreans made numbers the elements of more than just concrete physical objects. Aristotle seems to know of statements which attribute number to justice, soul, mind, opportunity, and marriage; and these are only examples.[9] If concrete objects, though, are made of numbers in the sense that "each such object consisted of a definite number of unit-point atoms,"[10] how would the same numbers add up to justice, or to mind, or marriage? It is an objection that has been made often from Aristotle onward,[11] and has never been satisfactorily answered.

Indivisible Magnitudes

Gregory Vlastos writes,[12] "Our best clue to the whole meaning of the theory that 'things are numbers' is surely the Pythagorean discovery of the numerical formulae for the concordant intervals in music which must have been the scientific source of the whole theory. Here there could be no question of number-atomism. Thus the $\frac{1}{2}$ ratio for the octave would only mean that the numbers 1, 2 would be assigned to *any* pair of homogeneous strings the first of which was half the length of the second (cf. Van der Waerden, 'Die Harmonielehre der Pythagoreer,' *Hermes* 78, 1943, 163*ff*.). It would be absurd to suggest that the numbers 1, 2 could be considered by any mind, no matter how bemused by numerology, the numbers of the 'spatially extended units' composing the strings." It is not so implausible, of course, that 1, 2 should be the numbers of the "spatially extended units" of the strings, if the units may be feet or meters or whatever.[13] What is fantastic (I agree wholeheartedly with Vlastos) is that these should be the numbers of *atomic* units *composing* the strings.

It is clear, I think, that the Pythagorean method relied on finding proportions, and not on counting atomic constituents. It is the proportion 2:1 which constitutes the octave, no matter what the units may be. It is still fairly obscure what proportion could determine justice or marriage, but it is very much less difficult to conceive of this than of a group of atoms which might perhaps cease to make up justice and instead make a pyramid or a brick.

The emphasis on proportion is also proved by the Pythagoreans' known interest in *particular* numbers. For an atomist, who believes that things are made of a number of indivisible pieces, there is no special magic about the first few numbers. If one man or brick is larger than another, it simply means that the larger has more atoms than the smaller. Since portions large enough to be *seen* are as a rule obviously divisible, atoms must as a rule be too small to be seen by themselves; hence concrete objects must be composed of rather large numbers of atoms. The Pythagoreans, however, were fascinated by particular numbers, especially the decad. The importance of the decad emerges from many passages, but particularly from the long quotation from a work by Speusippus called "Pythagorean Numbers," preserved in the *Theologoumena Arithmetica*.[14] Speusippus

Pythagorean "Atomism"

is said to have used the writings of Philolaüs as his source; his evidence is therefore rather late for the present purpose, but it probably gives a true picture of an original Pythagorean way of thinking. "Ten," he says, "is a perfect number, and rightly and naturally all of us, Greeks and all mankind, end at ten whenever we are counting. . . ." Aristotle confirms[15] that for the Pythagoreans "ten is thought to be something perfect and to embrace in itself the whole nature of number." The reasons for this view of the number ten are set out by Speusippus; they are well known, and need not be repeated here.[16] It is not suggested in any of them that the magic of the number ten derives from or extends to concrete objects made of ten "unit-point-atoms": the reasons have to do with shapes and proportions.

Early Pythagorean cosmogony, in so far as it can now be discovered, also seems incompatible with atomism. As I have shown above, the thesis that the Pythagoreans were atomists depends on the assumption that the monad is for them something that has magnitude *and* is altogether indivisible. Yet this monad with magnitude is something created; and when the first of them is created the first action that it performs is to divide into two. At least, this appears to be the case; Aristotle says,[17] "When the one was composed (whether out of planes or surface or seed or elements they cannot describe), at once the nearest part of the Infinite was drawn in and limited by Limit." Elsewhere,[18] he observes that the void enters the cosmos from the Infinite, being in fact breathed in, and separates things off, "on the ground that void is a kind of separation and distinction between adjacent things; and this" (said the Pythagoreans) "happens first in number, for the void distinguishes their natures." Alexander, possibly quoting from Aristotle's lost work *On the Pythagoreans*, reports[19] that the monad first divided to form the dyad, and so on to form the triad, and the other numbers in succession. These witnesses and others who might be quoted leave many gaps in our knowledge, but it seems fairly clear that the number series was not regarded as primitive or elementary by the Pythagoreans: the numbers were somehow generated, in succession, by the imposition of Limit upon the Infinite, and the first limiting agent appears to have been the first Monad. "The first unit," Raven

Indivisible Magnitudes

writes,[20] "begins to breathe in and limit the Unlimited, and the first outcome of its activity is, *by its own division and extension*, the generation of the number 2" (the italics are mine). So much for the alleged axiom that the unit is absolutely indivisible.

The number two, for the Pythagoreans, is also the line, and three is the plane and four the solid; hence the generation of the number series is also the generation of solid bodies. This confusion between arithmetic and geometry, as it has often been said, is explained more easily when one remembers the habit of writing numbers by arranging dots or alphas in patterns. This habit is amply described by Cornford and Raven and needs no further elaboration; but the question arises whether this feature of Pythagoreanism itself proves that they were atomists. The answer is clearly no. Three is the triangle in the sense that any triangle presupposes the number three: it has three elements in it. There is nothing in the theory that requires the elements to be atoms.

If all the contrary evidence is ignored and it is still insisted that the Pythagoreans were atomists, then it must be asked how their theory was supposed to account for change in the natural world. We know that there was a cosmogony: the atoms were generated, not original. The original monad was not an atom, since it divided in order to produce two. None of the units first produced were atoms, if they went on dividing, as it seems they did. Eventually, however, these productive units must have died, as it were; they ceased breathing void in and ceased dividing; atoms were finally produced. At this stage it seems that a completely different set of processes must have taken over. If natural change was to be explained at all (and surely that must have been a feature of any cosmology after Anaximander?), it could only be by rearrangement of atoms. It seems to me quite extraordinary that we should hear nothing at all about these features of their philosophy. There is, after all, an enormous quantity of Pythagorean literature: I have never seen any mention of a distinction between monads which are productive and divisible and monads which are atomic, nor any account of natural change which differs from their cosmogony. I find the conclusion inescapable that there were no such distinctions.

One further point should perhaps be cleared away. The dis-

Pythagorean "Atomism"

covery of incommensurables is well known to have caused the Pythagoreans some embarrassment: the discoverer is sometimes said to have been drowned in punishment for some indiscreet revelation connected with this subject.[21] It should be observed that their embarrassment does not entail that they were atomists. Probably the discovery was first made through studying the pentagram, according to the arguments of von Fritz, Junge, and Heller. It was proved that each diagonal was cut by another in a ratio which could not be expressed in whole numbers of any units whatever. But this is true, and equally embarrassing to those who believe that "all is number," whatever the unit may be; it makes no difference whether the unit is atomic or not.

As a matter of fact, the earliest known method of determining proportion, which was probably the method by which incommensurability was first discovered, itself points to the use of varying, non-atomic units. The method is called ἀνταναίρεσις, or "reciprocal subtraction."[22] To determine the proportion between two lengths A and B, of which A is the greater, first subtract B from A as many times as possible, leaving a remainder C. Then subtract C from B in the same way leaving a remainder D. Then subtract D from C . . . until no remainder is left. The first length which can be subtracted thus without leaving any remainder is the unit in terms of which the proportion $A:B$ can be expressed. Clearly the unit will vary according to what these lengths A and B are; and (to clinch the point that these units are not atoms) the units composing A may be different if A is compared not to B but to a different length Z.

To sum up this chapter, then, I conclude that the Pythagoreans were no more atomists than Aristotle was. In some contexts, they held that the unit had magnitude; but this, I have argued, does not make them atomists, since they used variable units.

But this chapter has left out of account what has always been the main prop for the structure of Pythagorean atomism—Zeno. We must now turn to the Eleatics.

Indivisible Magnitudes

NOTES TO CHAPTER 3

1. Heidel (1940), Vlastos (1953 and 1959a), Owen (1957-58).
2. *Metaphysics* A5, 986 a 15.
3. Theophrastus (*Metaphysics* 6 a 19) tells us that the authority for attributing this to Eurytus is Archytas.
4. Kirk and Raven (1957), pp. 247-248.
5. Tannéry (1887), pp. 250-251.
6. My analysis of this passage is a little different from the usual one and requires some minor alterations to the punctuation given in Ross's text: see note 8.
7. My analysis may be contrasted with Raven's (1948), pp. 53-57.
8. See note 6. My paraphrase assumes that $ἀδιαιρέτων$ in line 15 is taken by Aristotle to be entailed by $οὐ \ldots μέγεθος\ ἔχουσιν$ in the previous line. The mutual entailment of "indivisible" and "without magnitude" is a commonplace for Aristotle.
9. *Metaphysics* A 5, 985 b 26; M 4, 1078 b 21.
10. Kirk and Raven (1957), p. 249.
11. *Metaphysics* A 8, 990 a 22.
12. Vlastos (1953), p. 33.
13. Raven (Kirk and Raven, 1957, p. 247) writes: "the Pythagoreans did indeed assume, even though the assumption was only tacit, that units are spatially extended." The evidence seems to show that Pythagorean units were sometimes but *not always* regarded as spatially extended.
14. Conveniently accessible in DK 44 A 13.
15. *Metaphysics* A 5, 986 a 8.
16. See Kirk and Raven (1957), pp. 229-230.
17. *Metaphysics* N 3, 1091 a 15.
18. *Physics* Δ 6, 213 b 22.
19. *Metaphysics* 512.37.
20. Raven (1948), p. 50.
21. DK 18 A 4.
22. See Junge (1958) for a very clear explanation of this.

CHAPTER 4

THE ELEATIC CONCEPT OF AN INDIVISIBLE BEING

THE first undoubted assertion of an indivisible being was made by Parmenides. Melissus, his supporter, gave a lead to the Atomists, as has often been observed, when he said: "If there were many things, they would have to be of the same description as I say the One is."*[1] How would Melissus describe his "One"? Was its indivisibility the same as that which belonged to Parmenides' "One"?

Parmenides announced his intention of proving that Being is a "single whole" in the opening lines of the "Way of Truth."[2] He kept his promise later:

> Nor is it divisible, since it *is*, all alike; it is not any *more* here, which would prevent it holding together, nor any *less*, but all is full of being. So being is continuous (holds together); for being is next to being.[a]

If I understand Parmenides' argument correctly, he tried to show first that there could be no coming-to-be or passing-away, and hence that there could be no degrees of being; a thing must either *be* in a total sense, or not be. Then he picked up this conclusion; if it *is* in a total sense, then there can be no differentiation in it at all. There is nothing but total being everywhere.[3] Thus a would-be divider can find nothing on which he can get a purchase. Wherever he considers what exists, it is all exactly the same.

> Study confidently things distant, as being all similarly present to the mind; for you will not cut off being from its clinging to being,

* Please see end of chapter for numbered references.

[a] οὐδὲ διαιρετόν ἐστιν, ἐπεὶ πᾶν ἐστιν ὅμοιον·
οὐδέ τι τῇ μᾶλλον, τό κεν εἴργοι μιν συνέχεσθαι,
οὐδέ τι χειρότερον, πᾶν δ' ἔμπλεόν ἐστιν ἐόντος.
τῷ ξυνεχὲς πᾶν ἐστιν· ἐὸν γὰρ ἐόντι πελάζει. (Parmenides B 8, 22-25.)

Indivisible Magnitudes

either as scattering itself everywhere in order, or as compacting itself.[b]

I think this means that there are no differentiations of density in the real, and so again no possible differentiation for the divider to get a purchase on. It is interesting that, although Parmenides used a word that means *physical* division ("cut off"), he clearly meant to refer to theoretical division; it is the *mind* which cannot make any distinctions between far and near.

If this is what Parmenides meant, could he at the same time have asserted that the real is a sphere? Perhaps not. One would think that the shape of a sphere must give a purchase to the divider, since at least the center can be distinguished from the circumference. For this reason among others, many scholars have refused to take literally Parmenides' words at the end of the "Way of Truth":

> Since there is a bounding limit, it is complete in every direction, like the mass of a well-rounded ball, equally balanced in all directions from the center. . . .[c]

Perhaps they are right not to take it literally—though a problem then arises about Empedocles, who appears to have taken it literally.[4] This question can fortunately be shelved, since Melissus came between Parmenides and the Atomists, and Melissus' position on this subject is much clearer. Melissus must be considered next, in spite of Zeno's chronological priority, because he had positive things to say about the Eleatic One, whereas Zeno was essentially negative and destructive.

According to the reports of his arguments by Simplicius, Melissus began, as Parmenides did, by arguing that being has no beginning or end, and so it must always exist.[5] This is clearly a point about temporal continuity, but Melissus seems to slip from temporal to spatial continuity in much the same mysterious way as Par-

[b] λεῦσσε δ' ὅμως ἀπεόντα νόῳ παρεόντα βεβαίως·
οὐ γὰρ ἀποτμήξει τὸ ἐὸν τοῦ ἐόντος ἔχεσθαι
οὔτε σκιδνάμενον πάντῃ πάντως κατὰ κόσμον
οὔτε συνιστάμενον. (Parmenides B 4.)

[c] αὐτὰρ ἐπεὶ πεῖρας πύματον, τετελεσμένον ἐστί
πάντοθεν, εὐκύκλου σφαίρης ἐναλίγκιον ὄγκῳ,
μεσσόθεν ἰσοπαλὲς πάντῃ. (Parmenides B 8, 42-44.)

The Eleatic Concept of an Indivisible Being

menides did (or so I think). Simplicius puts it in this way:

> Just as he says that "what came-to-be" is limited in substance, so also he says that "what always is" is infinite in substance; he has made this clear in these words: "but as it *is* always, so it must always be infinite in magnitude." [d]

After explaining that he takes the word "magnitude" in the sense of "substance" here, Simplicius continues:

> He made "infinite in substance" follow immediately upon "everlasting," in the following words: "Nothing that has a beginning or an end is either everlasting or infinite"—and so what has not, is infinite. And he deduced "one" from "infinite" in this way: "If it be not one it will have a boundary with something else." [e]

In another place Simplicius gives a fuller version of the last argument:

> If it were infinite, it would be one; for if it were two, they could not be infinite, but would have boundaries with respect to each other. [f]

J. E. Raven writes about these arguments of Melissus:[6] "He argues for the unity of the One, in other words, from its infinity. But that his real object was rather to prove its infinity from its unity is obvious enough even in these fragments. . . ." I cannot understand this at all. It is perfectly plain that the argument is from "infinite" to "one."[7]

The fact that he made the transition from "everlasting" to "infinite" apparently with no more elaborate argument than that anything without a beginning or an end *must* be infinite suggests, as Owen has observed,[8] that he thought of himself as agreeing with Parmenides, not as opposing him. However that may be, Eleatic

---

[d] ὅτι δὲ ὥσπερ τὸ ποτὲ γενόμενον πεπερασμένον τῇ οὐσίᾳ φησίν, οὕτω καὶ τὸ ἀεὶ ὂν ἄπειρον λέγει τῇ οὐσίᾳ, σαφὲς πεποίηκεν εἰπών "ἀλλ' ὥσπερ ἔστιν ἀεί, οὕτω καὶ τὸ μέγεθος ἄπειρον ἀεὶ χρὴ εἶναι." (Simplicius *Physics* 109.29ff. = Melissus B 3.)

[e] καὶ ἐφεξῆς δὲ τῷ ἀιδίῳ τὸ ἄπειρον κατὰ τὴν οὐσίαν συνέταξεν εἰπών "ἀρχήν τε καὶ τέλος ἔχον οὐδὲν οὔτε ἀίδιον οὔτε ἀπειρόν ἐστιν," ὥστε τὸ μὴ ἔχον ἄπειρόν ἐστιν. ἀπὸ δὲ τοῦ ἀπείρου τὸ ἓν συνελογίσατο ἐκ τοῦ "εἰ μὴ ἓν εἴη, περανεῖ πρὸς ἄλλο." (*Ibid.* 110.2ff. = Melissus B 4 and 5.)

[f] εἰ γὰρ ⟨ἄπειρον⟩ εἴη, ἓν εἴη ἄν· εἰ γὰρ δύο εἴη, οὐκ ἂν δύναιτο ἄπειρα εἶναι, ἀλλ' ἔχοι ἂν πείρατα πρὸς ἄλληλα. (Simplicius *De Caelo* 557.16 = Melissus B 6.)
⟨ ⟩ Burnet.

Indivisible Magnitudes

doctrine, as interpreted by Melissus, included the proposition that Being was infinite.

But was it infinite in magnitude? And if so, how could it have been indivisible? Simplicius was troubled by this problem, and we must return to his comments on Melissus. He could not conceal the fact that Melissus *said* that it was infinite in magnitude; but in introducing this quotation (as we have seen) Simplicius was careful to amend this to "infinite in substance." And at once he explains:

> By "magnitude" he [Melissus] does not mean extended magnitude, because he himself shows that being is indivisible: "if it has been divided," he says, "it moves; and if it moves it cannot *be*." No, by "magnitude" he means just the sublimity of its existence. For he intends being to be incorporeal, as he declared: "If it were existing, it must be one; being one it must have no body. If it had πάχος, it would have parts, and would no longer be one."[g]

Simplicius thus suggests two reasons why he refuses to ascribe to Melissus the proposition that the real is infinite in *magnitude*: first, that he said it was indivisible, and second, that he said it was incorporeal, had no πάχος, and had no parts.

Simplicius was not the last to be puzzled about these points; there has been a long debate among modern scholars. Three positions can be distinguished. One follows Simplicius in saying that when Melissus wrote "μέγεθος," he did not mean spatial extension; this course has recently been adopted by Gregory Vlastos,[9] who differs from Simplicius, however, in thinking that it means *temporal* extension or continuity. This interpretation seems to me very difficult to maintain without further evidence that "μέγεθος" can have this sense.

A second course is to attack the other horn of the dilemma, and to say that the proposition "if it had πάχος, it would have parts, and would no longer be one" was polemical in intent, and referred

---

[g] μέγεθος δὲ οὐ τὸ διαστατόν φησιν· αὐτὸς γὰρ ἀδιαίρετον τὸ ὂν δείκνυσιν· "εἰ γὰρ διῄρηται," φησί, "τὸ ἐόν, κινεῖται. κινούμενον δὲ οὐκ ἂν εἴη." ἀλλὰ μέγεθος τὸ δίαρμα αὐτὸ λέγει τῆς ὑποστάσεως. ὅτι γὰρ ἀσώματον εἶναι βούλεται τὸ ὄν, ἐδήλωσεν εἰπών "εἰ μὲν ὂν εἴη, δεῖ αὐτὸ ἓν εἶναι· ἓν δὲ ὂν δεῖ αὐτὸ σῶμα μὴ ἔχειν." (Simplicius *Physics* 109.32ff. = Melissus B 10 and 9.)

"ἓν ἐόν," φησί, "δεῖ αὐτὸ σῶμα μὴ ἔχειν. εἰ δὲ ἔχοι πάχος, ἔχοι ἂν μόρια καὶ οὐκέτι ἓν εἴη." (*Ibid.* 87.6ff. = Melissus B 9.)

The Eleatic Concept of an Indivisible Being

only to the alleged "ones" of a plurality; Melissus nevertheless believed that *his* "one" had body, either not observing or not caring that this left him open to his own attack. This is the solution preferred by Zeller and Burnet, and, more recently, by N. B. Booth.[10] It seems to me less plausible than the first, since it attributes an astounding blindness to Melissus *and* Simplicius, and is unsupported by any other evidence.

The third course is to attribute to Melissus *both* the proposition that the One Being had spatial extension *and* the proposition that it had no body, πάχος, or parts. This view has been defended recently by Raven and Owen,[11] and I think it is correct. "Body," on this view, means not just three-dimensional existence, but solidity; similarly, "πάχος" does not mean depth but bulk. Melissus denies that his Being has this kind of "body," and so is able to deny that it has parts. It will be asked how it was possible to say that something with magnitude had no parts. One reason was certainly that its incorporeality allowed no internal distinctions to be made. Was another reason that its infinity offered no starting point for a division? Probably so, since this concept features in Melissus' arguments, as we have seen.[12]

Notes to Chapter 4

1. B 8.
2. B 8, 4 οὖλον μουνογενές τε ... This reading is certainly preferable to ἔστι γὰρ οὐλομελές, which is printed in both DK and Kirk and Raven (1957). The γάρ is an importation of Plutarch's, and has no place in Parmenides' argument.
3. I follow G. E. L. Owen (1960) in referring πᾶν ἔστιν ὅμοιον (22) to πάμπαν πελέναι (11), and I think the argument has gained enormously in clarity since he pointed this out. But I find it hard to follow him in making the whole of this section (22-33) refer only to *temporal* distinctions. I think Parmenides moves from temporal to spatial distinctions in the same way as Melissus does (see below, p. 58).
4. Empedocles B 27, 28, 29.
5. Simplicius *Physics* 109.20. See the excellent discussion of this and other passages on Melissus by Harold Cherniss (1935), pp. 68*ff*.
6. Kirk and Raven (1957), p. 300.
7. Raven's quotation from Aristotle (*De Generatione et Corruptione* A 8, 325 a 14) proves nothing, since even if it does refer to Melissus it is clearly not a summary of these arguments.

Indivisible Magnitudes

8. Owen (1960), p. 100.
9. Vlastos (1953), pp. 34-35.
10. Booth (1958).
11. Raven in Kirk and Raven (1957), p. 303; Owen (1960), p. 101; see now Guthrie (1965), 110-113.
12. See Simplicius *Physics* 110.2*ff.*, quoted on p. 59.

CHAPTER 5

ZENO

THE arguments of Zeno are probably the most important part of Eleatic philosophy for this history. This chapter has two main purposes: to show that these arguments do not require us to believe in Pythagorean atomism, and to explain the background against which Leucippus and Democritus must be seen. We must also consider whether Zeno's arguments require us to make any modifications in our account of Eleatic Being—and this is a problem, because at first sight some of his destructive arguments appear to destroy the Eleatic One along with other "ones." I shall argue that Eleatic Being had in Zeno's eyes a saving quality which exempted it from his attacks.

This is not the occasion for a detailed presentation of the whole of Zeno's philosophy; I wish to examine only those arguments which I think are relevant to the origins of atomism. I have learned most about Zeno from H. D. P. Lee, Hermann Fränkel, G. E. L. Owen, and Gregory Vlastos.*[1] I accept Vlastos' interpretation of the argument against Plurality, and I agree with Owen about the overall tendency of Zeno's polemics. If anything new is added in this chapter, it is only in the interpretation of the Moving Rows paradox, and possibly in the assessment of Zeno's historical position.

Zeno's purpose is explained to us by Plato. In the *Parmenides*[2] it is said that Zeno's writings were intended to support Parmenides against ridicule by showing that the consequences of believing in the existence of Many were still more ridiculous than those of believing only in One. It is not always clear how the paradoxes that we hear of were supposed to serve this purpose; but in the following argument (Zeno B 2 and 1) this is clear enough.

The argument (which for convenience I will call "Argument

* Please see end of chapter for numbered references.

Indivisible Magnitudes

A") is preserved in disconnected pieces by Simplicius; it was reassembled convincingly by H. Fränkel and runs as follows (I use Fränkel's lettering of the sections of the argument):

If there are many things in existence:

(a) [Each of the many] has no magnitude, since each is the same as itself, and one.[a]

(b) [Simplicius first summarizes this step in the following words: "If a thing has no magnitude or bulk (πάχος) or mass, it would not exist." Then he gives the reasoning in full.] For if it were added to something else that does exist, it would make it no greater; for if it were of no magnitude, and were added, it could not contribute anything to magnitude. So it would follow that what was added was nothing. If when it is taken away the other thing is to be no smaller, and is to be no bigger when it is added, it is clear that what was added or taken away was nothing.[b]

(c) If it exists, each must necessarily have some magnitude and bulk; and one part of it must be distinct from another part. And the same story holds good for the outstanding part—it too will have magnitude and part of it will stand out. Indeed to say this once is to say it always, since no such part of it will be last or not related as one part to another part.[c]

(d) Hence if there are many things in existence, they must be both large and small—so small as to have no magnitude, and so large as to be infinite.[d]

For the detailed interpretation of this argument I must refer to the commentaries of Fränkel, Owen, and Vlastos. In the present

---

[a] [... προδείξας ὅτι] οὐδὲ ἔχει μέγεθος ἐκ τοῦ ἕκαστον τῶν πολλῶν ἑαυτῷ ταὐτὸν εἶναι καὶ ἕν. (Simplicius *Physics* 139.18-19.)

[b] δείκνυσιν, ὅτι οὗ μήτε μέγεθος μήτε πάχος μήτε ὄγκος μηθείς ἐστιν, οὐδ' ἂν εἴη τοῦτο. "εἰ γὰρ ἄλλῳ ὄντι," φησί, "προσγένοιτο, οὐδὲν ἂν μεῖζον ποιήσειεν· μεγέθους γὰρ μηδενὸς ὄντος, προσγενομένου δέ, οὐδὲν οἷόν τε εἰς μέγεθος ἐπιδοῦναι. καὶ οὕτως ἂν ἤδη τὸ προσγινόμενον οὐδὲν εἴη. εἰ δὲ ἀπογινομένου τὸ ἕτερον μηδὲν ἔλαττον ἔσται, μηδὲ αὖ προσγινομένου αὐξήσεται, δῆλον ὅτι τὸ προσγενόμενον οὐδὲν ἦν οὐδὲ τὸ ἀπογενόμενον." (Ibid. 10-15.)

[c] εἰ δὲ ἔστιν, ἀνάγκη ἕκαστον μέγεθός τι ἔχειν καὶ πάχος καὶ ἀπέχειν αὐτοῦ τὸ ἕτερον ἀπὸ τοῦ ἑτέρου. καὶ περὶ τοῦ προύχοντος ὁ αὐτὸς λόγος. καὶ γὰρ ἐκεῖνο ἕξει μέγεθος καὶ προέξει αὐτοῦ τι. ὅμοιον δὴ τοῦτο ἅπαξ τε εἰπεῖν καὶ ἀεὶ λέγειν· οὐδὲν γὰρ αὐτοῦ τοιοῦτον ἔσχατον ἔσται οὔτε ἕτερον πρὸς ἕτερον οὐκ ἔσται. (Ibid. 141.2-6.)

[d] οὕτως εἰ πολλά ἐστιν, ἀνάγκη αὐτὰ μικρά τε εἶναι καὶ μεγάλα, μικρὰ μὲν ὥστε μὴ ἔχειν μέγεθος, μεγάλα δὲ ὥστε ἄπειρα εἶναι. (Ibid. 6-8.)

Zeno

context I hope it will suffice if I offer a summary of Zeno's meaning, and a few comments on points of particular interest.

Zeno takes his opponents' premise, "many exist"—that is to say, what exists is not all one and indivisible, as the Eleatics said, but is divided up—and proves contradictory conclusions from it.

First (a) he argues that if this division of what exists is carried through, each one of the resultant plurality can have no magnitude. His reasons for asserting this are given in brief by Simplicius, and I shall return to them in a moment.

(b) Now he takes up the conclusion of the first step, and deduces from it that each one of a plurality thus arrived at would not even exist, because if added to or subtracted from what exists it would make no difference to it. This step seems to follow only if it is assumed that what *is* must have magnitude; and it has sometimes been objected that this is an illegitimate assumption for Zeno to make at this point. But the assumption has been made initially by the opponents who have stated that what *is* can be *divided up* to make a plurality. Zeno's point is that if a thing is a part of some whole, it must be of the same nature as that whole. If the original whole was something that had parts and so had divisible magnitude, then the parts themselves must be of the same type. Hence the unit arrived at in (a), which has been shown to have *no* magnitude, cannot be a part of the original whole.

(c) Hence it follows that if the unit in question exists, it must have divisible magnitude and distinguishable parts. And the same is true of any one of these parts, and so on for ever.

(d) Hence the alleged unit has infinite magnitude, since it is composed of an infinite number of parts, each having magnitude—and it has already been shown that it must have *no* magnitude.

Simplicius' account of the first step (a) in this argument is unfortunately omitted from some of the editions most widely used; so it may be worth repeating the reasons for believing that it does in fact fill this position. After quoting step (b), he continues:

> Zeno says this, not by way of abolishing the One, but meaning that each of the many actually has *infinite* [reading ἄπειρον for ἀπείρων] magnitude, since there must always be something before the part that is taken, because of infinite divisibility; and this he

65

Indivisible Magnitudes

shows after showing first [step (a)] that it has no magnitude since each of the many is the same as itself and one.[e]

The reading ἄπειρον (proposed by H. Fränkel) seems to me almost certain. The manuscript text "each of the many and infinite" has no place in the argument. With the amended reading it becomes clear that Simplicius is merely summarizing step (c)—Zeno's attempt to prove that a divisible magnitude must have infinite magnitude. So in this passage Simplicius quotes (b), follows it with a summary of (c), and then says this was preceded by (a).

But (a) is still obscure in itself; Simplicius' very brief summary must be supplemented from elsewhere.

The combination of (a) and (b) puzzled the ancient commentators; Simplicius' comment in the passage just quoted, "not by way of abolishing the one," is a reflection of this. Taken together, they apparently prove that if there is a One it must have no magnitude, and therefore it must be non-existent; and this, it seemed, would demolish the Eleatic One as well as the opponents' plurality. Eudemus, apparently, knew a tale of Zeno himself saying that if someone would tell him what the One is, he would be able to speak about "things which exist" (i.e., a plurality). Eudemus commented that Zeno's doubt probably arose because every *sensible object* can be said to be "many," either by having different predicates or by division, and he would not allow that the *point* is a "one" at all— and Eudemus referred to step (b) in support of this last assertion. (In passing, it should be noted that Zeno was not necessarily talking about points; he was talking about any unit without magnitude, and there is no need to assume any special reference to geometry. It was Aristotle (*Metaphysics* B 4, 1001 b 7) who mentioned the point and the monad in connection with this argument, and no doubt Eudemus followed him.) Eudemus himself apparently said that Zeno's argument "did away with" the One. But Alexander interpreted him as meaning that the argument attacked a plurality of real beings, rather than the One, "on the ground that there is no *one* among the existing things, and the many are a plurality composed of ones."[3]

[e] καὶ ταῦτα οὐχὶ τὸ ἓν ἀναιρῶν ὁ Ζήνων λέγει, ἀλλ' ὅτι μέγεθος ἔχει ἕκαστον τῶν πολλῶν καὶ ἄπειρον, τῷ πρὸ τοῦ λαμβανομένου ἀεί τι εἶναι διὰ τὴν ἐπ' ἄπειρον τομήν· ὃ δείκνυσι προδείξας ὅτι οὐδὲν ἔχει μέγεθος ἐκ τοῦ ἕκαστον τῶν πολλῶν ἑαυτῷ ταὐτὸν εἶναι καὶ ἕν. (*Ibid.* 139 16-19.)

Zeno

What seems to emerge from all this is a Zenonian argument approximately as follows. To be one is not to be many. If a thing is divisible into parts, it is many, and therefore not one.[4] So each one of the alleged plurality (for a plurality is a collection of ones) must be indivisible and have no parts. But it is only by having the same kind of being as the whole that these alleged units have a claim to be parts of the whole: and that means that they ought to have *divisible* being. Hence these indivisible units cannot be parts of the whole. But the whole is, on the pluralists' hypothesis, "what exists." Hence these units cannot be parts of what exists.

But if this, or something like it, was Zeno's argument, is it possible that it was not at once seen to be equally damaging to the Eleatic One as to the Ones of the opponents' plurality? The Eleatic One was certainly said to be one, and certainly had magnitude; yet this argument seems to require that the two properties are incompatible. Vlastos writes[5] of Zeno's assumption "that anything which does have size is at least *logically* divisible and has at least logically discriminable parts." Owen observes[6] that Zeno assumes without argument that the conjunction of size with theoretical indivisibility would be a contradiction. Are we to suppose, then, that Zeno overlooked the contradiction between this proposition and his own most cherished tenet? Such blindness or inconsistency seems as unlikely in Zeno as in Melissus, whom I have already discussed.[7] There must be some way of avoiding the contradiction.

It is probable *a priori* that Zeno took the same line as Melissus on this subject. We have already seen that Melissus believed in a One Being with magnitude but with no parts, and that the saving feature of *his* One Being was that it lacked bulk or solidity ($\pi\acute{\alpha}\chi os$). There is a strong hint in the fragments of Zeno that he would have based his defense on the same ground; for the word $\pi\acute{\alpha}\chi os$ appears twice in significant positions in Argument A: it occurs in Simplicius' summary of step (b), and in his verbatim report of step (c). In each case the word is a gratuitous addition, unless it has the important function I want to assign to it; for on the usual view magnitude alone is significant, so that "$\mu\acute{\epsilon}\gamma\epsilon\theta os\ \kappa\alpha\grave{\iota}\ \pi\acute{\alpha}\chi os$" must be a piece of unnecessary rhetoric.

Zeno's strategy, then, if I am right, was to attack the Pluralists

Indivisible Magnitudes

on the ground that their "Beings," having magnitude and *bulk*, could be shown to be both reducible to nothing and infinitely large. Eleatic Being would be exempt from this attack because it lacked bulk and therefore gave the divider no starting point for his division. The Pluralists' idea of Being included various kinds of qualitative differentiation, such as those attacked by Parmenides in the "Way of Truth" (B 8, especially 22-25, quoted at the beginning of ch. 4). The later Eleatics seem to use σῶμα and πάχος as compendious expressions for this property of the Pluralists' Being. Such Being must always allow differentiation, and must always be divisible into parts which have this same property; but the Eleatic Being allows no differentiation at all. (We shall see later that the Atomists found an answer in the assertion of indivisible and undifferentiated *units*, making up a differentiated and divisible whole.)

So far I have concentrated on the first half of Zeno's antinomy in Argument A: his "proof" that the units of a plurality must have no magnitude and bulk and so cannot be numbered among the things that exist. Now I turn briefly to the second half, in which he argues that the units must have infinite magnitude.

Step (c) appears to prove that each of the many is infinitely *divisible*. But this is not the same as the conclusion ascribed to Zeno, that each is infinitely *large*. Hermann Fränkel observes that this conclusion is "an obvious fallacy," and he therefore tries to find a meaning for "so large as to be infinite" such that the phrase does not imply infinite extension, but only the lack of a limit (πέρας). Whenever we think we may have reached the surface of a thing, we observe that this surface can still be subdivided; we never reach the true surface, the limit; hence the object is "limitless" or infinite. Nevertheless, "the total extension, as the modern mathematicians express it, converges to a certain sum." F. Solmsen recently has proposed taking "large" and "infinite" to describe each of the many in relation to the decrease *ad infinitum* of its parts which the progressive division brings into existence.[8]

To adopt a solution like this would be to accuse the ancient commentators of a great misunderstanding; for they certainly thought Zeno meant infinitely *large*. But more seriously, it would also be to rob Zeno's objection of all its force, except the purely verbal success

Zeno

of forcing the Pluralists to use the word ἄπειρον of their units. So long as they were not committed to infinite extension they might well be willing to make this concession.[9]

If we suppose that the commentators are right after all, and the argument is intended to show the infinite size of each unit produced by the division of a real thing, then clearly some premise has been omitted, either by Zeno or by the commentators, presumably on the ground that it is self-evident. The missing premise is one which Epicurus used in his argument for theoretical indivisibles (C 1—see ch. 1): "When someone once says that there are infinite parts in something, however small they may be, it is impossible to see how this can still be finite in size."

Gregory Vlastos, in a recent article,[10] has observed how very close together a false statement and a true statement can be on this subject. He contrasts the following two statements:

(1) The sum of an infinite number of terms, each of which has finite size, is infinitely large.
(2) The sum of an infinite number of terms, the smallest of which has finite size, is infinitely large.

The first of these is false; the second is true. Zeno's mistake is understandable enough. Aristotle was the first, so far as the records show, to understand the principle of the infinite convergent series. And even he did not explain it so well that mistakes were no longer possible, for he did not convince Epicurus, as we have seen, and even Simplicius seems to assent to the first statement.[11]

Argument A, then, attacks the proposition that the Real might be divided up spatially into a plurality of real things, and that such a division might be completed. Zeno tried to prove that such things must be both without any magnitude, and infinite in magnitude. Insofar as it is effective, the argument is a refutation of atomism, as well as other forms of pluralism. This is therefore an argument which Leucippus and Democritus had to evade or refute. How they did so will be explained later.

FOUR famous arguments by Zeno are grouped together by Aristotle, our only authority, under the heading "arguments about motion."[12]

Indivisible Magnitudes

This heading need not, however, be taken too seriously; it may well be Aristotle's own.[13] If it is possible to interpret these arguments as attacks on pluralism, such an interpretation should be preferred, if we are to follow the guidance of Plato about Zeno's purpose.[14]

The first paradox is the Dichotomy (sometimes called the Stadium).[15] It states that before you reach the end of the stadium you must reach a half-way mark, then the next half-way mark . . . and so on for ever, so that the end is never reached. (Alternatively, the argument may mean that you cannot even start, let alone finish, because you must first reach a half-way mark, before that, a mark half-way to *that* mark, . . . and so on. But this is for the moment unimportant.)

The Achilles paradox[16] points out that if the tortoise has a start on Achilles, Achilles can never catch up; for while Achilles covers the distance that initially separates them, the tortoise advances a little, and so on for ever.

Aristotle remarks that the Achilles paradox is the same as the Dichotomy, except that the former does not confine itself to division into halves. The point of both arguments, it might be said, is to draw a ridiculous conclusion from the supposition that divisibility goes on *ad infinitum*. This is the alternative to the concept of a division that can be completed. A question arises about the range of application of these paradoxes. Clearly they are parables in some sense: Zeno did not wish to make a point only about the stadium or only about Achilles and the tortoise (actually in the latter case Aristotle implies that Zeno used the terms "the quickest" and "the slowest"). I want to suggest that they were intended to be interpreted very generally indeed, as applicable to *anything* infinitely divisible in magnitude, and to *any* kind of division. There is confirmation of this suggestion in a passage from the pseudo-Aristotelian treatise *On Indivisible Lines*, which deserves quotation. One of the arguments for the existence of indivisible lines runs as follows:

> According to Zeno's argument there must be a magnitude without parts, if it is impossible in a finite time to touch an infinite number of things one by one, and if it is necessary that anything that moves arrives at the half-way point first, and if there *is* a half-way point in everything that is not without parts. [The reference

to the Dichotomy is clear enough.] But if something moving on a line touches an infinite number of things in a finite time, and something moving more rapidly traverses more than something slower in an equal time, and the motion of thought is most rapid, then thought could touch upon an infinite number of things one by one in a finite time; so if thought's touching one by one is the same thing as counting, it is possible to count an infinite number of things in a finite time. If this is impossible, there must be an indivisible line.[f]

It is interesting, at least, that the movement of *thought* is the example chosen here. The choice would be explained if this were the common and perhaps the original way of interpreting the Dichotomy paradox.

Probably we have in these paradoxes of Zeno an early reference to what Epicurus calls μετάβασις:[17] that is, the process of "running over" or "scanning" an object mentally from side to side. When Epicurus says that we have to do away with infinite μετάβασις, he must have Zeno's arguments, or some repetition of them, in mind. Zeno would suggest to him that if the mind must touch upon an infinite number of divisions as it runs over an object, it can never reach the end of its task; moreover, according to the second part of Zeno's Argument A, the object itself must be infinitely large.

The third of the "arguments about motion" is called the Flying Arrow.[18] The text of this is doubtful. Roughly, the argument states that when a thing occupies a place equal to itself, it is at rest; but a flying arrow is always occupying a place equal to itself "now"—that is, at any given moment; so the flying arrow must be motionless. The point is that if the arrow is at rest at *every* moment in a stretch of time, then it is at rest throughout that stretch of time.

"It is easy to see," J. E. Raven writes,[19] "that this argument, unlike the two that precede it, treats time and space alike as composed of indivisible minima." I disagree. It certainly treats time as

---

[f] ἔτι δὲ κατὰ τὸν Ζήνωνος λόγον ἀνάγκη τι μέγεθος ἀμερὲς εἶναι, εἴπερ ἀδύνατον μὲν ἐν πεπερασμένῳ χρόνῳ ἀπείρων ἅψασθαι, καθ' ἕκαστον ἁπτόμενον, ἀνάγκη δ' ἐπὶ τὸ ἥμισυ πρότερον ἀφικνεῖσθαι τὸ κινούμενον, τοῦ δὲ μὴ ἀμεροῦς πάντως ἐστὶν ἥμισυ. εἰ δὲ καὶ ἅπτεται τῶν ἀπείρων ἐν πεπερασμένῳ χρόνῳ τὸ ἐπὶ τῆς γραμμῆς φερόμενον, τὸ δὲ θᾶττον ἐν τῷ ἴσῳ χρόνῳ πλεῖον διανύει, ταχίστη δ' ἡ τῆς διανοίας κίνησις, κἂν ἡ διάνοια τῶν ἀπείρων ἐφάπτοιτο καθ' ἕκαστον ἐν πεπερασμένῳ χρόνῳ, ὥστε εἰ τὸ καθ' ἕκαστον ἅπτεσθαι τὴν διάνοιαν ἀριθμεῖν ἐστίν, ἐνδέχεται ἀριθμεῖν τὰ ἄπειρα ἐν πεπερασμένῳ χρόνῳ. εἰ δὲ τοῦτο ἀδύνατον, εἴη ἄν τις ἄτομος γραμμή. (*On Indivisible Lines* 968 a 18ff.)

Indivisible Magnitudes

containing indivisible moments. But these moments cannot have any magnitude at all without destroying the plausibility of the arrow's being stationary, and hence they cannot be minima. On the nature of *space* I cannot see that it has anything to say at all. The point seems to be to draw a ridiculous conclusion from the mere fact of making distinctions *in time*. If you distinguish one moment of time from another, then Zeno will prove that at either of these moments, and then at *all* of them in a stretch of time, "the flying arrow is stationary." Since Parmenides was anxious to rule out temporal as well as spatial distinctions, Zeno's support would seem to be well enough directed.

The fourth of the arguments about motion will detain us longer, because it is the most misunderstood.[20] The Moving-Rows paradox (sometimes called "the Stadium") is reported by Aristotle, but perhaps most easily expounded with the help of Simplicius' diagram.

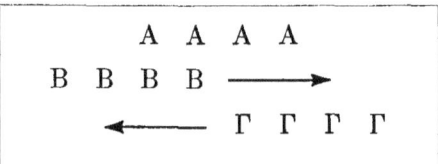

The A's represent four bodies of equal size, stationary; the B's are four bodies of this same size moving right, and the Γ's four equal bodies moving left at the same speed. The diagram represents the opening stage of the problem: at the end of the problem the leading B has passed the right A, and the leading Γ has passed the left A. At the end, says Aristotle,[21]

> ... it follows that the leading B and the leading Γ are at the end simultaneously, moving past each other. And it follows that this Γ has gone past all the B's, but the leading B has gone past half the A's; so that the time is half, since each is an equal time opposite each. And at the same time it follows that the B's have passed all the Γ's, since the leading Γ and the leading B will be simultaneously at their opposite ends, being the same time (says Zeno) opposite each of the B's as opposite each of the A's, since both lots are an equal time opposite the A's.[g]

[g] συμβαίνει δὴ τὸ πρῶτον Β ἅμα ἐπὶ τῷ ἐσχάτῳ εἶναι καὶ τὸ πρῶτον Γ, παρ' ἄλληλα κινουμένων. συμβαίνει δὲ καὶ τὸ Γ παρὰ πάντα τὰ Β διεξεληλυθέναι, τὰ δὲ Β παρὰ τὰ ⟨Α⟩ ἡμίση· ὥστε ἥμισυν εἶναι τὸν χρόνον· ἴσον γὰρ ἑκάτερόν ἐστι παρ'

Zeno

This argument, according to Aristotle, was to prove that "half the time is equal to double."[22] As a matter of Greek idiom, this may mean either $t/2=t$, or $t/2=2t$. It appears to be the latter that Aristotle has in mind. There is first the proof that "the time is half." "The time" is four time units (in our diagram)—the time taken by the leading Γ to pass all four B's. But in that time the leading B has passed only 2 A's. Therefore "the time is half, since each is an equal time opposite each" (the reasoning of this last clause will be discussed in a moment). If the proof were simply that $t=t/2$, it would now be completed—but Aristotle continues. H. D. P. Lee, in his very lucid and detailed exposition of this problem, argues for the interpretation $t=t/2$. I disagree with him without relish; but even though Aristotle did not say explicitly "so the time is double" at the end of it, it seems to me that he thought the second part was out to prove something new, since he made the second part *follow* his statement "the time is half."

Now it is generally agreed that this argument of Zeno's has no force at all *unless it is directed against a theory of indivisible magnitudes*. Once this condition is granted, it is clever and to the point; without it, it is puerile. Aristotle remarks,[23] "There is a mistake in supposing that to move past a stationary magnitude and an equal magnitude in motion takes an equal time." But suppose all these magnitudes are atoms, and there are also indivisible units of time. Then to move the distance of half an atom, or to take half a time unit, will both be logically impossible. Then there would be a real problem in knowing how the leading B has moved past four Γ's, but only two A's.

This is an attractive idea, because Zeno is a popular hero, and we want to hear nothing but good of him. But there is no sign whatever in our texts that these units were supposed to be indivisible; the mere use of the word "ὄγκος" certainly does not prove it, as some have argued. Moreover, it certainly did not occur to Aristotle that Zeno was speaking of indivisible units, even though he was well

---

ἕκαστον. ἅμα δὲ συμβαίνει τὰ Β παρὰ πάντα τὰ Γ παρεληλυθέναι· ἅμα γὰρ ἔσται τὸ πρῶτον Γ καὶ τὸ πρῶτον Β ἐπὶ τοῖς ἐναντίοις ἐσχάτοις, ἴσον χρόνον παρ' ἕκαστον γινόμενον τῶν Β ὅσον περ τῶν Α, ὥς φησι, διὰ τὸ ἀμφότερα ἴσον χρόνον παρὰ τὰ Α γίγνεσθαι. (*Physics* Z 9, 240 a 9ff.)

Indivisible Magnitudes

aware of the existence of such a theory in his own times, and also knew quite well that it was open to objections similar to those allegedly brought against it here by Zeno.[24]

But it is not enough merely to say that Aristotle may be right after all. Did the argument never have any plausibility at all? If so, it would be unique among Zeno's paradoxes, all of which have a certain persuasiveness. N. B. Booth,[25] who rightly, I think, rejects the atomistic view of this argument, can only suggest that "the idea of relative motion . . . at a time when motion had hardly been thought of, . . . cannot have been at all easy." But this is quite inadequate: it is enough to remark that the author of the Achilles paradox must have done *some* thinking about relative motion. Before the atomistic interpretation is killed, we must find some other analysis of the paradox which gives it an appearance of plausibility. This can, I think, be done.

There is a clue to Zeno's probable meaning in Aristotle's text, though it is often obscured by tendentious translations and emendations. The first half of the argument, as set out by Aristotle, depends on the premise "ἴσον γὰρ ἑκάτερόν ἐστι παρ' ἕκαστον," and the second on the premise "ἴσον χρόνον παρ' ἕκαστον γιγνόμενον τῶν Β ὅσονπερ τῶν Α, ὥς φησι, διὰ τὸ ἀμφότερα ἴσον χρόνον παρὰ τὰ Α γίγνεσθαι."[26] Lee translates the first premise "since each takes an equal time in passing each body"; in the second (following Ross) he omits the first part, as far as "ὥς φησι," as being a gloss, and translates "since both take an equal time in passing the A's." But the whole point, I think, lies in the use of a *static* vocabulary (ἐστι, γίγνεσθαι παρὰ ἕκαστον): the object "is opposite to," "lies against" the other—not "passes" the other. Zeno's argument was this. As the B's move past the A's, each B "is opposite to" each A for a certain time (call it m). Each Γ is also opposite to each A for the same time m, since the B's and the Γ's are moving at equal speeds. It follows that each Γ must be opposite to each B for the same time, *since they are both opposite to an A for this time*. Now the leading Γ passes all the B's in $4m$ (since it "is opposite to" each of the four for m): this Γ has been at it for $4m$. Meanwhile, though, the leading B has passed only two A's; it has only been at it for $2m$. So the time ($4m$) is half ($2m$); $t=t/2$. We have now proved that the

Zeno

time t is only $2m$; but during this time the leading B has passed all four Γ's—$4m$ again. So the time ($2m$) is double ($4m$); $t = 2t$.

The structure of this argument is reminiscent of the argument against plurality analyzed above. (There Zeno makes a case for thinking that units have no size: but in that case, they could not exist—so they must have size. But in that case they would be infinite.) The force of the argument, it seems to me, does not in any way depend on the indivisibility of the ὄγκοι, or the indivisibility of units of time. It depends only on the idea that a length can be divided up into sections, such that to traverse the length is to "be opposite to" each section in turn for a period of time, and that time can be divided up into such periods.

It is not, of course, a cogent argument. The essential step is that since a B and a Γ are opposite to the same A for the same time, they must be opposite to each other for that time; and this is fallacious. But it seems to me to have enough plausibility to stand alongside some others of Zeno's arguments.

I hope this interpretation of the Moving Rows will prove acceptable. It allows full weight to be given (for the first time, I think) to all the words of Aristotle's report; it frees Aristotle from a charge of gross misunderstanding; and it does not depend on any special assumption about Zeno's opponents. The purpose of the paradox is to show an unacceptable consequence of making temporal distinctions—but clearly it has something to say about spatial distinctions as well.

If my analysis of Zeno's arguments is approximately correct, only one of the arguments is directed against a theory of indivisible magnitudes, and that is Argument A. I doubt if the nature of this argument requires us to believe that someone before Zeno must have held an atomistic theory. The argument, as we have seen, seems to form one of a set, dealing with the alternative possibilities that the Real may be *completely* divided and that it may be divided *ad infinitum*. These features seem to be more like the result of an attempt to be exhaustive than the result of aiming at particular targets. At least, it must be conceded that the existence of one argument in

Indivisible Magnitudes

Zeno's philosophy which is directed against a completed division of the Real, is an inadequate foundation on which to rest the whole hypothesis of Pythagorean atomism.

But it is commonly stated that the Pythagoreans were not simply atomists but "unit-point-atomists"; that is, that they confused the geometrical point with the arithmetical unit and both with the physical atom[27] and that Zeno aimed to show up this confusion. The case against this view is put with great pungency by G. E. L. Owen:[28] The Pythagoreans, he observes, are credited "with failing to distinguish physical bodies from geometrical solids, and with holding about these solids *both* that they are infinitely divisible *and* that they are divisible into atomic bits, which bits *both* have magnitude *and* have the properties of points without magnitude. Zeno's arguments cannot have been directed against such a theory unless his whole program was misconceived. For in order to provide his arguments with a target a theory had to be produced which housed every or nearly every incompatible view on the divisibility of bodies. But the direct refutation of such a theory would be to show the absurdity of holding any two or more of these views concurrently. What Zeno does is to distinguish each view and refute it in isolation. In brief, his arguments seem designed to close not some but all avenues of escape to anyone holding the unremarkable belief that there is more than one thing in existence."

What avenues of escape were now left to the Pluralists? It is often supposed that one of them was to *accept* the hypothesis that the Real is infinitely divisible. Thus it is usually assumed that Anaxagoras' theory of the infinite divisibility of matter was an *answer* to Zeno and the other Eleatics.[29] I doubt this. Zeno pointed out some of the difficulties in infinite divisibility: if the parts reached have any magnitude at all, the object must be infinitely large—but if they have no magnitude, they cannot contribute anything at all to the sum. It seems to me that Anaxagoras had no answer to this dilemma—we shall see, in fact, that even Aristotle had some difficulty in finding one.[30] And it does not seem reasonable that Anaxagoras should blandly take over from Zeno as a prop for his philosophy something that Zeno had shown to be riddled with holes.

So I prefer to think that Zeno was answering Anaxagoras. The

Zeno

chronology of the two philosophers is so vague that I doubt if any objections can be brought on that account. It is perhaps significant that the two scholars who have done most work recently on the subject of divisibility, Luria and Mau, both take Anaxagoras to be *before* Zeno. The evidence connecting Zeno and Anaxagoras is fairly convincing,[31] but so far as I can see there is no certain answer to the question which of the two was answering the other. But perhaps it is not necessary to decide this question here.

Two escape routes were in fact tried. One was the assertion of a plurality of indivisible magnitudes, which will be investigated in the next chapter. The other was Aristotle's theory of the infinite divisibility of matter—not now the naïve theory of Anaxagoras, but a theory hedged carefully around with qualifications. This, too, will be explained in the next chapter.

Notes to Chapter 5

1. See Bibliography. I am particularly grateful to Professor Vlastos for sending me his duplicated notes on Zeno, as well as for his published articles.
2. 128 c = Kirk and Raven (1957), No. 365.
3. Eudemus quoted by Simplicius *Physics* 97 12*ff.* and 99.10*ff.* The passages are printed in DK 29 A 16 and 21.
4. For this part of the argument, cf. Melissus B 9, and Plato *Parmenides* 137 c 4–d 3.
5. Vlastos (1961), p. 29.
6. Owen (1957–58), p. 210.
7. Chapter 4, p. 60. Others attribute both of the contradictory propositions to Zeno, apparently with no qualms (e.g. Raven in Kirk and Raven (1957), p. 303).
8. Solmsen (1960), p. 172, n. 56.
9. If Zeno's argument is regarded as an *antimony*, it will not lose all its force, since there is still a contradiction between "of no magnitude" and "$ἄπειρον$ in this qualified sense." But its force as a *dilemma* will now be removed, since the Pluralists may now accept one of the alternatives.
10. Vlastos (1961).
11. Simplicius *Physics* 459.22; 462.3–5. See chapter 9 below.
12. *Physics* Z 9, 239 b 9*ff.* = DK 29 A 25 = Kirk and Raven (1957), No. 369.
13. It must be admitted, however, that although the heading "about motion" may be Aristotle's, the arguments must have been arranged in this *order* before *Physics* Z 9 was written; otherwise it would be hard to explain why Aristotle calls the Arrow argument the third (239 b 30), when he has already discussed it once by itself. Perhaps he could refer to a standard set of notes on Zeno: "$πρὸς\ τὰ\ Ζήνωνος$" is a title mentioned in the list of Aristotle's works in Diogenes Laertius (5.21.100).

14. See above, p. 63.
15. Kirk and Raven (1957), No. 370.
16. *Ibid.* No. 373.
17. C 2 in the passage discussed in Chapter 1.
18. Kirk and Raven (1957), No. 374.
19. *Ibid.* p. 295.
20. *Ibid.* Nos. 375-376.
21. I translate the text printed in Kirk and Raven (1957). For details of the various readings of the manuscripts, see W. D. Ross *ad loc.*
22. *Physics* Z 9, 240 a 1.
23. *Physics* Z 9, 240 a 2.
24. *Physics* Z 3, 234 a 24*ff*. The point is made by N. B. Booth (1957c, p. 195) and again by Vlastos (1961, p. 43, n. 1).
25. Booth (1957c), p. 194.
26. I take it that the antecedent of this participle is "$\tau\grave{o}\ \pi\rho\hat{\omega}\tau o\nu\ \Gamma$" in the preceding clause.
27. Kirk and Raven (1957), chs. 9 and 11.
28. Owen (1957-58), pp. 212-213.
29. This is defended by J. E. Raven (1954).
30. See chapter 11, especially pp. 150*ff*.
31. Kirk and Raven (1957), pp. 499-500.

CHAPTER 6

THE ATOMISTS' REPLY TO THE ELEATICS

ARISTOTLE discusses the composition of material substance in his *De Generatione et Corruptione*. In chapter 8 of the first book, he studies the views of earlier philosophers on the subject of the interaction of such substances (τὸ ποιεῖν καὶ πάσχειν). He mentions first those who believed that all interaction takes place through "pores," and then compares the pore theory with that of Leucippus and Democritus:

> Some, then, like Empedocles, held this theory with regard to *some* substances—not only those which interact with each other, but also they say that substances mix with each other if and only if their pores are commensurate. Leucippus and Democritus, on the other hand, held a theory which was supremely methodical and which applied to all substances; they began at the starting point given by nature.*[1]
>
> For some of the ancients had thought that what *is* must necessarily be one and motionless, since what is void is nonexistent, and there could be no motion without a separately existing void, and again there could be no plurality of existents without something to separate them. If someone thinks the universe is not continuous but consists of divided pieces in contact with each other, this is no different, they held, from saying that it is many, not one, and is void. For if it is divisible everywhere, there is no unit, and therefore no many, and the whole is void. If on the other hand it is divisible in one place and not another, this seems like a piece of fiction. For how far is it divisible, and why is one part of the whole like this—full—and another part divided?[a]

* Please see end of chapter for numbered references.

[a] οἱ μὲν οὖν ἐπί τινων οὕτω διώρισαν, ὥσπερ καὶ Ἐμπεδοκλῆς, οὐ μόνον ἐπὶ τῶν ποιούντων καὶ πασχόντων, ἀλλὰ καὶ μίγνυσθαί φασιν ὅσων οἱ πόροι σύμμετροι πρὸς ἀλλήλους εἰσίν· ὁδῷ δὲ μάλιστα καὶ περὶ πάντων ἑνὶ λόγῳ διωρίκασι Λεύκιππος καὶ

Indivisible Magnitudes

"Some of the ancients" are clearly of the Eleatic school. The argument that the non-existence of void entails the impossibility of motion belongs to Melissus, certainly, and probably to Parmenides.[2] It was Parmenides who said there could be no plurality without something to separate the units (at least, this seems to be one of a number of possible paraphrases of B 8, 25). The argument against a universe "divisible everywhere" but containing no void is, I think, Zeno's "Argument A," which I have discussed in chapter 5. At least the argument that if the universe is divisible everywhere there is no unit and therefore no "many" appears to be Zeno's; the further conclusion put into Eleatic mouths by Aristotle, that such a universe must therefore be *void*, is not expressed anywhere else, so far as I know.

I have quoted rather more of Aristotle's summary of the Eleatic position than is usually done by those who wish to explain the Atomists. The reason is that abbreviated quotation has suggested that the Atomists answered only the first two of these Eleatic arguments; and I want to show that in all probability they also answered the third, about divisibility. However, it is possible to omit the rest of Aristotle's remarks on the Eleatics without distortion, and I continue with his report of the Atomists' answer:

> But Leucippus thought he had arguments which would assert what is consistent with sense perception and not do away with coming-into-being and perishing and motion and the plurality of existents. He agrees with sensible appearances to this extent, but he concedes to those who maintain the One that there would be no motion without void, and says that what is void is not-being, and that no part of what *is* is not-being—for what *is* in the strict sense is wholly and fully being. But such being, he says, is not one; there is an infinite number of them, and they are invisible because of the smallness of their mass. They move in the

Δημόκριτος, ἀρχὴν ποιησάμενοι κατὰ φύσιν ἥπερ ἐστίν. ἐνίοις γὰρ τῶν ἀρχαίων ἔδοξε τὸ ὂν ἐξ ἀνάγκης ἓν εἶναι καὶ ἀκίνητον· τὸ μὲν γὰρ κενὸν οὐκ ὄν, κινηθῆναι δ' οὐκ ἂν δύνασθαι μὴ ὄντος κενοῦ κεχωρισμένου, οὐδ' αὖ πολλὰ εἶναι μὴ ὄντος τοῦ διείργοντος—τοῦτο δ' οὐδὲν διαφέρειν, εἴ τις οἴεται μὴ συνεχὲς εἶναι τὸ πᾶν ἀλλ' ἅπτεσθαι διῃρημένον, τοῦ φάναι πολλὰ καὶ μὴ ἓν εἶναι καὶ κενόν. εἰ μὲν γὰρ πάντῃ διαιρετόν, οὐθὲν εἶναι ἕν, ὥστε οὐδὲ πολλά, ἀλλὰ κενὸν τὸ ὅλον· εἰ δὲ τῇ μὲν τῇ δὲ μή, πεπλασμένῳ τινὶ τοῦτ' ἐοικέναι. μέχρι πόσου γάρ, καὶ διὰ τί τὸ μὲν οὕτως ἔχει τοῦ ὅλου καὶ πλῆρές ἐστι, τὸ δὲ διῃρημένον; (*De Generatione et Corruptione* A 8, 324 b 32–325 a 12.)

The Atomists' Reply to the Eleatics

void (for there *is* void), and when they come together they cause coming-to-be, and when they separate they cause perishing.[b]

The connection between the Eleatics and the Atomists, which John Burnet called "the most important point in the history of early Greek philosophy,"[3] is made in these famous words of Aristotle's, and confirmed by other writers, some of whom indeed say that Leucippus was a *pupil* of Zeno. It is unlikely that Leucippus ever sat at the feet of Zeno or any other Eleatic, but there is no reason to doubt that both he and Democritus consciously sought to reply to the Eleatics. It is generally agreed that Aristotle's account of their relation to the Eleatics on the subject of void, motion, and plurality is correct. But Aristotle mentions an argument about divisibility when he summarizes the Eleatic position. In the present passage he does not say anything at all about the Atomists' answer, but the implication that they *had* an answer is strong enough.

The implication is confirmed by something Aristotle says in the *Physics*:

> Some gave in to both of these [sc. Eleatic] arguments—to the argument that all is one if "what is" means one, by saying that not-being exists, and to the argument from Dichotomy, by positing atomic magnitudes.[c]

The ancient commentators, Alexander and Porphyry, who are quoted by Simplicius in his note on this passage, seem to have gone off on the wrong track here. They apparently took Aristotle's "some" to refer to Plato and Xenocrates: it was Plato who said that not-being exists, and Xenocrates who posited atomic magnitudes. They can quote in support of this attribution *Metaphysics* 1089 a 2-6, where the Platonic theory of not-being is related to

[b] Λεύκιππος δ' ἔχειν ᾠήθη λόγους, οἵτινες πρὸς τὴν αἴσθησιν ὁμολογούμενα λέγοντες οὐκ ἀναιρήσουσιν οὔτε γένεσιν οὔτε φθορὰν οὔτε κίνησιν καὶ τὸ πλῆθος τῶν ὄντων. ὁμολογήσας δὲ ταῦτα μὲν τοῖς φαινομένοις, τοῖς δὲ τὸ ἓν κατασκευάζουσιν ὡς οὐκ ἂν κίνησιν οὖσαν ἄνευ κενοῦ, τό τε κενὸν μὴ ὂν καὶ τοῦ ὄντος οὐθὲν μὴ ὂν φησιν εἶναι· τὸ γὰρ κυρίως ὂν παμπλῆρες ὄν. ἀλλ' εἶναι τὸ τοιοῦτον οὐχ ἕν, ἀλλ' ἄπειρα τὸ πλῆθος καὶ ἀόρατα διὰ σμικρότητα τῶν ὄγκων. ταῦτα δ' ἐν τῷ κενῷ φέρεσθαι (κενὸν γὰρ εἶναι), καὶ συνιστάμενα μὲν γένεσιν ποιεῖν, διαλυόμενα δὲ φθοράν. (Ibid. 325 a 23-32.)

[c] ἔνιοι δ' ἐνέδοσαν τοῖς λόγοις ἀμφοτέροις, τῷ μὲν ὅτι πάντα ἕν, εἰ τὸ ὂν ἓν σημαίνει, ὅτι ἔστι τὸ μὴ ὄν, τῷ δὲ ἐκ τῆς διχοτομίας, ἄτομα ποιήσαντες μεγέθη. (*Physics* A 3, 187 a 1-3.)

Indivisible Magnitudes

Parmenides. But it is much more likely that Aristotle was thinking of Leucippus and Democritus. The assertion that not-being (i.e. void) exists, and the relation of this assertion to the Eleatic One Being, are mentioned in the passage of the *De Generatione et Corruptione* which we have just examined, and the assertion is there attributed to Leucippus by name. Admittedly in that passage the argument for One Being is expressed differently, but I think that is of no importance: "all is one if 'what is' means one," in the *Physics*, looks to me like a summary of a large part of the Eleatic philosophy, rather than one particular argument. If, then, the Atomists are said to have "given in" to the first argument, it is almost certainly they who are mentioned in connection with the second: the sentence, after all, has only one subject, and it is no surprise to hear that they "posited atomic magnitudes."[4]

But what is "the argument from Dichotomy"? It has not been mentioned earlier in the *Physics*; Aristotle evidently felt that the name itself was enough to identify it. I suppose the obvious candidate is the first of Zeno's four arguments about motion, listed by Aristotle in *Physics* Z 9 (see above, ch. 5). Aristotle refers to this argument as "the Dichotomy" (τῇ διχοτομίᾳ 239 b 22, τῷ διχοτομεῖν b 19). It is not clear, however, whether he is using the expression as a technical name or merely as a convenient term for reference; his use of the word is certainly not confined to reports of Zeno. Alexander, quoted by Simplicius, did not think Aristotle meant this argument, but another—still Zeno's—which he gives in the following form: If what *is* has magnitude and is divided, what *is* would be many and not one; hence the one would be none of the things that *are*. This is a similar move to the one mentioned by Aristotle in *De Generatione et Corruptione* 325 a 8 (p. 79 above), which—as I have already pointed out—is derived from Zeno's Argument A.

In fact it does not matter much which of the two arguments Aristotle is supposed to have had in mind. Both arguments involve dichotomy, and both are invalidated if there are indivisible magnitudes. Argument A starts by supposing that what exists is divisible into ultimate units, and then claims that if such a division is completed, the resultant units have no magnitude and therefore cannot

The Atomists' Reply to the Eleatics

be parts of the original "what exists"; the argument called "Dichotomy" shows that if such a division can *never* be completed but goes on for ever, the whole can never be traversed. Both arguments are blocked if what exists is divisible into indivisible magnitudes.[5]

Further details of the Atomists' answer to the Eleatics can be recovered from another passage of Aristotle's *De Generatione et Corruptione*, where he gives at length what he describes as "the argument which appears to prove that there are indivisible magnitudes." There can be no doubt that Aristotle has Democritus and Leucippus in mind when he reproduces this argument: his conclusion contains a phrase which has been previously used in a summary of their theory,[6] and he begins it by praising Democritus for "having been persuaded by proper, physical arguments," as opposed to the abstract arguments used by the Platonists to establish their "indivisible planes." With due caution Harold Cherniss remarks:[7] "Aristotle outlines what he feels to be the reasoning which makes men think atomic bodies necessary; he does not say that it was the reasoning which led the Atomists to their theory, and it is not mentioned in what purports to be the historical account of the origin of Atomism." But in that historical account, which is of course the passage quoted at the beginning of this chapter, none of the Atomists' arguments are *described* at all; it is just mentioned that Leucippus thought he had some. So the absence of this particular argument from that account does not signify that the argument is a construction of Aristotle's and not a report of what the Atomists themselves wrote. Philoponus certainly took it to be Democritus' own argument,[8] and most commentators have followed him. Mau is one who has not.[9] He finds the whole argument to be permeated with Aristotelian concepts, and carefully tailored by Aristotle to suit the refutation which is to follow. He contrasts the hesitant optative with which Aristotle speaks here of Democritus with the confident indicative he uses elsewhere.[10] All this is true: Aristotle has certainly expressed the argument in his own terms. But I still think it probable that the logic of the argument belongs to Democritus. I cannot see why else Aristotle should begin as he does:

One group says that (otherwise) the Triangle-itself will be many, but Democritus would appear to have been persuaded by proper,

Indivisible Magnitudes

physical arguments. What we mean will become clear as we proceed.[d]

The argument is unmistakably reminiscent of Zeno's argument against plurality (Argument A), as Luria observed.[11] Suppose that a body is stated to be everywhere divisible, and (I take this to be an Aristotelian refinement) that there is no impossibility involved in its being *actually* divided.

> Suppose then that it *is* divided; now, what will be left? Magnitude? No, that cannot be, since there will then be something not divided, whereas it was *everywhere* divisible. But if there is to be no body or magnitude [left] and yet [this] division is to take place, then either the whole will be made of points and then the [parts] of which it is composed will have no size, or [that which is left will be] nothing at all. [In the latter case] it would come into being or be composed out of nothing and the whole would be nothing but an [illusory] appearance. Similarly if it is made out of points, it will not be a quantity. For when they were in contact and there was one magnitude and they were together, they did not increase the magnitude of the whole; for when it was divided into two or more, the whole was no larger or smaller than formerly. So if they are all put together, they will not make a magnitude.[e]

I have inserted some words in the translation to make the line of reasoning clearer.

Aristotle states two alternatives (a third possibility is dealt with later): either the products of this division must be points, or they must be nothing at all. In either case, such units cannot be the components of a magnitude. Zeno argued from "something having no size does not contribute to the size of the whole" to "something having no size is nothing." Aristotle's text distinguishes two cases: certainly a collection of "nothings" cannot be anything but an

---

[d] οἱ μέν φασιν αὐτὸ τὸ τρίγωνον πολλὰ ἔσται, Δημόκριτος δ' ἂν φανείη οἰκείοις καὶ φυσικοῖς λόγοις πεπεῖσθαι. δῆλον δ' ἔσται ὃ λέγομεν προϊοῦσιν. (*De Generatione et Corruptione* A 2, 316 a 11-14.)

[e] διῃρήσθω. τί οὖν ἔσται λοιπόν; μέγεθος; οὐ γὰρ οἷόν τε· ἔσται γάρ τι οὐ διῃρημένον, ἣν δὲ πάντῃ διαιρετόν. ἀλλὰ μὴν εἰ μηδὲν ἔσται σῶμα μηδὲ μέγεθος, διαίρεσις δ' ἔσται, ἢ ἐκ στιγμῶν ἔσται, καὶ ἀμεγέθη ἐξ ὧν σύγκειται, ἢ οὐδὲν παντάπασιν, ὥστε κἂν γίνοιτο ἐκ μηδενὸς κἂν εἴη συγκείμενον, καὶ τὸ πᾶν δὴ οὐδὲν ἀλλ' ἢ φαινόμενον. ὁμοίως δὲ κἂν ᾖ ἐκ στιγμῶν, οὐκ ἔσται ποσόν. ὁπότε γὰρ ἥπτοντο καὶ ἓν ἦν μέγεθος καὶ ἅμα ἦσαν, οὐδὲν ἐποίουν μεῖζον τὸ πᾶν· διαιρεθέντος γὰρ εἰς δύο καὶ πλείω, οὐδὲν ἔλαττον οὐδὲ μεῖζον τὸ πᾶν τοῦ πρότερον· ὥστε κἂν πᾶσαι συντεθῶσιν, οὐδὲν ποιήσουσι μέγεθος. (*Ibid.* 316 a 24-34.)

The Atomists' Reply to the Eleatics

illusion, but also a collection of points (i.e. *things*—not "nothings" —having no magnitude) cannot be a magnitude. There is a close similarity between Zeno's argument and the second of these two given by Aristotle. The latter argues that if a given line is divided in two the sum of its two parts remains the same as the length of the original whole; yet there are now two points, at the inner end of each of the two half-lines, where formerly there was only one; hence the extra point made no difference to the length—and so any number of points will make no difference to length. The distinction between "nothings" and points may be Aristotle's work; but because of its likeness to Zeno's argument we may confidently attribute to Democritus at least an argument that units having no magnitude cannot add up to a magnitude, and hence that no magnitude can be reduced to such units by division.

The argument reported by Aristotle then considers a third possibility: that the *results* of the division may be of no size, but the magnitude somehow disappears in the process of division, like sawdust. But if the sawdust is corporeal, then the problem of *its* divisibility arises, and we are faced with exactly the same dilemma as before. If it is not a body, but some kind of form or quality, then we are faced with the absurdity of a magnitude's being composed of elements without magnitude. After some further variations, which seem likely to be Aristotle's own,[12] the conclusion is stated: "there must be indivisible bodies and magnitudes."

So FAR in this chapter I have concentrated on establishing the conclusion that in Aristotle's view the theory of indivisible magnitudes was advanced by Leucippus and Democritus as an answer to certain Eleatic arguments, including Zeno's Argument A. The next step is to consider what kind of a theory would be needed to answer these arguments. Having done this we may look for further evidence that will either refute or confirm the hypothesis that they held a theory of this kind.

The first part of the program should present no difficulty. Nobody, so far as I know, has argued that the Eleatics were trying to defend a One Being that was only physically unsplittable. Their

Indivisible Magnitudes

arguments against the divisibility of what exists were aimed at *all* kinds of divisibility. I have mentioned above (chapter 4) that Parmenides *fr*. 4 is about theoretical divisibility. Melissus believed in a Being that was incorporeal and indivisible—and this must be theoretical indivisibility. Zeno's arguments have usually been taken as bearing on *mathematical* problems of divisibility; it may not indeed be the case that his attack was specifically directed against mathematical concepts, but it would be too much of a *volte-face* to say that the theoretical, as opposed to practical, divisibility of what exists was excluded from his target.

If this is so, a physically unsplittable atom which is still theoretically divisible will not meet the Eleatic arguments at all. Most English scholars have taken it almost for granted that Leucippus and Democritus were physical atomists only, perhaps following Sir Thomas Heath's question-begging dictum[13] that Democritus was "too good a mathematician" to believe in indivisible geometrical magnitudes. Thus Burnet remarked:[14] "We must observe that the atom is not mathematically indivisible, for it has magnitude." G. S. Kirk repeats this:[15] "They [sc. the atoms] were indivisible in fact, though not (since they had extension in space) in thought." But this will not do. A theoretically divisible atom would certainly not answer the argument from Dichotomy—whichever of Zeno's arguments Aristotle meant when he used the phrase. Argument A would show that an atom theoretically divisible to infinity must be infinite in magnitude; and the first of Zeno's "arguments about motion" would show that such an atom could never be traversed—that is, if one starts imagining it, one can never imagine the *whole* of it.

There is an *a priori* likelihood, then, that Leucippus and Democritus were more than physical atomists. We must now see whether this hypothesis will stand up to such tests as we can devise for it.

First, we can ask whether the Atomists' argument, as reported by Aristotle, tends to prove the existence of physically unsplittable bodies, or of theoretically indivisible ones; and this can perhaps be answered by studying Aristotle's criticism of the argument.

The Atomists' Reply to the Eleatics

Having gone through the steps of the argument and stated its conclusion, "it follows that there are indivisible bodies and magnitudes,"[16] Aristotle continues:

> However, those who assert this are involved in just as many impossibilities; these have been examined elsewhere.[f]

The reference, as Philoponus saw, is to *De Caelo* Γ and *Physics* Z (Philoponus also mentions *De Lineis Insecabilibus*, "which some attribute to Theophrastus").

In *De Caelo* Γ 4, Aristotle lists a number of objections to the theory of Leucippus and Democritus, including the following:

> Moreover, they must be in conflict with mathematics when they say there are indivisible bodies, and rule out many common opinions and sensible phenomena, which have already been discussed in the works on Time and Motion.[g]

This passage also refers to the *Physics*, then, for Aristotle habitually calls the later books of the *Physics* "the books on Motion." But before turning to what he says there, we must comment on this sentence of the *De Caelo*. When Aristotle says that the Democritean theory of indivisible magnitudes is in conflict with *mathematics*, can he mean anything other than *theoretically* indivisible magnitudes? How could physical atoms be in conflict with mathematics? We can see more clearly what Aristotle had in mind from something he says earlier in the same work, to illustrate the point that a small divergence from truth early in an argument is enormously multiplied as one proceeds:

> For example, suppose one were to say that there is a smallest magnitude: by introducing this "smallest" one upsets the greatest features of mathematics.[h]

The conflict consists in the fact that the hypothesis of indivisible magnitudes denies one of the principles of mathematics, and so

---

[f] οὐ μὴν ἀλλὰ καὶ ταῦτα θεμένοις οὐχ ἧττον συμβαίνει ἀδύνατα· ἔσκεπται δὲ περὶ αὐτῶν ἐν ἑτέροις. (*Ibid.* 316 b 16-18.)

[g] πρὸς δὲ τούτοις ἀνάγκη μάχεσθαι ταῖς μαθηματικαῖς ἐπιστήμαις ἄτομα σώματα λέγοντας, καὶ πολλὰ τῶν ἐνδόξων καὶ τῶν φαινομένων κατὰ τὴν αἴσθησιν ἀναιρεῖν, περὶ ὧν εἴρηται πρότερον ἐν τοῖς περὶ χρόνου καὶ κινήσεως. (*De Caelo* Γ 4, 303 a 20-24.)

[h] οἷον εἴ τις ἐλάχιστον εἶναί τι φαίη μέγεθος· οὗτος γὰρ τοὐλάχιστον εἰσαγαγὼν τὰ μέγιστα κινεῖ τῶν μαθηματικῶν. (*Ibid.* A 5, 271 b 9-11.)

Indivisible Magnitudes

destroys the structure built on these principles. Simplicius, commenting on these two passages, fills in the detail: the Atomists' assumption means the denial of the principle that any given line may be divided into two. And this interpretation is confirmed by a scholium on Euclid Book 10:

> That there is no smallest magnitude, as the Democriteans say, is proved also by this theorem, that it is possible to obtain a magnitude smaller than any given magnitude.[1]

One more passage in the *De Caelo* is worth some attention. In Γ 7, Aristotle groups together some criticisms of Empedocles, Democritus, and the Platonists on the subject of the transformation of the simple bodies (earth, air, fire, and water) into each other. At the relevant point, where he speaks of "indivisible bodies," it is chiefly Plato that he has in mind, since he argues against the theory that the simple bodies are reducible to planes; but then he generalizes his comment so as to combat any theory which distinguishes its simple bodies by shape:

> They are compelled to deny that every body is divisible, and so to be in conflict with the most exact sciences. For the mathematical sciences take even the *intelligible* to be divisible, whereas these philosophers do not even allow that every *sensible* body is divisible, in their anxiety to save their theory. For all those who allot a shape to each of the elements and distinguish their natures by shapes are compelled to say that they are indivisible, since when a pyramid or a sphere is divided in some way the remainder is not a sphere or pyramid. So either the part of fire will not be fire, and there will be something prior to the element (since everything is either an element or a product of elements), or not every body is divisible.[j]

---

[1] ὅτι οὐκ ἔστιν ἐλάχιστον μέγεθος, ὡς οἱ Δημοκρίτειοί φασιν, καὶ διὰ τούτου τοῦ θεωρήματος δείκνυται, εἴ γε παντὸς τοῦ ἐκκειμένου μεγέθους δυνατὸν ἔλαττον λαβεῖν. (DK 68 A 48a.)

[j] ἀνάγκη μὴ πᾶν σῶμα λέγειν διαιρετόν, ἀλλὰ μάχεσθαι ταῖς ἀκριβεστάταις ἐπιστήμαις· αἱ μὲν γὰρ καὶ τὸ νοητὸν λαμβάνουσι διαιρετόν, αἱ μαθηματικαί, οἱ δὲ οὐδὲ τὸ αἰσθητὸν ἅπαν συγχωροῦσι διὰ τὸ βούλεσθαι σώζειν τὴν ὑπόθεσιν. ἀνάγκη γὰρ ὅσοι σχῆμα ποιοῦσιν ἑκάστου τῶν στοιχείων καὶ τούτῳ διορίζουσι τὰς οὐσίας αὐτῶν, ἀδιαίρετα ποιεῖν αὐτά· τῆς γὰρ πυραμίδος ἢ τῆς σφαίρας διαιρεθείσης πως οὐκ ἔσται τὸ λειπόμενον σφαῖρα ἢ πυραμίς. ὥστε ἢ τὸ τοῦ πυρὸς μέρος οὐ πῦρ, ἀλλ' ἔσται τι πρότερον τοῦ στοιχείου, διὰ τὸ πᾶν εἶναι ἢ στοιχεῖον ἢ ἐκ στοιχείων· ἢ οὐχ ἅπαν σῶμα διαιρετόν. (*De Caelo* Γ, 306 a 26-b 2.)

The Atomists' Reply to the Eleatics

There is one point here which should alert us at once to a difference between Aristotle's outlook and ours. He alters what seems to us the natural emphasis. His opponents, he says, do not *even* allow every sensible body to be divisible—as if the indivisibility of a sensible body were *more incredible* than that of a conceptual magnitude. We may contrast this Aristotelian viewpoint with that of Sir Thomas Heath, for example, who found it incredible that Democritus should believe in an indivisible mathematical magnitude, but saw no difficulty in the concept of a physical atom. Aristotle believed that every physical body was potentially divisible everywhere in exactly the same way as every mathematical body: matter, or the substratum of physical bodies, was continuous, and so all the laws of the mathematical continuum could be applied to it. It will be important to bear this in mind when we come back to the criticism of the Atomists' argument in *De Generatione et Corruptione* A 2.[17]

It is the *Physics* to which Aristotle refers, as we have seen, for a full discussion of the problem of "indivisible magnitudes." He referred to this book in connection with Leucippus and Democritus: the question before us is whether the discussion in the *Physics* concerns physically unsplittable atoms or theoretically indivisible magnitudes. Fortunately there is no need to take long about answering it. It is abundantly clear that Aristotle discusses theoretically indivisible magnitudes. There cannot be anything continuous, he says,[18] made of indivisibles, e.g., a line made of points. The reason is that things are continuous if and only if "their extremities are one," and an indivisible has no extremities. It is clear at once that this has nothing to do with physical atoms; for unless the object is theoretically indivisible there is no reason why it should not have extremities.

But this argument is the basis of the whole discussion in *Physics* Z. Aristotle begins chapter 2 with a summary: "since every magnitude is divisible into magnitudes (for we have shown that nothing continuous can be made of indivisibles, and all magnitude is continuous) . . .," and proceeds to make some points about motion and change. (We shall examine some of his arguments in ch. 8.) He argues, for instance, that a "partless body" (i.e. an indivisible body) cannot move or change at all.[19] This is the kind of objection that is meant

Indivisible Magnitudes

in the *De Caelo* 303 a 20 (p. 87 above), where Aristotle says that those who believe in indivisible bodies "have to rule out many sensible phenomena."

To sum up the argument of the last few pages, then: Aristotle begins his criticism of the "indivisible magnitudes" of Democritus, in *De Generatione et Corruptione*, by saying that the resultant impossibilities have been examined elsewhere. We have seen reason to believe that the reference must be to the *De Caelo* and *Physics*. In these two works, the "indivisible magnitudes" discussed are theoretically indivisible magnitudes, not merely physical atoms, and the alleged impossibilities result from this. It is perhaps worth saying at this point that the traditional Democritus, "too good a mathematician to believe in indivisible magnitudes," should have agreed with every word of Aristotle's criticisms of him.

I RETURN now to *De Generatione et Corruptione* A 2:

> We must try to solve these problems; so we must restate the case from the beginning.
>
> That every sensible body should be divisible at any point and be indivisible is nothing out of the way—it will be the former in potentiality, the latter in actuality. But that it should be divisible everywhere *simultaneously* in potentiality would seem to be impossible. For if it were possible, it would happen; ... so there will be nothing left, and the body will have been destroyed into what is not body, and would come into being either out of points or out of nothing at all. And how is this possible?[k]

This is a tricky passage. The difficulty is to know which clauses belong to Aristotle's stage directions, so to speak, and which to his formulation of the Atomists' argument.[20] The opening sentence of the second paragraph, I think, is introductory. Aristotle wishes to

---

[k] ἀλλὰ ταῦτα πειρατέον λύειν, διὸ πάλιν ἐξ ἀρχῆς τὴν ἀπορίαν λεκτέον.

τὸ μὲν οὖν ἅπαν σῶμα αἰσθητὸν εἶναι διαιρετὸν καθ' ὁτιοῦν σημεῖον καὶ ἀδιαίρετον οὐδὲν ἄτοπον· τὸ μὲν γὰρ δυνάμει, τὸ δ' ἐντελεχείᾳ ὑπάρξει. τὸ δ' εἶναι ἅμα πάντῃ διαιρετὸν δυνάμει ἀδύνατον δόξειεν ἂν εἶναι. εἰ γὰρ δυνατόν, κἂν γένοιτο ... οὐδὲν ἄρα ἔσται λοιπόν, καὶ εἰς ἀσώματον ἐφθαρμένον τὸ σῶμα, καὶ γίγνοιτο δ' ἂν πάλιν ἤτοι ἐκ στιγμῶν ἢ ὅλως ἐξ οὐδενός. καὶ τοῦτο πῶς δυνατόν; (*De Generatione et Corruptione* A 2, 316 b 18-27.)

The Atomists' Reply to the Eleatics

point out that the problem cannot be solved simply by introducing potentiality and actuality; so he begins by showing how far these concepts can go. "Divisible everywhere" and "indivisible" need not be incompatible predicates, if the former belongs potentially, the latter actually. So far as that goes, Democritus might agree with Aristotle. The trouble is that "divisible everywhere" seems an impossible predicate even in a potential sense—that is the first proposition in Aristotle's formulation of the Atomist argument. "For if it were possible, it would happen," and then the result would be exactly what Aristotle described in his first statement of the argument (text *e*, p. 84).

> But it is clear that it is divided into separate magnitudes, and always into smaller ones, and into pieces which are distinct and separated. But when one divides step by step, neither would the process of breaking the thing up be infinite, nor could it be divided simultaneously at every point (since that is impossible); it would only go so far and no further. Hence there must be indivisible magnitudes in it, which cannot be seen—especially if generation and destruction take place through association and dissociation respectively.
>
> This then is the argument which seems to prove the existence of indivisible magnitudes.[1]

When an extended body is actually divided, it is divided into smaller parts which are in actual existence, separate from each other. But *actual* division like this cannot be continued infinitely, nor can the thing be actually divided simultaneously at every point in it. So far as I can see, Aristotle would accept the argument up to this point—even the statement that the process of division cannot be continued infinitely. For this statement seems to mean only that "division to infinity" cannot take place in actuality. Aristotle would agree to this, but he goes on to point out that the impossibility of infinite division *in this sense* does not entail indivisible magnitudes.

[1] ἀλλὰ μὴν ὅτι γε διαιρεῖται εἰς χωριστὰ καὶ ἀεὶ εἰς ἐλάττω μεγέθη καὶ εἰς ἀπέχοντα καὶ κεχωρισμένα, φανερόν. οὔτε δὴ κατὰ μέρος διαιροῦντι εἴη ἂν ἄπειρος ἡ θρύψις, οὔτε ἅμα οἷόν τε διαιρεθῆναι κατὰ πᾶν σημεῖον (οὐ γὰρ δυνατόν), ἀλλὰ μέχρι του· ἀνάγκη ἄρα ἄτομα ἐνυπάρχειν μεγέθη ἀόρατα, ἄλλως τε καὶ εἴπερ ἔσται γένεσις καὶ φθορὰ ἡ μὲν διακρίσει ἡ δὲ συγκρίσει. ὁ μὲν οὖν ἀναγκάζειν δοκῶν λόγος εἶναι μεγέθη ἄτομα οὗτός ἐστιν. (*Ibid.* 316 b 28–317 a 1.)

Indivisible Magnitudes

Having thus restated the argument, Aristotle proceeds with the refutation:

> Let us now explain that this argument contains a fallacy, and where the fallacy is. Since point is not next to point, there is a sense in which the predicate "divisible everywhere" belongs to magnitudes and a sense in which it does not. When this is asserted [sc. that magnitudes are divisible everywhere], it seems that there is a point anywhere and everywhere, so that the magnitude must have been divided up into nothing—since there is a point everywhere, and so it will be made either of points or of contacts. Yet there is a sense in which there is a point everywhere, in that there is one point anywhere, and all of them are there if you take them one by one. But there is not more than one (since they are not consecutive to each other), and so they are not everywhere.[m]

The refutation of the Atomists' argument depends on Aristotle's analysis of the concepts of "point," "next to," "contact," etc., which he offers in full in *Physics* E 3. It is impossible to divide a magnitude "at every point," because points are not next to each other; between *any* two points there is a magnitude. But this does not entail that there are indivisible magnitudes; every magnitude has points on it, at which it may be divided.

It must be conceded that the whole of this discussion is about sensible magnitudes. Does that entail that it is about physical atoms? I. Hammer-Jensen, who was the first modern scholar, I think, to show that this was Aristotle's report of a genuine argument of the Atomists, thought it referred only to physical divisibility. "Als Einleitung wird stark betont, dass hier, wo es sich um Teilung von Körpern (nicht von mathematischen Grössen) handelt, von einer abstrakten Möglichkeit keine Rede ist, sondern von einer Möglichkeit, die jeden beliebigen Augenblick als sinnliche Wirklichkeit hervortreten kann; daher wird man auch daran erinnert, dass unendlich mehr ist als zehntausendmal zehntausend."[21]

Is this true? Certainly Aristotle does mention "ten thousand

---

[m] ὅτι δὲ λανθάνει παραλογιζόμενος, καὶ ᾗ λανθάνει, λέγωμεν. ἐπεὶ γὰρ οὐκ ἔστι στιγμὴ στιγμῆς ἐχομένη, τὸ πάντῃ εἶναι διαιρετὸν ἔστι μὲν ὡς ὑπάρχει τοῖς μεγέθεσιν, ἔστι δ' ὡς οὔ. δοκεῖ δ', ὅταν τοῦτο τεθῇ, καὶ ὁπηοῦν καὶ πάντῃ στιγμὴν εἶναι, ὥστ' ἀναγκαῖον εἶναι διαιρεθῆναι τὸ μέγεθος εἰς μηδέν—πάντῃ γὰρ εἶναι στιγμήν, ὥστε ἢ ἐξ ἀφῶν ἢ ἐκ στιγμῶν εἶναι. τὸ δ' ἔστιν ὡς ὑπάρχει πάντῃ, ὅτι μία ὁπηοῦν ἐστι καὶ πᾶσαι ὡς ἑκάστη· πλείους δὲ μιᾶς οὐκ εἰσίν (ἐφεξῆς γὰρ οὐκ εἰσίν), ὥστ' οὐ πάντῃ. (Ibid. 317 a 1-9.)

The Atomists' Reply to the Eleatics

times ten thousand divisions," but his purpose is not quite what Hammer-Jensen takes it to be:

> If [a body or magnitude] is divisible everywhere, and this is possible, then it might be simultaneously divided, even if the acts of dividing were not simultaneous; and if this happened, nothing impossible would result. So in the same way, if [a body] is divisible everywhere, whether by [progressive] bisection or in any other way, then nothing impossible will have taken place if it *is* divided. For even if it is divided into ten thousand times ten thousand divisions, this is nothing impossible, even though I suppose no one would actually do it.[n]

Aristotle's purpose here is to point out that the "impossibility" which is an essential element in the Atomists' argument is not merely a question of human limitations. If a body is everywhere divisible, then nothing impossible will have happened if it is everywhere divided; of course no one is likely to try, but nothing *logically* impossible will have happened.

Other details of Aristotle's language in this passage, like this one, leave it doubtful whether he is considering the physical or theoretical division of physical bodies. The only way in which we can make any progress is by taking the whole passage—the statement and restatement of the argument, and Aristotle's solution of the difficulty—and try to read it as applying only to atomism in the limited sense, physical but not theoretical. This is the traditional Democritean atomism. The Democritus of tradition understands that his physical atoms are theoretically divisible to infinity. He applies the Eleatic "argument from dichotomy" to *physical* divisibility, and cannot answer it except by positing indivisible magnitudes. But either he does not apply it at all to theoretical divisibility (although this was its original application), or else he applies it and *solves the problem differently*—solves it, in fact, in much the same way as Aristotle does. Aristotle, on this hypothesis, takes Democritus' argument for physical atomism, applies to it his own theory of

---

[n] εἰ γὰρ πάντῃ διαιρετόν, καὶ τοῦτο δυνατόν, κἂν ἅμα εἴη τοῦτο διῃρημένον, καὶ εἰ μὴ ἅμα διῄρηται· κἂν εἰ τοῦτο γένοιτο, οὐδὲν ἂν εἴη ἀδύνατον. οὐκοῦν καὶ κατὰ τὸ μέσον ὡσαύτως, καὶ ὅλως δέ, εἰ πάντῃ πέφυκε διαιρετόν, ἂν διαιρεθῇ, οὐδὲν ἔσται ἀδύνατον γεγονός, ἐπεὶ οὐδ' ἂν εἰς μυρία μυριάκις διῃρημένα ⟨διαιρεθ⟩ῇ, οὐδὲν ἀδύνατον· καίτοι ἴσως οὐδεὶς ἂν διέλοι. (*Ibid.* 316 a 17-23.)
⟨ ⟩ Joachim.

Indivisible Magnitudes

continuity, and thus shows that the argument is not cogent; and he does so without ever mentioning that Democritus too did not think the argument cogent at the theoretical level. He does so, in fact, without apparently being conscious that any distinction is necessary or possible.

There are too many paradoxes here. It seems much simpler to believe that neither Democritus nor Aristotle made any distinction between physical and theoretical divisibility. Just as Aristotle thought his own theory of continuity held good at the physical level as well as the theoretical level, so Democritus thought of his indivisible magnitudes as being theoretically as well as physically indivisible.[22]

So much for the evidence of Aristotle. I turn now to other sources. The hypothesis that Democritus believed in theoretically indivisible magnitudes is confirmed by Simplicius:

> Leucippus and Democritus think that the cause of the indivisibility of the primary bodies is not merely their imperviousness (*apatheia*) but also their smallness and partlessness; Epicurus, later, does not think they are partless, but says they are atomic because of their imperviousness.[º]

In another context, Simplicius again refers to "the school of Leucippus and Democritus, who say that the atoms, atomic because of their smallness and hardness, are elements."[23]

A pause must be made here to refute a heresy. Cyril Bailey writes:[24] "It is certain that the Leucippean argument from size is nowhere attributed to Democritus and indeed cannot have been used by him." This is an unaccountable mistake, since this argument plainly *is* attributed to Democritus, at least twice, in these passages of Simplicius; and unfortunately it is an influential one.[25] Bailey built quite an edifice of theory on this alleged difference between Leucippus and Democritus.

Three pieces of evidence *for* the difference may be considered. First, Bailey quotes a statement of Galen[26] which distinguishes the

---

º Λεύκιππος μὲν καὶ Δημόκριτος οὐ μόνον τὴν ἀπάθειαν αἰτίαν τοῖς πρώτοις σώμασι τοῦ μὴ διαιρεῖσθαι νομίζουσιν, ἀλλὰ καὶ τὸ σμικρὸν καὶ ἀμερές, Ἐπίκουρος δὲ ὕστερον ἀμερῆ μὲν οὐχ ἡγεῖται, ἄτομα δὲ αὐτὰ διὰ τὴν ἀπάθειαν εἶναί φησι. (Simplicius *Physics* 925·13ff. = DK 67 A 13.)

The Atomists' Reply to the Eleatics

Epicureans, who believed the atoms to be unbreakable because of their hardness, from "the school of Leucippus," who believed them to be unbreakable because of their smallness. But in the context of course Galen would include Democritus in "the school of Leucippus."

Secondly, Simplicius himself contradicts the statements I have quoted above. Commenting on Aristotle's use of the word "indivisible," he distinguishes three senses of "undivided."[27] There is (a) that which is divisible but not yet divided, like any continuous quantity; (b) the absolutely indivisible, because it has no parts, like a point or monad; (c) that which has parts and magnitude, but is impervious through hardness and compactness, *like Democritus' atoms*. But it is clear, I think, that Simplicius is assuming here that magnitude entails "having parts," as it did to all good Aristotelians. His hasty reference here should not be preferred to what he says when he explicitly distinguishes two different positions held by the Atomists.

Thirdly, there is the undeniable fact that Democritus certainly said his atoms had magnitude, and there are texts which suggest that some atoms had quite considerable magnitude. For there is a report, of rather doubtful authority, that distinguishes between Epicurus, who held that "all the atoms are very small and therefore imperceptible," and Democritus, who said that some atoms are very large.[28] Could Democritus have suggested that atoms are indivisible because of their smallness, and yet that some of them are "very large"? Could he in fact have held (as he undoubtedly did) that atoms differed from each other in size, and claimed also that they had no distinguishable parts?

From this point on we may forget Bailey's erroneous distinction between Leucippus and Democritus, and treat the matter more generally. What could be the reasoning behind the assertion that smallness is a cause of indivisibility? Simplicius ties smallness to partlessness, and if the Atomists were answering the Eleatics, this must be correct. The most likely line of argument, then, is the one used by Epicurus, which has been studied in chapter 1—that is, from the analogy with perception. There is a minimum perceptible quantity within which no parts can be distinguished by a perceiver. The

Indivisible Magnitudes

mind's eye, as it were, functions as a microscope: it can distinguish much smaller parts than the senses can, but there is still a lower limit beyond which it cannot make any distinctions. I can find no proof that this was the reasoning of Leucippus and Democritus, but I think it is suggested by fragment 11 of Democritus. There he distinguishes between "genuine knowledge" and "darkling knowledge." The fragment breaks off in the middle, but it is virtually certain that it says that the former, which is a product of the mind, takes over when the latter, which is sense perception, "can no longer see into smaller detail nor hear nor taste," etc.[29] Since Democritus seems to have drawn a general analogy between sense perception and thought, and since the concept of something too small to be seen was certainly familiar to him, it seems quite likely that he might have used the idea of something so small that no parts can be distinguished even by the mind.

But what are we to say about the "very large" atoms attributed to Democritus? The evidence for the attribution is not very good, and it may be that it can be explained away. Epicurus[30] disputed Democritus' assertion that the shapes of atoms are infinitely varied, on the ground that this would mean that some of them were infinitely large. It is very likely that later writers, contrasting Epicurus with Democritus, would carelessly write as though Democritus himself had spoken of infinitely large atoms. It seems to me that this would explain the testimony of Dionysius, quoted above, and also the single, unrelated mention of "world-sized" atoms by Aëtius.[31] Diogenes Laertius' statement that "the atoms are infinite in size and number"[32] seems too careless to be worth anything. On the other hand we have some reliable evidence from Aristotle's lost work *On Democritus*, quoted by Simplicius:

> Democritus thinks of his substances [i.e. the atoms] as being so small that they escape our senses; they have all sort of shapes and figures and differences of magnitude.[p]

This makes much better sense, as well as having much better authority.[33]

---

[p] νομίζει δὲ εἶναι οὕτω μικρὰς τὰς οὐσίας ὥστε ἐκφυγεῖν τὰς ἡμετέρας αἰσθήσεις· ὑπάρχειν δὲ αὐταῖς παντοίας μορφὰς καὶ σχήματα παντοῖα καὶ κατὰ μέγεθος διαφοράς. (Aristotle *On Democritus* fr. 1 Ross = Simplicius *De Caelo* 295. 5ff.)

The Atomists' Reply to the Eleatics

The probability is, then, that Democritus' atoms were supposed to be so small that distinctions could not be made inside them. Yet they had some magnitude, and many variations in shape and size. There seems to be an inescapable contradiction here. If we take together a smaller atom and a larger one, we can always distinguish in the larger one that part which is covered by the smaller and that which is not. Even within the limits of a single atom, supposing it to be of a complex shape (say hook-shaped), we can always distinguish one part of the shape from another (say the hook from the shaft). S. Luria, in his learned and pioneering paper, accepted the evidence of Aristotle as proving that Democritus' theory included the idea of theoretically indivisible units: but he was so daunted by the thought of the magnitude of the atoms that he decided Democritus' theory was the same as Epicurus'; that is, that atoms are physically unsplittable, but divisible theoretically into smaller, absolutely indivisible parts. Against Luria, Jürgen Mau correctly insists on the evidence of Aristotle. Aristotle shows no signs whatever of distinguishing between two kinds of indivisible units in Democritean theory. To my mind this is nearly conclusive: but there is one piece of evidence which may be added to strengthen Mau's case. It is in fact used by Luria to support his thesis, but I think it can be turned against him.

In the *De Caelo*[34] Aristotle mentions that Leucippus and Democritus "did not define clearly what shape each of the elements had, except that they allotted the sphere to fire." Later he adds a remarkable criticism:

> Even according to their own assumptions, the elements would not seem to be infinite, if the bodies differ in shape and all shapes are composed of pyramids, straight-edged ones of straight-edged pyramids, and the sphere out of eight pieces. For there must be certain *archai* of the shapes. So if they (sc. the *archai*) are one or two or some larger number, the simple bodies also must come to the same number.[q]

At first sight this seems to tell in favor of Luria's position: Aristotle does indeed say "according to their own assumptions"

---

[q] ἔτι οὐδὲ κατὰ τὴν τούτων ὑπόληψιν δόξειεν ἂν ἄπειρα γίγνεσθαι τὰ στοιχεῖα, εἴπερ τὰ μὲν σώματα διαφέρει σχήμασι, τὰ δὲ σχήματα πάντα σύγκειται ἐκ πυραμίδων, τὰ μὲν εὐθύγραμμα ἐξ εὐθυγράμμων, ἡ δὲ σφαῖρα ἐξ ὀκτὼ μορίων. ἀνάγκη γὰρ εἶναί τινας ἀρχὰς τῶν σχημάτων. ὥστε εἴτε μία εἴτε δύο εἴτε πλείους, καὶ τὰ ἁπλᾶ σώματα τοσαῦτα ἔσται τὸ πλῆθος. (*De Caelo* Γ 4, 303 a 29–b 3.)

Indivisible Magnitudes

and continues "if . . . all shapes are composed of pyramids," etc. I feel convinced, however, that this appearance is misleading. The Atomists' assumptions are that material substances differ in quality because of the differences in the shapes of their component atoms, and that such differences are innumerable. The second clause ("if all shapes are composed of pyramids," etc.) is not one of their assumptions; Aristotle gives this away by adding as a piece of justification "there *must* be certain *archai* of the shapes," not "they said these were the *archai*." Simplicius confirms this in his paraphrase: if the Atomists said the atoms are infinite because they differ in shape and shapes are infinite, then, "*if some argument shows* that the primary shapes are finite," then the elements will be finite too.³⁵ Aristotle himself, in the next chapter, reveals that the reduction of all shapes to elementary pyramids is a widespread assumption; for there he attributes it to some thinkers (Simplicius in his note says they were Pythagoreans) who believed that fire is characterized by a pyramidal shape.³⁶ The Atomists thought fire atoms were spherical.

I think, therefore, that this part of Luria's case can be turned against him. If Aristotle applied someone else's idea, that all shapes are composed of elementary pyramids, to the Atomists' doctrine with hostile intent, it must follow that the Atomists themselves had no idea that their atoms were not of elementary, irreducible shape, or at any rate that Aristotle did not know of such an idea of theirs. For he could have used their own theory against them much more effectively.

The most direct piece of evidence Luria can quote is from Alexander's commentary on *Metaphysics* A. Aristotle observes that Leucippus and Democritus neglected to say anything about the origin of motion.³⁷ Alexander says that they explained how atoms moved by collision, but not how they moved naturally:

> For they do not even explain how atoms get their weight. They say that the partless units which are conceptually present in the atoms and which are parts of them are without weight; and how could weight come about through the association of weightless units?ʳ

ʳ οὐδὲ γὰρ τὸ πόθεν ἡ βαρύτης ἐν ταῖς ἀτόμοις λέγουσι· τὰ γὰρ ἀμερῆ τὰ ἐπινοούμενα ταῖς ἀτόμοις καὶ μέρη ὄντα αὐτῶν ἀβαρῆ φασιν εἶναι. ἐκ δὲ ἀβαρῶν συγκειμένων πῶς ἂν βάρος γένηται; (Alexander *Metaphysics* 36.25-27.)

The Atomists' Reply to the Eleatics

This says explicitly that Democritean atoms had parts which were themselves partless; in fact it identifies Democritean and Epicurean atoms. That is probably the explanation, though it is hard to prove it—and I am not sure that what Alexander reports is true even of Epicurean atoms. We have to strike a balance between conflicting evidence: against this statement of Alexander's we must set the contradictory statements of Simplicius (see pp. 94-95), and the (to my mind) overwhelming consideration that Aristotle does not distinguish between "partless units" and atoms. Theophrastus evidently knew nothing of the doctrine reported by Alexander; for he could hardly have failed to mention it in his account of the weight of Democritean atoms, which we possess.[38] Alexander's seems to be a unique testimony. The only possible conclusion is that it is mistaken.[39]

Luria quotes the text of Simplicius which we have examined on p. 94 (text *o*), where it is said that Leucippus and Democritus gave two causes of the indivisibility of atoms—their imperviousness (*apatheia*) and their partlessness. Simplicius failed to understand, Luria maintains, that these causes apply to *two different kinds* of atom. This will hardly carry conviction—particularly as the Epicurean theory is contrasted explicitly with the Democritean in the same sentence. However, it might be as well to pursue the question: Why did Democritus stress the hardness and imperviousness of the atoms, and the fact that they contained no void, as causes of their indivisibility? He certainly did so; yet to meet the Eleatics' arguments it was a *partless* unit that was required, rather than a hard one. The answer can be found, I think, in the first passage of *De Generatione et Corruptione* quoted at the beginning of this chapter. The Eleatics, says Aristotle, objected to the pluralists that if the universe is divisible in one place and not in another, this seems like a piece of fiction. Why should it be so? We have the Atomists' answer in the hardness of the atoms. What *is*, they said, is indivisible (as the Eleatics claimed): each atom is absolutely solid, packed with being and nothing else. There is no void, or not-being, in an atom; hence nothing can penetrate it, so as to divide it.[40] The universe as a whole is divisible, however, in the sense that there is a plurality of existents separated by void.

✱

Indivisible Magnitudes

ALL the evidence I have produced so far has been in second-hand reports. Clearly some attempt must be made to clinch the argument by means of the original fragments of Democritus. But they are unfortunately quite inconclusive. Only one of them, so far as I can see, says anything to the point at all; that is the fragment which discusses the problem of slicing a cone in a plane parallel to the base. It is quoted by Plutarch, who was interested in Chrysippus' answer to the problem and did not think Democritus' solution was worth mentioning (supposing that he knew it in the first place).

> If a cone is cut along a plane parallel to its base, what must we think of the surfaces of the two segments—that they are equal or unequal? If they are unequal, they will make the cone uneven, with many step-like indentations and roughnesses: if they are equal, then the segments will be equal, and the cone will turn out to have the same properties as a cylinder, being composed of equal and not of unequal circles—which is quite absurd.[8]

The cone-fragment has sometimes been taken for proof that Democritus did not believe in indivisible magnitudes, but I do not see that it proves this at all. It could well be that he adopted the first of his alternatives: the two faces *are* unequal, and the cone does taper not smoothly but in steps. His theory of knowledge can perfectly well account for this: for "darkling knowledge" the cone is smooth, but for "genuine knowledge," which knows that if the cone is anything at all it must be made of indivisible magnitudes, it is stepped.

The only other direct evidence about Democritus on this subject is furnished by the titles of some of his books.[41] These show at least that he interested himself in geometry, and particularly in the problems of irrational proportions and others which involve the concept of a limit. But, as with the cone problem, the fact that he discussed the problem does not tell us how he attempted to solve it. We know that attempts were made in antiquity to handle the problems of

---

[8] εἰ κῶνος τέμνοιτο παρὰ τὴν βάσιν ἐπιπέδῳ, τί χρὴ διανοεῖσθαι τὰς τῶν τμημάτων ἐπιφανείας, ἴσας ἢ ἀνίσους γιγνομένας; ἄνισοι μὲν γὰρ οὖσαι τὸν κῶνον ἀνώμαλον παρέξουσι πολλὰς ἀποχαράξεις λαμβάνοντα βαθμοειδεῖς καὶ τραχύτητας, ἴσων δ' οὐσῶν ἴσα τμήματα ἔσται καὶ φανεῖται τὸ τοῦ κυλίνδρου πεπονθὼς ὁ κῶνος, ἐξ ἴσων συγκείμενος καὶ οὐκ ἀνίσων κύκλων, ὅπερ ἐστὶν ἀτοπώτατον. (Plutarch *De Communibus Notitiis* 1079 E = DK 68 B 155.)

The Atomists' Reply to the Eleatics

irrationals by using approximations which could be made as near as you please.[42] If Democritus regarded geometry as the science of measuring bodies, then all his geometry could well have been adapted to an atomistic view of the composition of bodies; and there seems to be no evidence that he did not adapt it in this way. It is worth observing that in the title of his book *On Irrational Lines and Solids* (περὶ ἀλόγων γραμμῶν καὶ ναστῶν) there is a startling juxtaposition of mathematics and physics: "ναστός" is Democritus' own word for "solid," in the sense in which a physical atom is solid.

The balance of the evidence, then, supports the view that Leucippus and Democritus were more than physical atomists. They believed their atoms to be theoretically as well as physically indivisible. There is no evidence, so far as I have noticed, that they also regarded space as composed of indivisible minima. I think this was an innovation by Epicurus.[43]

Notes to Chapter 6

1. An alternative reading "ᾗπερ ἔστιν," suggested by Joachim, would mean "beginning at the natural starting point, viz. that it *is*." This would be a reference to the Eleatic doctrine reported in the next sentence. This is ingenious, but seems to me implausible. What Aristotle means by "the starting point given by nature" is not, I think, Eleatic monism, but the observed facts of change, motion, and plurality (cf. 325 a 25, below).
2. See Kirk and Stokes (1960). Melissus B 7, §7.
3. Burnet (1930), p. 334.
4. I have the support of Sir David Ross on this point: see his edition of *Physics*, p. 480.
5. It is sometimes said that Zeno's arguments *proved* infinite divisibility. If so, then they could not be blocked merely by asserting finite divisibility; it would have been necessary to refute his proof first. But since his whole aim was to prove that "what exists" is *indivisible*, he can hardly have claimed to prove that it is infinitely divisible.
6. 316 b 33; cf. 315 b 6.
7. Cherniss (1935), p. 113.
8. *In De Generatione et Corruptione*, ad loc.
9. Mau (1954), pp. 25-26.
10. The potential optative is probably to be explained by connecting it with the adjectives. Aristotle is qualifying his assertion that Democritus' arguments were "proper, physical ones."
11. Luria (1933), pp. 130*ff*.

Indivisible Magnitudes

12. Note the use of δυνάμει in 316 b 12.
13. Heath (1921), I, 181.
14. Burnet (1930), p. 336.
15. Kirk and Raven (1957), p. 408.
16. 316 b 15 ἀνάγκη εἶναι σώματα ἀδιαίρετα καὶ μεγέθη. It hardly needs pointing out that in Aristotle's usage "σώματα καὶ μεγέθη" does not necessarily mean two sets of objects, (a) physical solids, *and* (b) mathematical magnitudes.
17. Professor Vlastos kindly drew my attention to this passage of *De Caelo* Γ in a letter. He observed that the phrase "μάχεσθαι ταῖς ἀκριβεστάταις ἐπιστήμαις" is used here, and explained by Simplicius, to mean something like "holding a physical doctrine which is out of step with a mathematical doctrine," not "holding a mathematical doctrine which is inconsistent with mathematical principles."

    Up to a point I can agree with this. But I do not think it carries any damaging implications for my argument about *De Caelo* 303 a 20, on p. 87. Aristotle seems to have believed that the infinite divisibility of the geometrical continuum entails the infinite divisibility of matter. Hence he was able to regard any denial of the infinite divisibility of matter as being contrary to mathematical principles (not merely "out of step with" them).

    It must be admitted that this consideration weakens the force of Aristotle's evidence about Democritus. For it might be held that it was only Aristotle's own conviction that mathematical and physical divisibility must march in step which enabled him to accuse Democritus of being in conflict with mathematics. However, I should argue against this (1) that in any case the indivisible magnitudes required to meet the Eleatic arguments are still indivisible in the stronger sense; (2) that Aristotle must have been guilty of more than ordinary disingenuousness or ignorance if he had failed to mention or notice a distinction in Democritus' work between physical and conceptual divisibility; and (3) that there is no good reason for thinking that Democritus was clearer on the subject of this distinction than Aristotle was.
18. 231 a 24.
19. *Physics* Z 10, 240 b 8*ff*.
20. Verdenius and Waszink (1946) argue that the passage has been interpolated by "a zealous but not very intelligent Aristotelian." They would bracket b 20 καὶ ἀδιαίρετον, b 21 τὸ μὲν γὰρ δυνάμει, τὸ δ' ἐντελεχείᾳ ὑπάρξει, b 22 δυνάμει, and b 23-5 οὐχ ὥστε . . . ὁτιοῦν σημεῖον. They may be right; I admit that I can make nothing of the last of these, even on Joachim's hypothesis that it was originally a marginal note. I have omitted it from my translation, but I have thought it best to try to make sense of the rest.
21. Hammer-Jensen (1910), p. 104.
22. I am tempted to quote an additional piece of Aristotelian evidence, *De Anima* A 4, 409 a 10-16. Here Aristotle appears to draw a parallel between Xenocrates' theory that soul is a number, and therefore (according to Aristotle) made of monads, and Democritus' theory that soul is composed of "little corpuscles." This parallel might well suggest that Aristotle thought of Democritean soul atoms as being *partless*, like monads. But unfortunately I do not fully understand Aristotle's argument here: "a very difficult passage," as Ross observes in his commentary.

The Atomists' Reply to the Eleatics

Somewhat similar is *Metaphysics* M 8, 1084 b 26. Here again Aristotle seems to compare the Atomists (ἕτεροί τινες, but the identification is fairly sure), who composed things out of "the minimum" (τὸ ἐλάχιστον), with the Pythagoreans who used "the one" or "the monad" in this way. See Cherniss (1944), p. 130.

23. Simplicius *De Caelo* 609.17.
24. Bailey (1928), p. 126.
25. See Mau (1954), pp. 19-20; Kirk and Raven (1957), p. 408, n. 1.
26. *De Elementis secundum Hippocratem* 1, 2 = DK 68 A 49 (Vol. II, 97, 25).
27. Simplicius *Physics* 82.1.
28. Dionysius, reported by Eusebius, DK 68 A 43.
29. DK 68 B 11.
30. See Lucretius, 2.481-521 and Epicurus *Letter to Herodotus* §55.
31. DK 68 A 47.
32. DK 68 A 1 (Vol. II, 84.13).
33. I note Jürgen Mau's ingenious argument (1954, p. 24) that the size of atoms had something to do with the commensurability problem: astronomical calculations, having a large common measure, might admit "world-sized atoms." But I doubt if this ingenuity is necessary.
34. Γ 4, 303 a 12.
35. Simplicius *De Caelo* 613.12-16. Note the indefinite "ἐὰν δείξῃ τις λόγος."
36. Γ 5, 304 a 10.
37. *Metaphysics* A 4, 985 b 19.
38. Theophrastus, *De Sensibus* 61 = DK 68 A 135: βαρὺ μὲν οὖν καὶ κοῦφον τῷ μεγέθει διαιρεῖ Δημόκριτος. εἰ γὰρ διακριθὲν ἓν ἕκαστον κατὰ σχῆμα διαφέρει σταθμῷ, τῷ μεγέθει διαφέρειν. That this or something like it is the true reading is cogently argued by John B. McDiarmid (1960).
39. In rejecting this testimony I can claim the support of Diels and Kranz, Kirk and Raven, Burnet, and all those who believe that Democritus was only a physical atomist.

   Luria also quotes Themistius *De Caelo* 186.26, which seems to suggest that there is found in the atoms something which admits division conceptually into seven (sic) parts. This is a Latin version of a Hebrew version of an Arabic version of the Greek; the text is also corrupt.

   He claims also that there is support for his case in Simplicius *Physics* 82.1, *De Caelo* 648.26 and 649.2 ff. The first of these has been dealt with on p. 95; the last two explain Aristotle's criticism, and are not necessarily derived from Democritus at all.
40. Cf. the similar argument in Lucretius 1.528-539, and Epicurus *Letter to Herodotus* §41.
41. DK 68 B 11 1: περὶ διαφορῆς γωνίης (for this reading, see Heath (1921), I, 178-179) ἢ περὶ ψαύσιος κύκλου καὶ σφαίρης. 11p περὶ ἀλόγων γραμμῶν καὶ ναστῶν.
42. See Plato *Republic* 546 c, and the many commentaries on this passage, along with Heath (1921), 1.305 ff.
43. Guthrie (1965), 503-507, has independently reached the same conclusion about the atoms of Democritus.

CHAPTER 7

INDIVISIBLE MAGNITUDES IN THE ACADEMY

WE are faced with the conclusion that Democritus believed there were minute particles of matter which were not merely unsplittable but also theoretically indivisible. Yet they certainly had size and shape. How could this be?

Perhaps it will help to make this conclusion more plausible if we examine some other theories which seem to involve "indivisible magnitudes" of a similar type. Aristotle attributed such a theory to Plato himself:

> Plato used to attack this whole class [sc. the class of points] as being a belief of the geometricians; he used to call the starting point (ἀρχή) of a line (and he used to make this statement often) the indivisible lines.[a]

This, as Sir David Ross has observed in his most helpful note on this sentence, is the only direct attribution of the theory of indivisible lines to Plato, though it was frequently assigned to his pupil Xenocrates. Still, it is as explicit as one could wish, and one would need powerful reasons for discounting it. It does not matter very much for our present purpose whether Plato himself worked with such a theory or not; it will be enough to observe that it was current in the early Academy. I wish to stress two points: that the theory in question *is* a theory of theoretically indivisible units having extension in space, and that it was held by people who were in contact with the best mathematicians of the day.

The second of these points will hardly be disputed: one has only to think of Theaetetus and Eudoxus. Theaetetus worked on irra-

---

[a] τούτῳ μὲν οὖν τῷ γένει καὶ διεμάχετο Πλάτων ὡς ὄντι γεωμετρικῷ δόγματι, ἀλλ' ἐκάλει ἀρχὴν γραμμῆς—τοῦτο δὲ πολλάκις ἐτίθει—τὰς ἀτόμους γραμμάς. (*Metaphysics* A 9, 992 a 20 ff.)

Indivisible Magnitudes in the Academy

tional numbers and classified "irrational lines" according to different types.*[1] This is particularly significant, in that the existence of irrational lines raises the problem of divisibility very acutely. Eudoxus is believed to have worked out the method of exhaustion in geometry, which involves making a series of approximations to a limit, and thus seems to demand the infinite divisibility of geometrical magnitudes. It would seem that any members of the Academy who wished to maintain a theory of indivisible magnitudes would not have lacked expert criticism.

We must return to the first point, and see what kind of a theory it was. This can be done best by looking at the arguments used in its support, some of which, fortunately, are preserved at the beginning of the Peripatetic treatise *On Indivisible Lines*. (I have no special theory about this disappointing work; I imagine it is post-Aristotelian, and written in opposition to Xenocrates.)

The five arguments may be summarized as follows:[2]

(1) If we accept that there is a real difference between the large and the small, and if the large admits practically (σχεδόν) an infinite number of divisions, then the small must admit only a finite number of divisions. And this applies to all types of quantity.
(2) If there is an idea of line, and if the idea is prior to everything which shares its name, then the Line-itself must be indivisible; for otherwise, since parts are prior to their whole, there would be something prior to the Line-itself.
(3) If bodies are made of elements, and nothing is prior to the elements, the elements must be indivisible, since (again) parts are prior to their whole.
(4) Zeno's argument, that something moving along a line must always reach the half-way point first, proves that there are indivisible lines. [This argument has already been discussed above, chapter 5.]
(5) [This is an argument which attempts to prove the existence of indivisible lines and planes from the mathematicians' own assumptions about commensurability. I have not yet been able to understand it. The text is corrupt, and I doubt whether either Joachim or Schramm has explained it correctly.]

These five arguments, with the exception of the third, are all concerned not with physical but with theoretical divisibility. More-

* Please see end of chapter for numbered references.

Indivisible Magnitudes

over, it is clear that there is no discrepancy between a theory of indivisible *lines* and a theory of indivisible *planes* or *solids*; indeed the treatise opens with these words: "Are there indivisible lines, and in general is there a partless unit in all quantitative things, as some say?" Indivisible lines are simply the most basic of all the indivisibles. The indivisible line is the unit of measurement in one dimension, but it has *no* extension at all in the other two. The indivisible plane is the unit of measurement in two dimensions, and the indivisible solid in three. The indivisible solid is not *divisible* into indivisible planes (nor the indivisible plane into indivisible lines) since no amount of planes could make up a solid; the plane does not have a very small extension in the third dimension; it has none whatever.

It may be objected that if someone holds a theory of indivisible solids, and if this is not merely about physical possibilities but about theoretical possibilities, then he *cannot* believe in the existence of indivisible planes or lines. For he is saying that nothing smaller than his indivisible solid is conceivable; no distinctions in it are possible. But the plane would be one face of his solid, as opposed to the other faces. So in speaking about the plane he is transgressing his own law, and making distinctions within the indistinguishable.

The answer to this objection is that the theory states only that there is a minimum unit of *measurement*. The indivisible solid is not divisible into solids of smaller dimensions. The plane is not a smaller solid, since it is not a solid at all. It has *no* third dimension.

We can now see why Plato might have objected to the point as being just "a belief of the geometricians." The indivisible solid is the unit of cubic measurement, the indivisible plane the unit of square measurement, and the indivisible line the unit of linear measurement. The point is nothing at all. If you have a line then it must be at least one unit long; in this sense the indivisible line is the ἀρχὴ γραμμῆς. The point has no claim to be an ἀρχή since it is "destroyed along with"[3] the line (to use the Academy's technical term) and therefore is not prior to the line.

My intention in raising the subject of "indivisible lines" was simply to point out that such a theory could and did co-exist in the old Academy with expert mathematical knowledge. But while we are on the subject, I should like to consider as briefly as possible

Indivisible Magnitudes in the Academy

whether any such theory could have been held by Plato himself without inconsistency.

Cherniss has argued[4] that Aristotle did not understand Plato's theory of indivisible lines to mean that there is a lower limit to the divisibility of a line in space. "He [Aristotle] has just remarked that, since it is not difficult to overthrow the theory of indivisible lines, it can be shown that spatial magnitude is infinitely divisible (*Physics* 206 a 16–18); then, after setting forth his theory of the infinite by division and inversely by addition, he remarks that Plato set up two infinities (i.e. the great and the small) because there seems to be no limit to the progressions of increase and diminution. The fact that this is merely a reconstruction of Aristotle's . . . does not alter the obvious fact that he could not have ascribed to Plato the doctrine of indivisible lines mentioned in this chapter, for he shows that he is aware that such a theory must deny the possibility of the spatially infinite by division. Nor does the fact that he adds that Plato did not use his 'two infinities' imply a lower limit to spatial division, for this assertion is supported by the remark that *in the number series* Plato made the unit the minimum and the decad the maximum. That he had to take recourse to the number theory here is evidence that he knew nothing of a limit set by Plato to spatial division."

This subtle argument is persuasive; but it must not induce us to overlook the facts. Aristotle *did* attribute to Plato a theory of indivisible lines, and he *did* understand this to mean that there is a lower limit to the divisibility of extended magnitude. It is surely the other part of this alleged contradiction that we must scrutinize. Does Plato's concept of "the great and small" entail the infinite divisibility of spatial magnitudes? This is a highly speculative business, and only a very bold man will be dogmatic. But it should be observed that "the great and the small," otherwise known as "the Indefinite Dyad," played the part of a first principle of all being in Plato's theory, along with "the One." The One and the Dyad are the origin of numbers, and hence of Ideas, and hence of everything else. But the indefinite Dyad itself is of course *not* a determinate being; a determinate being arises only from the imposition of the One on to the Dyad. It seems to me, therefore, perfectly possible that Plato spoke of the Great and Small as infinite in both directions,

Indivisible Magnitudes

and yet imagined that all determinate being (including everything having spatial magnitude) had limits imposed upon it by the One. As Aristotle observed, Plato did not *use* his two infinities. (Cherniss's last argument seems to me insignificant; Aristotle probably chose the number series rather than spatial extension simply because Plato regarded the former as prior, and because in this case there was a limit in *both* directions.)

Apart from the theory of Indivisible Lines, another type of indivisible unit may be attributed to Plato. Nothing here is certain or universally agreed: again, I must be brief, and therefore fail to do justice to many learned counter arguments.

I think the theory of the elementary bodies, earth, water, air, and fire, in Plato's *Timaeus* involves the use of indivisible planes. I follow Cornford's interpretation of the passage; A. E. Taylor, in his *Commentary*, took a different view, but in his review of Cornford's book stated that he found Cornford's arguments convincing.

When the time comes in the *Timaeus* to describe the structure of the primary bodies, Plato first announces that they are made up of two basic units, both right-angled triangles. One is the right-angled isosceles triangle, or half-square; the other is the triangle whose angles are 90°, 60°, 30°, which is half an equilateral triangle. The half-square is used to make up cubes, which is the characteristic shape of earth particles. The half-equilateral is used to make up regular pyramids, octahedrons, and icosahedrons, which are the characteristic shapes of the particles of fire, air, and water respectively.

Now nothing is said about the indivisibility of these triangles. But it seems to me that Plato's theory entails their indivisibility, and that he probably had this in mind. The crucial point is this: fire, air, and water can change into each other; for instance, the half-equilaterals which form an icosahedron of water may re-form into pyramids and thus become fire. But earth cannot become anything else, because the half-square is peculiar to it. It is clear from this that the basic triangles are taken to be indivisible. It is not difficult to construct a figure in which a square is divided into 12 half-equilaterals and a smaller square (see Ahlvers *Zahl und Klang* 56ff., where this point is very fully developed). It seems that there is nothing to

Indivisible Magnitudes in the Academy

prevent the cube of earth from turning into pyramids of fire (say), with a smaller residue of earth—unless the basic triangles are taken to be indivisible in principle.

But if the triangles are indivisible, what kind of indivisibility would they have? At first sight it appears that these must be physical units, like atoms, so that they might be *physically* unsplittable but theoretically divisible to infinity. Plato's words lend themselves to this interpretation:

> When earth meets with fire and is dissolved by the sharpness of fire, it might wander about—either in fire itself or in a mass of air or water, as it happened to be when dissolved—until its parts happen to come together somehow, when they would fit together with each other and become earth, since they could not change into another kind of thing.[b]

The "parts" of earth mentioned here are the elementary half-squares, of which earth is composed. So Aristotle has some justification, it seems, when he objects that Plato allows plane figures the kind of existence that belongs only to physical bodies.

But this will not do. Plato has often been defended against Aristotle's attack with the plea that his plane figures are not physical units in this sense. Taylor, in his *Commentary* (p. 408), compares Timaeus' picture of the changing elements to the modern notion of "the 'propagation' of wave-motion, e.g. when we talk of a wave as passing from end to end of a sheet of water." Cornford, in *Plato's Cosmology* (p. 229), remarks that "the picture of plane surfaces being broken up and the fragments drifting about till they find others to combine with... cannot be taken literally"; later (p. 274) he implies that a solution to this problem is found if the "fragments" can be thought of as combining in the meantime into *irregular* solids.

We cannot have it all ways at once. If the elementary triangles are *physical* units, then we must concede that their indivisibility may be merely physical—a concession which Taylor seems to be claiming on p. 405. If on the other hand they are not physical units but some

---

[b] γῇ μὲν συντυγχάνουσα πυρὶ διαλυθεῖσά τε ὑπὸ τῆς ὀξύτητος αὐτοῦ φέροιτ' ἄν, εἴτ' ἐν αὐτῷ πυρὶ λυθεῖσα εἴτ' ἐν ἀέρος εἴτ' ἐν ὕδατος ὄγκῳ τύχοι, μέχριπερ ἂν αὐτῆς πῃ συντυχόντα τὰ μέρη, πάλιν συναρμοσθέντα αὐτὰ αὑτοῖς, γῆ γένοιτο—οὐ γὰρ εἰς ἄλλο γε εἶδος ἔλθοι ποτ' ἄν. (Plato *Timaeus* 56 d 1 ff.)

Indivisible Magnitudes

kind of abstraction, as Taylor claims on p. 408, then, their indivisibility must be of the same non-physical order. Since the latter seems more consistent with Plato's argument, it seems that there is a reasonable case for believing that Plato held a theory of theoretical indivisibles. I do not wish to make much of this, however, since the *Timaeus* is such slippery ground, and I doubt whether all my inferences in this argument are as secure as they should be.

Notes to Chapter 7

1. Pappus *Commentary on Euclid* X; see Heath (1921), I, 209.
2. Throughout, I follow Joachim's interpretation, *Oxford Translation of Aristotle*, VI.
3. συναναιρεῖν. This is a conjectural explanation. If it is correct, we must assume that the Academy, and probably Plato himself, later rehabilitated the point. Alexander tells (*Metaphysics* 55.20ff. = Aristotle *Fragmenta*, περὶ τἀγαθοῦ fr. 2 Ross) that Plato and the Pythagoreans held the point to be prior to the line by the criterion of συναναίρεσις. This is confirmed by Aristotle's *Topics* 141 b 5, which is generally thought to reflect Academic doctrine.
4. Cherniss (1944), p. 128.

CHAPTER 8

ARISTOTLE'S CRITICISMS AND EPICURUS' ANSWERS

If the reasoning of the preceding chapters is correct, we have reached this position: Democritus' theory of "indivisible bodies" was not merely a theory of unsplittable atoms but also asserted theoretically indivisible particles of matter. In principle these ultimate particles might have differed from atoms; they might have been parts of atoms. But the evidence shows that Democritus made no such distinction: his physical atoms were also theoretically indivisible particles.

Now we come to Epicurus; the theory of atomism is a century older. Epicurus, as we have seen in Part I of this study, believed in physical atoms which *contained* indivisible parts. He believed also, as we shall see, in indivisible units of time and space. What caused this modification in atomism?

The answer is unquestionably to be sought in Aristotle's criticism of the earlier versions of atomism, as Simplicius saw. I have already quoted Simplicius' description of the difference between the Democritean and the Epicurean atom (see ch. 6, text *o*); this description is at once followed by an explanation:

> Aristotle often refuted the doctrine of Democritus and Leucippus; because of these refutations, perhaps, as they were directed against the concept of the "partless," Epicurus, a later adherent of the doctrine of Democritus and Leucippus about the primary bodies, retained their imperviousness but dropped their partlessness, since they had been refuted on this ground by Aristotle.[a]

[a] καὶ πολλαχοῦ μὲν τὴν Λευκίππου καὶ Δημοκρίτου δόξαν ὁ Ἀριστοτέλης διήλεγξεν, καὶ δι' ἐκείνους ἴσως τοὺς ἐλέγχους πρὸς τὸ ἀμερὲς ἐνισταμένους ὁ Ἐπίκουρος ὕστερον μὲν γενόμενος, συμπαθῶν δὲ τῇ Λευκίππου καὶ Δημοκρίτου δόξῃ περὶ τῶν πρώτων σωμάτων, ἀπαθῆ μὲν ἐφύλαξεν αὐτά, τὸ δὲ ἀμερὲς αὐτῶν παρείλετο, ὡς διὰ τοῦτο ὑπὸ τοῦ Ἀριστοτέλους ἐλεγχομένων. (Simplicius *Physics* 925.17ff.)

Indivisible Magnitudes

It was probably what Aristotle had to say about the motion of a partless body that exerted the decisive influence on Epicurus. It is worth quoting at length:

> We assert that a thing without parts cannot move except incidentally, for example by being present in a body or a magnitude which is in motion, as when a thing in a boat is moved by the boat's being moved, or a part is moved by the motion of its whole. (By "a thing without parts" I mean something that is quantitatively indivisible.)
>
> There *is* a difference between the movements of parts considered by themselves, and their movements considered in relation to the movement of the whole. You can see the difference most clearly in the case of a sphere: there is a difference in speed between the parts near the center, the parts on the outside, and the whole; and this is because there is not just one movement.
>
> As we say, then, a thing without parts *may* move like a man who is sitting in a boat while the boat moves, but considered by itself it cannot move. Let us assume that it changes from *AB* to *BC* (it can be from one magnitude to another, from one form to another, or from one contradictory to another); and let the primary time taken by the change be *D*. Now at the time when the change happens it must be either in *AB*, or in *BC*, or partly in one and partly in the other; this is true of everything which changes. But it cannot be partly in each of the two, because then it would have parts. Nor can it be in *BC*, since it will then have changed, whereas our hypothesis is that it *is* changing. It remains that it is in *AB* at the time in which it changes. So it will be at rest, for to be in the same place or state for a time is what we mean by "to rest."
>
> It follows that a thing without parts cannot move, or indeed change at all. The only way in which it *could* move is if time were composed of "nows"; for in any "now" it would *have moved* or *have changed*, and so it would never move but always have moved. But the impossibility of this has already been demonstrated; time is not composed of "nows", nor a line of points, nor motion of jerks—for anyone who asserts this [sc. that a partless thing can move] is in fact saying that motion is composed of partless units, as if time were composed of "nows" or length were composed of points.[b]

[b] λέγομεν ὅτι τὸ ἀμερὲς οὐκ ἐνδέχεται κινεῖσθαι πλὴν κατὰ συμβεβηκός, οἷον κινουμένου τοῦ σώματος ἢ τοῦ μεγέθους τῷ ἐνυπάρχειν, καθάπερ ἂν εἰ τὸ ἐν τῷ πλοίῳ κινοῖτο ὑπὸ τῆς τοῦ πλοίου φορᾶς ἢ τὸ μέρος τῇ τοῦ ὅλου κινήσει. (ἀμερὲς δὲ λέγω τὸ κατὰ ποσὸν ἀδιαίρετον.)

Aristotle's Criticisms and Epicurus' Answers

This argument of Aristotle's bears such a close relation to the theories of Epicurus that a causal connection must be suspected. But there is a difficulty. A proof that a partless body could not move would be fatal to the Democritean atom, as Simplicius saw, if the Democritean atom was, as I have been arguing, a theoretically indivisible unit (not, of course, if it was merely unsplittable, with distinguishable parts; for in that case it could be "partly in one place and partly in another" and would thus escape from Aristotle's argument). Hence there is a strong *prima facie* case for thinking that Epicurus had this argument in mind when he announced that the atom was not, after all, partless.

The difficulty is that Aristotle argued that a partless body could not move *except by a series of jerks*. So a theory of motion which adopted this principle would make it unnecessary to modify the Democritean atom. But there is evidence that Epicurus did in fact hold such a theory of motion.

The clearest ascription of this doctrine to Epicurus is made by the Aristotelian commentators; unfortunately Epicurus' own works on the subject are ambiguous in the form in which they have survived. Themistius writes:

> But our clever friend Epicurus is not ashamed to use a remedy more severe than the disease—and this in spite of Aristotle's

καὶ γὰρ αἱ τῶν μερῶν κινήσεις ἕτεραί εἰσι κατ' αὐτά τε τὰ μέρη καὶ κατὰ τὴν τοῦ ὅλου κίνησιν. ἴδοι δ' ἄν τις ἐπὶ τῆς σφαίρας μάλιστα τὴν διαφοράν· οὐ γὰρ ταὐτὸν τάχος ἐστὶ τῶν τε πρὸς τῷ κέντρῳ καὶ τῶν ἐκτὸς καὶ τῆς ὅλης, ὡς οὐ μιᾶς οὔσης κινήσεως.

καθάπερ οὖν εἴπομεν, οὕτω μὲν ἐνδέχεται κινεῖσθαι τὸ ἀμερὲς ὡς ὁ ἐν τῷ πλοίῳ καθήμενος τοῦ πλοίου θέοντος, καθ' αὑτὸ δ' οὐκ ἐνδέχεται. μεταβαλλέτω γὰρ ἐκ τοῦ AB εἰς τὸ BΓ, εἴτ' ἐκ μεγέθους εἰς μέγεθος εἴτ' ἐξ εἴδους εἰς εἶδος εἴτε κατ' ἀντίφασιν· ὁ δὲ χρόνος ἔστω ἐν ᾧ πρώτῳ μεταβάλλει ἐφ' οὗ Δ. οὐκοῦν ἀνάγκη αὐτὸ καθ' ὃν μεταβάλλει χρόνον ἢ ἐν τῷ AB εἶναι ἢ ἐν τῷ BΓ, ἢ τὸ μέν τι αὐτοῦ ἐν τούτῳ τὸ δ' ἐν θατέρῳ· πᾶν γὰρ τὸ μεταβάλλον οὕτως εἶχεν. ἐν ἑκατέρῳ μὲν οὖν οὐκ ἔσται τι αὐτοῦ· μεριστὸν γὰρ ἂν εἴη. ἀλλὰ μὴν οὐδ' ἐν τῷ BΓ· μεταβεβληκὸς γὰρ ἔσται, ὑπόκειται δὲ μεταβάλλειν. λείπεται δὴ αὐτὸ ἐν τῷ AB εἶναι, καθ' ὃν μεταβάλλει χρόνον. ἠρεμήσει ἄρα· τὸ γὰρ ἐν τῷ αὐτῷ εἶναι χρόνον τινὰ ἠρεμεῖν ἦν.

ὥστ' οὐκ ἐνδέχεται τὸ ἀμερὲς κινεῖσθαι οὐδ' ὅλως μεταβάλλειν· μοναχῶς γὰρ ἂν οὕτως ἦν αὐτοῦ κίνησις, εἰ ὁ χρόνος ἦν ἐκ τῶν νῦν· αἰεὶ γὰρ ἐν τῷ νῦν κεκινημένον ἂν ἦν καὶ μεταβεβληκός, ὥστε κινεῖσθαι μὲν μηδέποτε, κεκινῆσθαι δ' ἀεί. τοῦτο δ' ὅτι ἀδύνατον, δέδεικται καὶ πρότερον· οὔτε γὰρ ὁ χρόνος ἐκ τῶν νῦν οὔθ' ἡ γραμμὴ ἐκ στιγμῶν οὔθ' ἡ κίνησις ἐκ κινημάτων· οὐδὲν γὰρ ἄλλο ποιεῖ ὁ τοῦτο λέγων ἢ τὴν κίνησιν ἐξ ἀμερῶν, καθάπερ ἂν εἰ τὸν χρόνον ἐκ τῶν νῦν ἢ τὸ μῆκος ἐκ στιγμῶν. (*Physics* Z 10, 240 b 8–241 a 6.)

Indivisible Magnitudes

demonstration of the viciousness of the argument. The moving object, he says, *moves* over the whole distance, but over each of the indivisible units of which the whole is composed it does not move but *has moved*.^c

This is confirmed by Simplicius' comment on the same Aristotelian passage.*¹

The position is this, then. Aristotle showed that an indivisible body could not move except on the supposition that time, motion, and extension are themselves all composed of indivisible units; and he claimed to have demonstrated the impossibility of this. Epicurus accepted the conclusion that *all* these things must be composed of indivisibles if any are, but asserted that this is in fact the case. We must now look more closely into Aristotle's demonstration of the impossibility of indivisible units of extension, time, and motion and try to see how Epicurus met it. We can then return to the problem of why Epicurus identified the unit of extension, not with the atom itself, but with its *minimae partes*.

THE important part of Aristotle's argument is at the beginning of *Physics* Z. It is impossible for anything continuous to be made of indivisibles, e.g. for a line to be made of points: for two things are said to be continuous "if their extremities are one," and points *have* no extremities. It is impossible to distinguish the extremity from another part of an indivisible. Nor could a continuous line be made up of points *in contact*. Contact is either of one whole with another, or of a part with a part, or of a part with a whole. Since the indivisible *has* no parts, contact between indivisibles must be of whole with whole. But a whole in contact with a whole cannot form a continuum, since a continuum has *different* parts and is divisible into parts which differ from each other by being spatially distinct.

---

^c ἀλλ' ὁ σοφώτατος ἡμῖν Ἐπίκουρος οὐκ αἰσχύνεται χρῆσθαι φαρμάκῳ τῆς νόσου χαλεπωτέρῳ καὶ ταῦτα Ἀριστοτέλους τὴν μοχθηρίαν τοῦ λόγου προεπιδείξαντος. ἐπὶ μὲν γὰρ τῆς ὅλης τῆς ΑΒΓ κινεῖται, φησί, τὸ κινούμενον, ἐφ' ἑκάστου δὲ τῶν ἀμερῶν, ἐξ ὧν σύγκειται, οὐ κινεῖται, ἀλλὰ κεκίνηται. (Themistius *Physics* 184.9 = Usener 278.)

* Please see end of chapter for numbered references.

Aristotle's Criticisms and Epicurus' Answers

The Epicurean answer to this argument is given in the passages I have examined in detail in Part I.

> If the finite body has an extremity which is distinguishable, even though it cannot be thought of in isolation, it must be that one thinks of the similar part next to this. . . .[d]
> We see that there exists in everything that last extremity which is seen to be the minimum with respect to our senses, so that you may infer from this that the last extremity of those things which you cannot see is the minimum ⟨with respect to the mind⟩.[e]

Apparently the first move in the Epicurean argument was to insist that "the extremity" of a physical body must have dimensions. You can *see* the extremity of a physical body; but you can only see what has physical existence; hence the extremity of a visible body has physical existence, and therefore has dimensions. By analogy, you can infer that the same is true of "the things you cannot see," i.e. the atoms; they too have extremities which have dimensions.

> We study these parts in succession, beginning from the first, and not all within the same area nor as touching each other part to part, but in their own proper nature measuring out the sizes [of bodies], more of them for a larger one, fewer for a smaller.[f]

Here Epicurus answers Aristotle with an echo of his own words. These indivisible units are ranged in order in the continuum, and their contact is neither of whole with whole (i.e. "within the same area") nor of part with part.

But Aristotle said that contacts *must* be either of whole with whole or of part with part or of part with whole. Epicurus clearly envisages another possibility altogether. His indivisibles, he explains, are to be *units of measure*: that is to say, they are to have extension. So although they have no parts, in the sense that they cannot be

---

[d] ἄκρον τε ἔχοντος τοῦ πεπερασμένου διαληπτόν, εἰ μὴ καὶ καθ' ἑαυτὸ θεωρητόν, οὐκ ἔστι μὴ οὐ καὶ τὸ ἑξῆς τούτου τοιοῦτον νοεῖν . . . (*Letter to Herodotus* §57 = C 2.)

[e] cum videamus id extremum cuiusque cacumen
esse quod ad sensus nostros minimum esse videtur
conicere ut possis ex hoc, quae cernere non quis
extremum quod habent, minimum consistere ⟨menti⟩. (Lucretius 1.749–752.)
For the supplement, see chapter 2, p. 29.

[f] ἑξῆς τε θεωροῦμεν ταῦτα ἀπὸ τοῦ πρώτου καταρχόμενοι καὶ οὐκ ἐν τῷ αὐτῷ, οὐδὲ μέρεσι μερῶν ἁπτόμενα, ἀλλ' ἢ ἐν τῇ ἰδιότητι τῇ ἑαυτῶν τὰ μεγέθη καταμετροῦντα, τὰ πλείω πλεῖον καὶ τὰ ἐλάττω ἔλαττον. (*Letter to Herodotus* §58 = D 3.)

Indivisible Magnitudes

divided into units having smaller dimensions, this does not entail that there is *no* distance between one surface of his unitary solid and another. In such a unitary solid, he might have added, it is perfectly legitimate to speak of one surface as opposed to another. Surfaces are not parts.

Thus the Epicurean theory attempts to slip through a gap in Aristotle's net. Aristotle has shown that a continuous magnitude cannot be composed of indivisible units *which have no size at all*; but he has not shown here that an indivisible unit *must* have no size. It would have been clearer, I think, if the Epicureans had not made a mistake in their treatment of the concept of "an extremity." "The indivisible," said Aristotle, "does not have an extremity and some other part." The Epicureans could have pointed out that the extremity is not a *part*: a surface is not a *part* of a solid, and a point is not a *part* of a line.[2] So an indivisible *may* have extremities without thereby having parts. However, they chose a different course. They accepted Aristotle's view that the extremity is a part. They identified it with the indivisible part. They were then left without a word for the edges of the indivisible part; but the existence of its edges was a necessary consequence of their theory, and need not have caused them embarrassment.

Their theory might be clarified (if any clarification is needed) with the help of the analogy of a drawing made on a piece of graph paper by filling in some squares of the grid and leaving others blank. There is no third alternative; so there is no room for talk of any fraction of a square, or of the diagonal of a square. The squares are all considered as wholes. They can be arranged in rows, one next the other. This means that the right edge of one is in contact with the left edge of the next; but there is no question of (say) filling in the edge and leaving the rest blank; the squares are still indivisible wholes. If the squares are small enough, and numerous enough, complex shapes can be built up within small overall dimensions. The Epicurean atom, which was itself too small to be seen, was supposed to exist in a kind of three-dimensional grid of this kind. The grid need not be *squared*, to satisfy the requirements of the theory. Any arrangement of shapes which can fill the whole of space without leaving any interstices will do, and I have not noticed

Aristotle's Criticisms and Epicurus' Answers

any evidence which points to one arrangement rather than another.[3]

Now I continue with Aristotle's argument in *Physics* Z 1. He sums up the first stage in these words:

> Obviously every continuum is divisible into parts which are always divisible, since if it is divisible into indivisibles there will be one indivisible in contact with another; for in things which are continuous the extremities are one and in contact.[g]

He proceeds then to a demonstration that either magnitude, time, and motion are all three composed of indivisibles, or none is. The structure of this demonstration is not transparently clear, and since otherwise it is impossible to evaluate Epicurus' answer to it, we must look at it in some detail.

> If magnitude is composed of indivisibles, motion over it will be composed of an equal number of indivisible motions: e.g. if the magnitude *ABC* is composed of *A*, *B*, and *C*, each of these being indivisible, the motion *DEF*, which is the motion of an object *X* moving over *ABC*, will have each part indivisible.[h]

This seems self-evidently true, since "a motion" is clearly being regarded here as meaning "traversing a distance." I think Aristotle regarded it as self-evidently true, and that what follows now is *not* part of the demonstration that indivisibility of motion stands or falls with the indivisibility of magnitude, but is a new argument to exhibit the difficulties involved in the concept of an indivisible motion.[4] It rules out indivisible motions, and thus, since indivisible magnitudes have now been shown to entail indivisible motions, it provides another argument against indivisible magnitudes.

> If something must move when there is a motion, and vice versa, moving will also be composed of indivisibles.

Now *X* moved distance *A* when it moved with motion *D*, distance *B* with motion *E*, and distance *C* with motion *F*. If something moving from one place to another cannot simultaneously *be moving* and *have moved* to the place to which it was

---

[g] φανερὸν δὲ καὶ ὅτι πᾶν συνεχὲς διαιρετὸν εἰς αἰεὶ διαιρετά· εἰ γὰρ εἰς ἀδιαίρετα, ἔσται ἀδιαίρετον ἀδιαιρέτου ἁπτόμενον· ἓν γὰρ τὸ ἔσχατον καὶ ἅπτεται τῶν συνεχῶν. (*Physics* Z 1, 231 b 15-18.)

[h] εἰ γὰρ τὸ μέγεθος ἐξ ἀδιαιρέτων σύγκειται, καὶ ἡ κίνησις ἡ τούτου ἐξ ἴσων κινήσεων ἔσται ἀδιαιρέτων, οἷον εἰ τὸ ΑΒΓ ἐκ τῶν ΑΒΓ ἐστὶν ἀδιαιρέτων, ἡ κίνησις ἐφ' ἧς ΔΕΖ, ἣν ἐκινήθη τὸ Ω ἐπὶ τῆς ΑΒΓ, ἕκαστον τὸ μέρος ἔχει ἀδιαίρετον. (*Ibid.* 231 b 21-25.)

Indivisible Magnitudes

moving when it was moving (e.g. if someone is walking to Thebes, he can't simultaneously *be walking* to Thebes and *have walked* to Thebes), and X was moving distance A, which is partless, when it had motion D, then, if it *had traversed* the distance later than when it *was traversing* it, the motion would be divisible (for when it was traversing, neither was it at rest nor had it traversed it; it was in between).

If, on the other hand, it *is traversing* and *has traversed* the distance simultaneously, then the walker *while walking* will have arrived at the destination.

If, again, something moves over the whole distance ABC, and *its motion is DEF*, and if over the indivisible distance A it does not move but has moved, than motion would be composed not of motions (κινήσεις) but of jerks (κινήματα), and by virtue of something having moved without moving; for it has traversed A without traversing it. So there will be a case of having walked without walking; he has walked this distance without walking it.

Now if everything must be either at rest or moving, X is at rest in each of the sections A, B, C; so we shall have something continuously at rest and simultaneously moving, for it *was* moving over the whole ABC, and it is at rest in each part of the whole and therefore in all of it.

And if the indivisible parts of the motion DEF are motions, then it will be possible, when motion is present, for the thing not to move but be at rest. If the parts are *not* motions, then it will be possible for motion not to consist of motions.[1]

[1] εἰ δὴ παρούσης κινήσεως ἀνάγκη κινεῖσθαί τι, καὶ εἰ κινεῖταί τι, παρεῖναι κίνησιν, καὶ τὸ κινεῖσθαι ἔσται ἐξ ἀδιαιρέτων. τὸ μὲν δὴ Α ἐκινήθη τὸ Ω τὴν τὸ Δ κινούμενον κίνησιν, τὸ δὲ Β τὴν τὸ Ε, καὶ τὸ Γ ὡσαύτως τὴν τὸ Ζ. εἰ δὴ ἀνάγκη τὸ κινούμενόν ποθέν ποι μὴ ἅμα κινεῖσθαι καὶ κεκινῆσθαι οὗ ἐκινεῖτο ὅτε ἐκινεῖτο (οἷον εἰ Θήβαζέ τι βαδίζει, ἀδύνατον ἅμα βαδίζειν Θήβαζε καὶ βεβαδικέναι Θήβαζε), τὴν δὲ τὸ Α τὴν ἀμερῆ ἐκινεῖτο τὸ Ω, ᾗ ἡ τὸ Δ κίνησις παρῆν· ὥστ' εἰ μὲν ὕστερον διελήλυθει ἢ διῄει, διαιρετὴ ἂν εἴη (ὅτε γὰρ διῄει, οὔτε ἠρέμει οὔτε διελήλυθει, ἀλλὰ μεταξὺ ἦν).

εἰ δ' ἅμα διέρχεται καὶ διελήλυθε, τὸ βαδίζον, ὅτε βαδίζει, βεβαδικὸς ἐκεῖ ἔσται καὶ κεκινημένον οὗ κινεῖται.

εἰ δὲ τὴν μὲν ὅλην τὴν ΑΒΓ κινεῖταί τι, καὶ ἡ κίνησις ἣν κινεῖται τὰ ΔΕΖ ἐστι, τὴν δ' ἀμερῆ τὴν Α οὐθὲν κινεῖται ἀλλὰ κεκίνηται, εἴη ἂν ἡ κίνησις οὐκ ἐκ κινήσεων ἀλλ' ἐκ κινημάτων καὶ τῷ κεκινῆσθαί τι μὴ κινούμενον· τὴν γὰρ Α διελήλυθεν οὐ διεξιόν. ὥστε ἔσται τι βεβαδικέναι μηδέποτε βαδίζον· ταύτην γὰρ βεβάδικεν οὐ βαδίζον ταύτην.

εἰ οὖν ἀνάγκη ἢ ἠρεμεῖν ἢ κινεῖσθαι πᾶν, ἠρεμεῖ καθ' ἕκαστον τῶν ΑΒΓ, ὥστ' ἔσται τι συνεχῶς ἠρεμοῦν ἅμα καὶ κινούμενον. τὴν γὰρ ΑΒΓ ὅλην ἐκινεῖτο καὶ ἠρέμει ὁτιοῦν μέρος, ὥστε καὶ πᾶσαν.

καὶ εἰ μὲν τὰ ἀδιαίρετα τῆς ΔΕΖ κινήσεις, κινήσεως παρούσης ἐνδέχοιτ' ἂν μὴ κινεῖσθαι ἀλλ' ἠρεμεῖν· εἰ δὲ μὴ κινήσεις, τὴν κίνησιν μὴ ἐκ κινήσεων εἶναι. (Ibid. 231 b 25–232 a 17.)

Aristotle's Criticisms and Epicurus' Answers

That is the argument. It considers the concept of an indivisible motion by studying the application of two phrases: P "it is moving," and Q "it has moved." There are three possibilities. The first is that P is true *before* Q; this is said to entail the divisibility of the motion. The second is that P and Q are true simultaneously; this is refuted as being contradictory—one cannot, logically, simultaneously be en route and have arrived. The third is that P is *never* true in the case of an indivisible motion. In that case, says Aristotle, there are all sorts of troubles: a thing may have moved without ever moving; a thing may be simultaneously at rest and moving; and motion may be composed of non-motions.

Aristotle evidently thought that his objections to the third alternative were sufficient. Simplicius remarks that he was apparently mistaken:[5]

> It is clear that he has not found a completely convincing objection here, since in spite of his having proposed and refuted the idea the Epicureans said later that motion *does* happen in this way.[J]

What was Epicurus' escape route this time? I think his line of argument can be reconstructed from the wreckage of his writings; but the pieces which survive are not directly on indivisible motions but also involve questions of space and time. These questions, too, were discussed by Aristotle; and his discussion must be outlined first.

The first part of Aristotle's argument depends on the premise that something moving at a constant speed covers less ground in less time. If this is so, and if every motion is divisible, it follows that both time and distance are divisible too.[6]

The second part of the argument *assumes* that every distance is divisible, and assumes also that one thing may move faster than another, in the sense that it may reach its destination before the other.[7] From these premises Aristotle proves that the faster thing covers an equal distance in less time than the slower thing. Then he continues:

> Since every motion takes time, and a thing may move in any stretch of time, and since everything that moves may move faster

---

[J] ὅτι δὲ οὐ πάντῃ πιθανὸν (MSS ἀπίθανον) ταύτην τέθεικε τὴν ἔνστασιν, δηλοῖ τὸ καὶ θέντος αὐτὴν καὶ διαλύσαντος τοὺς περὶ Ἐπίκουρον ὅμως ὕστερον γενομένους οὕτω λέγειν τὴν κίνησιν γίνεσθαι. (Simplicius *Physics* 934.23-25.)

Indivisible Magnitudes

or slower, a thing may move faster or slower in any stretch of time. It follows from these premises that time is continuous (in the sense that it is divisible into parts that are always divisible). It has been shown that the faster covers an equal distance in less time: so let A be the faster and B be slower, and let B have moved distance CD in time FG. Now clearly the faster will move the same distance in *less* time than this: call it FH. Now again, since the faster has traversed the whole of CD in time FH, the slower will traverse *less* distance in the same time: call this distance CI. Since the slower, B, has traversed CI in time FH, the faster will traverse it in *less* time; so the time will have been divided again. And if the time is divided, so is the distance, in the same way; and if the distance is, so is the time. And this will go on for ever if we go from the faster to the slower, and then from the slower to the faster, using the proposition that we have proved about them; the faster will divide the time and the slower will divide the distance. So if this alternating procedure is always valid, and whenever we alternate there is a division, obviously all time will be continuous. At the same time it is clear that every magnitude is continuous; for time and distance are similarly divisible.[k]

It will be seen that this argument may either take as a premise the divisibility of *motion*, and prove the divisibility of time and distance, or else assume the divisibility of distance and prove the divisibility of time. The first sentence of Aristotle's chapter 2 pro-

---

[k] ἐπεὶ δὲ πᾶσα μὲν κίνησις ἐν χρόνῳ καὶ ἐν ἅπαντι χρόνῳ δυνατὸν κινηθῆναι, πᾶν δὲ τὸ κινούμενον ἐνδέχεται καὶ θᾶττον κινεῖσθαι καὶ βραδύτερον, ἐν ἅπαντι χρόνῳ ἔσται τὸ θᾶττον κινεῖσθαι καὶ βραδύτερον. τούτων δ᾽ ὄντων ἀνάγκη καὶ τὸν χρόνον συνεχῆ εἶναι. λέγω δὲ συνεχὲς τὸ διαιρετὸν εἰς αἰεὶ διαιρετά· τούτου γὰρ ὑποκειμένου τοῦ συνεχοῦς, ἀνάγκη συνεχῆ εἶναι τὸν χρόνον. ἐπεὶ γὰρ δέδεικται ὅτι τὸ θᾶττον ἐν ἐλάττονι χρόνῳ δίεισιν τὸ ἴσον, ἔστω τὸ μὲν ἐφ᾽ ᾧ Α θᾶττον, τὸ δ᾽ ἐφ᾽ ᾧ Β βραδύτερον, καὶ κεκινήσθω τὸ βραδύτερον τὸ ἐφ᾽ ᾧ ΓΔ μέγεθος ἐν τῷ ΖΗ χρόνῳ. δῆλον τοίνυν ὅτι τὸ θᾶττον ἐν ἐλάττονι τούτου κινήσεται τὸ αὐτὸ μέγεθος· καὶ κεκινήσθω ἐν τῷ ΖΘ. πάλιν δ᾽ ἐπεὶ τὸ θᾶττον ἐν τῷ ΖΘ διελήλυθεν τὴν ὅλην τὴν ΓΔ, τὸ βραδύτερον ἐν τῷ αὐτῷ χρόνῳ τὴν ἐλάττω δίεισιν· ἔστω οὖν ἐφ᾽ ἧς ΓΚ. ἐπεὶ δὲ τὸ βραδύτερον τὸ Β ἐν τῷ ΖΘ χρόνῳ τὴν ΓΚ διελήλυθεν, τὸ θᾶττον ἐν ἐλάττονι δίεισιν, ὥστε πάλιν διαιρεθήσεται ὁ ΖΘ χρόνος. τούτου δὲ διαιρουμένου καὶ τὸ ΓΚ μέγεθος διαιρεθήσεται κατὰ τὸν αὐτὸν λόγον. εἰ δὲ τὸ μέγεθος, καὶ ὁ χρόνος. καὶ ἀεὶ τοῦτ᾽ ἔσται μεταλαμβάνουσιν ἀπὸ τοῦ θάττονος τὸ βραδύτερον καὶ ἀπὸ τοῦ βραδυτέρου τὸ θᾶττον, καὶ τῷ ἀποδεδειγμένῳ χρωμένοις· διαιρήσει γὰρ τὸ μὲν θᾶττον τὸν χρόνον, τὸ δὲ βραδύτερον τὸ μῆκος. εἰ οὖν αἰεὶ μὲν ἀντιστρέφειν ἀληθές, ἀντιστρεφομένου δὲ αἰεὶ γίγνεται διαίρεσις, φανερὸν ὅτι πᾶς χρόνος ἔσται συνεχής. ἅμα δὲ δῆλον καὶ ὅτι μέγεθος ἅπαν ἐστὶ συνεχές· τὰς αὐτὰς γὰρ καὶ τὰς ἴσας διαιρέσεις ὁ χρόνος διαιρεῖται καὶ τὸ μέγεθος. (Physics Z 2, 232 b 20–233 a 12.)

Aristotle's Criticisms and Epicurus' Answers

mises to do the latter; but the conclusion seems to point to the former. There is a slight muddle here, but an unimportant one.

THE case which Epicurus had to answer can now be seen as a whole. Aristotle produced an argument to show that every magnitude must be divisible, based on the premise that no indivisible can be in contact with another: we have already seen Epicurus' answer to that. Aristotle had a second argument for the divisibility of magnitude, based on a study of motion: if there is an indivisible magnitude, then there must be an indivisible motion; and this is very difficult. There is then a third argument which employs the concept of faster and slower motion, and shows that time and distance must be divisible along with motion.

Epicurus' solution of these difficulties can be briefly summed up. He accepted Aristotle's conclusion that there must be indivisible units of time, distance, and motion if there are indivisible units of any one of these three. He asserted that there *are* indivisible units of motion and indivisible units of time, such that one unit of motion involves traversing one unit of space in one unit of time; and in this case (he agreed with Aristotle) it is *never* true to say "it is moving" but only "it has moved." And he accepted Aristotle's contention that faster and slower motion entails the divisibility of time and distance; he developed the theory that there are no *real* differences in speed, and undertook to explain away the apparent differences in the speeds of visible moving bodies.

The texts in which Epicurus explained this theory are extremely corrupt and difficult to understand. I think it would prolong this essay unduly to go into all the details of interpretation that have been suggested, and I shall therefore try to be brief. There are two passages of the *Letter to Herodotus* which have a bearing in this theory: §§46–47, and §§61–62. Bailey, following an argument of Giussani's, decided that the first of these was misplaced in the manuscripts and combined the two into one. Von der Muehll, Mau, and Arrighetti keep them separate, as they stand in the manuscripts. I agree with this latter view.

The later passage is the more directly relevant; it follows the

Indivisible Magnitudes

argument about indivisible units of magnitude examined in chapter 1, after a section which discusses the concept of "up and down" in an infinite universe.

> Furthermore, the atoms must all move at the same speed, when they travel through the void without collision; neither will the heavy ones move faster than the small, light ones, so long as nothing collides with them, nor will the small ones move faster than the large ones, since they all have a track that is big enough for them[8] when nothing collides even with the large ones. Nor ⟨will there be any difference between⟩ their motion upward or sideways through collisions, and their motion downward through their own weight. For as long as one of these two motions is in force the atom will move as quick as thought, until there is a counterblow, either from something outside, or else from its own weight acting against the force of the object which hit it.[1]

This seems to me clear enough in outline, even though the theory is an odd one. Epicurus states unequivocally that the atoms all move at the same speed, "as quick as thought," however their motion is caused. He *must* state this; otherwise the Aristotelians will prove that there are no indivisibles. Graziano Arrighetti is therefore wrong, when he writes in his note *ad loc.*: "E l'isotachia? È la condizione che si dà quando gli atomi si muovono nel vuoto; vale a dire, praticomente, mai." On the contrary: atoms *always* move in the void, since there is nothing else for them to move in; and Epicurus says, and means, that they always move at the same speed whether their motion is due to weight or collision.[9]

Two kinds of motion are mentioned here: motion downward, which is due to weight, and motion upward or sideways, which is due to collision. The last sentence of this passage may need explanation. Epicurus says that motion due to either one of these causes will go on at the same speed until it is countered. If it is downward motion, it can only be countered by collision with another atom

---

[1] καὶ μὴν καὶ ἰσοταχεῖς ἀναγκαῖον τὰς ἀτόμους εἶναι, ὅταν διὰ τοῦ κενοῦ εἰσφέρωνται μηθενὸς ἀντικόπτοντος· οὔτε γὰρ τὰ βαρέα θᾶττον οἰσθήσεται τῶν μικρῶν καὶ κούφων, ὅταν γε δὴ μηδὲν ἀπαντᾷ αὐτοῖς· οὔτε τὰ μικρὰ τῶν μεγάλων, πάντα πόρον σύμμετρον ἔχοντα, ὅταν μηθὲν μηδὲ ἐκείνοις ἀντικόπτῃ· οὔθ' ἡ ἄνω οὔθ' ἡ εἰς τὸ πλάγιον διὰ τῶν κρούσεων φορά, οὔθ' ἡ κάτω διὰ τῶν ἰδίων βαρῶν. ἐφ' ὁπόσον γὰρ ἂν κατίσχῃ ἑκάτερον, ἐπὶ τοσοῦτον ἅμα νοήματι τὴν φορὰν σχήσει, ἕως ἀντικόψῃ ἢ ἔξωθεν ἢ ἐκ τοῦ ἰδίου βάρους πρὸς τὴν τοῦ πλήξαντος δύναμιν. (*Letter to Herodotus* §61.)

Aristotle's Criticisms and Epicurus' Answers

coming up or across; if it is upward or sideways motion, it can be countered either by collision or by the reassertion of weight. In the latter case one would expect a slow deceleration, followed by acceleration in another direction, but this is ruled out. Motion at full speed in one direction is followed instantaneously by motion at full speed in the other direction. Of course variations in weight must cause variations in motion (Arrighetti is right to stress this). Variations may be of two kinds, in direction or in distance. If a falling heavy atom collides with a light atom, then the heavy atom may perhaps be only *slightly* deflected, or else it may be turned directly about but move upward through only a few space units before its weight reasserts itself.

This account of atomic motion leaves out two important points. The first is that atoms have a *third* source of motion in Epicurean theory: there is the swerve, as well as weight and collision. I do not know why Epicurus failed to mention it here. The second is that perceptible things certainly do exhibit obvious differences in speed. This is explained in the next section.

> But of course, in the case of compounds, one will be said to be faster than another, although atoms all move with equal speed, by virtue of the atoms in the compounds moving in one and the same direction even over the smallest *continuous* period of time, though in the times which are distinguishable only in thought they do *not* move in the same direction but have frequent collisions, until the continuous tendency of their motion comes within the scope of perception.[10] [m]

It is *compounds* which exhibit differences of speed. How are these differences to be explained, if the atoms which compose these compounds all move with the same speed? All compounds, in Epicurean theory, are composed of aggregations of atoms which jostle continually with one another in never-ceasing motion. A compound will move, if all its component atoms move in the same direction over a period of time. If they *never* move all in the same direction,

[m] ἀλλὰ μὴν καὶ κατὰ τὰς συγκρίσεις θάττων ἑτέρα ἑτέρας ῥηθήσεται, τῶν ἀτόμων ἰσοταχῶν οὐσῶν, τῷ ἐφ' ἕνα τόπον φέρεσθαι τὰς ἐν τοῖς ἀθροίσμασιν ἀτόμους καὶ κατὰ τὸν ἐλάχιστον συνεχῆ χρόνον, εἰ μὴ ἐφ' ἕνα κατὰ τοὺς λόγῳ θεωρητοὺς χρόνους, ἀλλὰ πυκνὸν ἀντικόπτουσιν, ἕως ἂν ὑπὸ τὴν αἴσθησιν τὸ συνεχὲς τῆς φορᾶς γίνηται. (Ibid. §62.)

Indivisible Magnitudes

the compound will be stationary. If they all have the same general direction only when a *long* period of time is considered, the compound will move slowly. It will move fast only if all the atoms move in the same direction in *the smallest period of continuous time*. Of course, the atoms in a compound do not all move in the same direction in *the indivisible units of time*: that would mean that the compound moved at atomic speed, "as quick as thought," and we see that compounds do not do that. When you consider those periods of time that are too short to be perceived, namely the indivisible units of time, which are distinguishable only in thought, the atoms in a compound must be supposed to be moving all over the place, because of collisions with each other. The motion of a compound is the overall tendency of its component atoms taken over a *continuous* period of time—that is, a multiple, large enough to be perceived, of indivisible units of time.

Such is Epicurus' argument, or so I believe. It will be seen that he mentions two somewhat mysterious units of time: "the smallest continuous period of time" and "the times which are distinguishable only in thought." There has been a long-lasting dispute about the meaning of these two phrases, the essentials of which were reviewed by Mau (1954). I agree with Mau's conclusion, that "the times which are distinguishable only in thought" are indivisible units of time—*periods* of time, of course, not instants or limits—within which an atom "has moved" (for you can never say "it *is* moving") over an indivisible unit of space. "The smallest continuous period of time" is clearly a multiple of indivisible units. According to Mau it is still too small for perception, and occupies in the time scale the same position as the atom in the magnitude scale. This may be right, though I do not see either why it should be below the level of perception, or what need there is in the theory for a unit of time corresponding to the atom. The essential point is that it is a period of time over which a *general* tendency of motion can be detected. Perhaps it consists of 10 indivisible units, and an atom moves upward for 4 of them and downward for 6; then it will have moved 2 space units downward in 10 time units. It will then *appear* (or would appear, if it were perceptible in isolation) to move more slowly than an atom which moves upward for 3 units

Aristotle's Criticisms and Epicurus' Answers

and downward for 7, and therefore moves 4 space units downward in 10 time units. Over this continuous period of time a difference of speed has appeared; but there is still no difference within each indivisible time unit. Epicurus in fact adds a warning that what is true of a continuous period of time is not true of indivisible units:

> The conjecture made about what is unseen, to the effect that the times distinguishable only in thought will also admit continuity of motion, is not true of such things; for everything that is studied in thought or grasped by apprehension *is* true.[n]

The last sentence is of importance for the Epicurean theory of knowledge, but need not concern us now. His warning against pressing an analogy between two kinds of time unit is reminiscent of his warning about different kinds of space unit in §59.[11] He points out there that the minimum in sensation is like a continuous stretch of sensible magnitude in that it *is* a stretch of sensible magnitude, but unlike it in that it has no parts. Similarly the indivisible unit of matter is like the atom of which it is a part, but unlike it in that it has no parts. Now we have a third set: the indivisible time unit is like a continuous stretch of time in that it *is* a stretch of time, but unlike it in that it has no parts.

The other passage of the *Letter to Herodotus* which deals with the topic of time and motion is clear up to a point, but beyond that point it remains, to me, incomprehensible. In §46, Epicurus explains that solid bodies give off streams of *eidola* from their surfaces into the surrounding void. The *eidola* are of extreme fineness but preserve the shape of their parent solid. Then he adds some remarks about the speed at which they move:

> Furthermore, their motion through the void, occurring without collision with things which *might* collide,[12] traverses every conceivable distance in an inconceivably short time. For slowness and quickness are just the appearance which collision and non-collision take on.[o]

[n] τὸ γὰρ προσδοξαζόμενον περὶ τοῦ ἀοράτου, ὡς ἄρα καὶ οἱ διὰ λόγου θεωρητοὶ χρόνοι τὸ συνεχὲς τῆς φορᾶς ἕξουσιν, οὐκ ἀληθές ἐστιν ἐπὶ τῶν τοιούτων· ἐπεὶ τό γε θεωρούμενον πᾶν ἢ κατ' ἐπιβολὴν λαμβανόμενον τῇ διανοίᾳ ἀληθές ἐστι. (Ibid. §62.)

[o] καὶ μὴν καὶ ἡ διὰ τοῦ κενοῦ φορὰ κατὰ μηδεμίαν ἀπάντησιν τῶν ἀντικοψόντων γινομένη πᾶν μῆκος περιληπτὸν ἐν ἀπερινοήτῳ χρόνῳ συντελεῖ. βράδους γὰρ καὶ τάχους ἀντικοπὴ καὶ οὐκ ἀντικοπὴ ὁμοίωμα λαμβάνει. (Ibid. §46.)

Indivisible Magnitudes

This is clear enough. The *eidola* move at atomic speed when there are no collisions, because atoms always *do* move at such speeds; apparent differences of speed are due to ἀντικοπή. Epicurus explains later *why* there are no collisions, but first he says something more about speed:

> Of course, the moving body[13] does not reach its many destinations *simultaneously* in the periods of time distinguishable in thought; that is unthinkable.[p]

The whole passage has to do with perception. Epicurus has just remarked that perceptible images travel inconceivably fast. It is an obvious fact that people at different distances from an object *appear* to receive visual impressions of it simultaneously. So it is entirely to be expected that in commenting on the speed at which these images move Epicurus should say that they travel so fast that differences in their time of arrival at different distances will be unobservable, though not non-existent. It is unthinkable, he says, that such an image reaches many places simultaneously—and I should have expected him to go on to point the contrast: though they may *appear* to do so. The next sentence does indeed seem to contrast a *perceptible* time interval with imperceptible ones, but not quite in the expected way:

> And this [sc. moving body—the *eidolon*?] when it *does* arrive simultaneously [or along with another?] in perceptible time will be departing, not from whatever place it is we apprehend as its source of motion, but from any place at all in the infinite. For it will be like ἀντικοπή, although up to this point we leave the speed of its motion as uncountered.[14] It is indeed useful to get hold of this principle.[q]

Does this mean that an image may get reflected somehow, and thus be delayed in its arrival, so as to arrive at an observer along with images that were actually produced earlier? Or are we to think now of different objects, instead of different observers? I have to confess myself baffled, and pass on to the next sentence.

[p] οὐ μὴν οὐδ' ἅμα κατὰ τοὺς διὰ λόγου θεωρητοὺς χρόνους αὐτὸ τὸ φερόμενον σῶμα ἐπὶ τοὺς πλείους τόπους ἀφικνεῖται—ἀδιανόητον γάρ. (Ibid. §47.)

[q] καὶ τοῦτο συναφικνούμενον ἐν αἰσθητῷ χρόνῳ ὅθεν δήποθεν τοῦ ἀπείρου οὐκ ἐξ οὗ ἂν περιλάβωμεν τὴν φορὰν τόπου ἔσται ἀφιστάμενον· ἀντικοπῇ γὰρ ὅμοιον ἔσται, κἂν μέχρι τοσούτου τὸ τάχος τῆς φορᾶς μὴ ἀντικοπὲν καταλίπωμεν· χρήσιμον δὴ καὶ τοῦτο κατασχεῖν τὸ στοιχεῖον. (Ibid. §47.)

Aristotle's Criticisms and Epicurus' Answers

Epicurus now explains how it is that the *eidola* are able to move so fast:

> Next, no observation falsifies the theory that the *eidola* are of maximum fineness: hence they have maximum speed, since they all have a path big enough to ensure that nothing collides, or few things collide. . . .[r]

At this point the text again seems unintelligible. But perhaps this is enough for my present purpose.

One point of interest may be worth an additional comment, on Epicurus' concept of maximum speed. In his view, atoms moving through the void move "*inconceivably* fast." This again seems to be related to an argument of Aristotle's. Aristotle held that the speed with which bodies move through a medium varies with the weight of the bodies and the density of the medium. Void has no density at all, so that the speed of motion through a void can have no ratio to other speeds at all. Since this is impossible, Aristotle argues that there is no void. Epicurus turns this argument upside-down (as Mau[15] points out): there *is* a void, so atoms move through it at "*inconceivable*" speed. They do not, of course, move at *infinite* speed; but their speed is such that it cannot be related at all to the speed of observable motion.

WE ARE now in a position to summarize the development of atomism from Leucippus and Democritus to Epicurus.

The founders of the atomic theory, as we have seen, looked for a way of escaping from the impasse to which physics had been brought by Parmenides, Zeno, and Melissus. The Eleatics had argued that the assertion of the divisibility of material being into parts led to intolerable contradictions; and hence the real world could contain no plurality or change or motion of any kind. The atomists realized that there was one hole through which they could escape—by postulating absolutely indivisible and solid pieces of matter, all below the level of visibility, containing no internal differences at all,

---

[r] εἶθ' ὅτι τὰ εἴδωλα ταῖς λεπτότησιν ἀνυπερβλήτοις κέχρηται οὐθὲν ἀντιμαρτυρεῖ τῶν φαινομένων· ὅθεν καὶ τάχη ἀνυπέρβλητα ἔχει, πάντα πόρον σύμμετρον ἔχοντα πρὸς τὸ ἀπείροις (?) αὐτῶν μηθὲν ἀντικόπτειν ἢ ὀλίγα ἀντικόπτειν. . . . (*Ibid.* §47.)

127

Indivisible Magnitudes

though differing from each other in shape and size. They held that provided these bodies had no internal differences, and therefore no parts, no sort of division of them was possible and so the Eleatic arguments were forestalled.

Aristotle, however, answered the Eleatics differently, by arguing that magnitudes might be potentially divisible to infinity, in the sense that they might be divided *anywhere*, though they could not be actually divided everywhere at the same time (there is a question about his answer to Zeno's "dichotomy," discussed, for example, in Sir David Ross's edition of the *Physics*, pp. 71*ff.*; but Aristotle seems to have thought his answer adequate). By providing a different answer Aristotle made the theory of indivisible magnitudes *unnecessary*. But he also tried to prove it false. A magnitude cannot be made of indivisibles, he argued, because *either* the indivisibles would coincide, and so not make up a magnitude, *or* they would be in contact part to part, and so they would be divisible after all. Moreover, if there is an indivisible magnitude, there must be an indivisible time and an indivisible motion. A partless body could only move by jerks, in such a way that absurdities would follow (e.g. "it has moved without moving").

Epicurus was unable to accept Aristotle's theory of continuity, because it involved the notion of potentiality and this was in conflict with his fundamental principles.[16] Like Leucippus and Democritus, therefore, he felt it necessary to accept the existence of indivisible magnitudes. To avoid Aristotle's refutation, he postulated that his indivisibles should be *minima*—not points without magnitude, but units of minimum extension. Such minima could, he thought, be arranged in succession, side by side, without being liable to Aristotle's objection that they must touch either whole to whole or part to part. He suggested that we have experience of such units in the extremity of any perceptible object: if it is divisible, it is not the extremity; but it must have magnitude, or it would not be perceptible.

Epicurus was now faced with further complications. Aristotle had demonstrated that indivisible magnitudes *in motion* require the assumption of indivisible units of space, time, and motion and, further, that there can be no real difference of speed. Epicurus

Aristotle's Criticisms and Epicurus' Answers

accepted these conclusions, and worked out a theory of motion which would incorporate these features and at the same time be consistent with phenomena.

But this still leaves it undecided why Epicurus chose to make his minimum units of extension into *parts* of atoms, and not into the atoms themselves (the hypothesis of physical atoms was, of course, adopted by him for reasons not discussed in this summary). I have not been able to find any direct evidence on this question; but it is possible to make a reasonable guess. Aristotle's careful analysis of the geometry of motion made it clear that the distance traversed by a moving body must be composed of indivisible minima, if there are indivisible magnitudes at all. So he made it necessary for Epicurus to consider, not merely the atoms, but the places successively occupied by moving atoms. It must then have become obvious that the units must all be equal (otherwise absurd consequences would follow, such as that an indivisible space was too small or too large for an indivisible atom to fit into it). But if this is so, then either all atoms must be equal in size, or else some atoms must occupy more than one unit of spatial extension. The first alternative, so Epicurus thought, did not square with phenomena. So he adopted the second.

Notes to Chapter 8

1. Simplicius *Physics* 934.24 = Usener 278, quoted on p. 119 below.
2. "A quantity or number making up with others a larger quantity or number" is one of the definitions of the word "part" in *Chambers's Twentieth Century Dictionary*. It is in this sense that the surface or edge of a volume is not a part of it. This is of course not the only possible sense of "part." See *Introduction*, p. 6.
3. See also Lucretius 2.476-499, discussed on pp. 41-43.
4. So I differ from Sir David Ross, who writes of 231 b 18 to 232 a 22: "This is a single argument to show that magnitude, time and motion must either all be composed of indivisibles, or none of them so composed." Themistius (183.15-18) and Simplicius (932.17-18) both apparently interpret the argument as I do.
5. I think $πιθανόν$ should be substituted for $ἀπίθανον$ in the first line. If we must retain $ἀπίθανον$, Simplicius says that Epicurus found Aristotle's objection "not wholly unpersuasive"—i.e. his argument that distance and motion must both be composed of indivisibles, if one of them is.
6. *Physics* Z 1, 232 a 18-22.

Indivisible Magnitudes

7. *Physics* Z 2, 232 a 23*ff*.
8. πάντα πόρον σύμμετρον ἔχοντα: "avendo ogni meato proporzionato" Arrighetti; "weil . . . ihrer aller Weg gleichermassen frei ist" Mau; "having their whole course uniform" Bailey—but Bailey's is a queer interpretation of σύμμετρον. See also §47.10, translated on p. 127.
9. Professor Guthrie is therefore too generous to Epicurus in saying that he "had the remarkable perspicacity to anticipate the finding of modern science that in a vacuum all bodies will fall at an equal speed, irrespective of their relative weights" (Guthrie, 1962, p. 18). It was not a question of perspicacity, but of doggedly wrestling with *Physics* Z.
10. I read τὸν ἐλάχιστον for τῶν ἐλαχίστων, in line 3, with Meibom and (I think) all other editors; and the indicative ἀντικόπτουσι for the subjunctive in line 5, with Gassendi. Otherwise I have kept the manuscript reading. Most editors make considerable alterations—perhaps rightly.
11. See above, chapter 1, p. 25.
12. Reading ἀντικοψόντων, with Usener, for ἀντικοψάντων.
13. Reading either αὐτὸ τὸ φερόμενον σῶμα, with von der Muehll, or τὸ καταφερόμενον σῶμα, with Mau, for κατὰ τὸ φερόμενον σῶμα.
14. Reading μὴ ἀντικοπὲν with von der Muehll, for the manuscripts' μὴ ἀντικοπέον or ἀντικοπτέον.
15. Mau (1954), p. 43.
16. This point is discussed in more detail in chapter 11, pp. 154*ff*.

CHAPTER 9

EPICURUS AND DIODORUS CRONUS

SOME sort of theory of indivisibles was advanced by the Megarian philosopher Diodorus Cronus. So much is certain, but the date of this Diodorus is obscure. Zeller gives the date of his death as 307 B.C. This would make it likely that he preceded Epicurus, since Epicurus was only 33, or thereabouts, in 307. Zeller's date reappears in most histories. But the basis of this chronology is remarkably shaky. According to Diogenes Laertius (2.111), Diodorus took part in a discussion with his colleague Stilpo at a symposium given by Ptolemy Soter. Stilpo presented him with a problem which he was unable to solve on the spot. The king was displeased, and Diodorus was derisively nicknamed "Kronos."*1 He wrote a treatise about the problem, and "died of despondency." Diogenes wrote an appalling epigram about him, which suggests that he committed suicide because he was unable to solve Stilpo's puzzle. But this encounter with Stilpo can be dated in 307, because Ptolemy Soter was in Megara then, and Stilpo, so we are told by Diogenes (2.115), never visited Egypt. Hence, Diodorus died in 307.

It seems clear that we could jettison this date if there were any compelling reason to suppose that Diodorus *followed* Epicurus. He might have spent 25 years trying to solve Stilpo's riddle, and *then* have died of despondency. Or the whole story may be a bit of romantic nonsense. However, it will perhaps be best to underrate the originality of Epicurus here rather than exaggerate it; so I shall assume, merely for the sake of argument, that Diodorus comes first.

Diodorus held a theory of "minimum, partless bodies." According to Dionysius of Alexandria (quoted by Eusebius *Praeparatio Evangelica* 14.23) it was a common opinion that Diodorus was responsible for substituting the name "partless bodies" for "atoms."

* Please see end of chapter for numbered references.

Indivisible Magnitudes

Whether or not there is any truth in the implication that Diodorus was a conscious innovator in this matter, it seems to be agreed among the doxographers that the use of the term "partless bodies" distinguished Diodorus from Democritus and Epicurus. The same is said by Sextus Empiricus (*Against the Mathematicians* 9.363 and *Outlines of Pyrrhonism* 3.32) and by Stobaeus (*Eclogae* 1 p. 128.10); "partless bodies" are attributed to Diodorus, without any explicit contrast with the Atomists, by Alexander (*De Sensu* 122.23 and 172.29) and Simplicius (*Physics* 926.20).

The most interesting point about Diodorus is that he apparently held a theory of motion remarkably like the Epicurean theory. It is reported at length by Sextus Empiricus (*Against the Mathematicians* 10.37-154). Sextus distinguishes three views which may be held about motion: that it exists, that it does not exist, and that "it exists no more than it does not exist." Those who hold the second view, he says, are Parmenides and Melissus—and Diodorus Cronus, "unless it ought to be said that according to him a thing *has moved* though nothing *is moving*."[2]

The argument by which Diodorus defended this position is similar to the Aristotelian argument we have already studied.[3] It runs like this. A partless body must occupy a partless place, and it cannot move *in* this place, since it fills it up. Nor can it move in another place, since it is not yet in it so as to move in it. So it cannot move at all. But we observe that a thing is in one place at one time and another at another; so it *has moved*. The missing step in this argument is supplied by Aristotle:[4] a *partless* thing cannot be partly in one place and partly in another, so there is no third alternative. Sextus clearly takes this for granted, since he introduces the argument with the remark that the assumption of indivisibles itself entails that nothing moves.

There is not much to show what use Diodorus made of his theory of motion, but there are a few points of interest in the subsequent development. Diodorus, it seems, did not merely assert, what Aristotle had thought too ridiculous to need refutation, that "it has moved" could be true of something of which it was *never* true to say "it is moving." He found some examples to make the concept more plausible.

Epicurus and Diodorus Cronus

Suppose that one man is married at one time and another married a year after him. Now the proposition 'they *have* married'—i.e. the perfect—is true, but 'they are marrying'—the present—is false; for when the first was marrying, the second was not yet marrying, and when the second was marrying, the first was no longer marrying. The proposition 'they are marrying' would only be true if they were marrying simultaneously.[a]

Similarly "Helen had three husbands" is true, though "Helen has three husbands" never was.

Sextus objects to these examples which, he says, depend on an ambiguity; for "these men married" may mean "these men married together," which is false, or "this man married and that man married," which is true.

Diodorus had a better example, however, says Sextus.

Let a ball be thrown on to an overhanging roof. Now during the time when the ball is in flight the proposition in the present "the ball is touching the roof" is false, since it is still moving. But when it touches the roof, the perfect becomes true: "it has touched the roof." So it is possible for the perfect to be true though the present is false, and hence a thing may *have moved*, in the perfect, though it does not *move*, in the present.[b]

Sextus' objection to this is that the present "it is touching the roof" becomes true when the ball *begins to touch* the roof, and the perfect becomes true when it ends its contact and returns.

There is another of Diodorus' arguments "against motion" which may perhaps have some relevance to Epicureanism, though I cannot profess to understand its significance fully. Diodorus, it appears, made a distinction between *motion by predominance* and *motion in totality*.[5] The former occurs when the greater number of parts of a body is in motion while the lesser number is at rest, the

---

[a] ἔστω γάρ τινα πρὸ ἐνιαυτοῦ γεγαμηκέναι καὶ ἕτερον μετ' ἐνιαυτόν. οὐκοῦν ἐπὶ τούτων τὸ μὲν "οὗτοι ἔγημαν" ἀξίωμα συντελεστικὸν ὂν ἀληθές ἐστιν, τὸ δ' "οὗτοι γαμοῦσι" παρατατικὸν καθεστὼς ψεῦδός ἐστιν· ὅτε γὰρ οὗτος ἐγάμει, οὔπω οὗτος ἐγάμει, καὶ ὅτε οὗτος ἐγάμει, οὐκέτι οὗτος ἐγάμει. τότε δ' ἂν ἦν ἀληθὲς ἐπ' αὐτῶν τὸ "οὗτοι γαμοῦσιν", εἰ ὁμόσε ἐγάμουν.(Sextus Empiricus *Against the Mathematicians* 10.97.)

[b] βαλλέσθω γάρ, φησί, σφαῖρα εἰς τὸν ὑπερκείμενον ὀροφον. οὐκοῦν ἐν τῷ μεταξὺ τῆς βολῆς χρόνῳ τὸ μὲν παρατατικὸν ἀξίωμα " ἅπτεται ἡ σφαῖρα τῆς ὀροφῆς" ψεῦδός ἐστιν· ἔτι γὰρ ἐπιφέρεται. ὅταν δὲ ἅψηται τῆς ὀροφῆς, γίνεται ἀληθὲς τὸ συντελεστικόν, τὸ "ἥψατο ἡ σφαῖρα τῆς ὀροφῆς." ἐνδέχεται ἄρα ψεύδους ὄντος τοῦ παρατατικοῦ ἀληθὲς ὑπάρχειν τὸ συντελεστικόν, καὶ διὰ τοῦτο μὴ κινεῖσθαι μέν τι παρατατικῶς κεκινῆσθαι δὲ συντελεστικῶς. (*Ibid.* 101.)

Indivisible Magnitudes

latter occurs when all parts are in motion. (The parts, as we see later on, are supposed to be indivisible.) But the former is prior to the latter, in the sense that the conception of the latter implies the former but not vice versa; for instance, one cannot become wholly grey without having been partly grey. Now suppose a body is composed of three indivisibles, two of them in motion, and one at rest. If we add a second motionless indivisible, the body will still move, because "the three indivisibles with which it moved formerly are stronger than the single added one." And so on, one by one, until we have 10,000 indivisibles, of which 9998 are motionless: the body will still be moving "by predominance"—which is ridiculous. So there is no motion by predominance; and therefore no motion in totality, since the former is prior to it.

This is a most peculiar argument, in which the fallacy seemed obvious to Sextus, as it does to me. I mention it here simply because I do not understand it. Perhaps it gives a clue to Diodorus' general position, if he had one. Zeller[6] regarded the argument as at least consistent with Diodorus' idea that a thing may have moved without ever moving, but it seems to me to be as valid against motion of this kind as against any other. It seems in fact to be nothing but an implausible sophistic argument "against motion." It makes one wonder whether Diodorus did after all believe in any positive theory of motion.[7]

I think it is possible, then, that Diodorus may have helped Epicurus by developing some of the ideas put forward by Aristotle on the subject of partless bodies and an atomic theory of motion. But I have not observed anything which Epicurus must have borrowed from Diodorus and could not have derived from Aristotle; and since on other grounds I believe that Aristotle was by far the most important force in the development of Epicureanism, I am inclined to discount the influence of Diodorus.

Notes to Chapter 9

1. Kronos was a common nickname for someone who was "past it," because of its supposed association with *Chronos* (time). See Plato *Euthydemus* 287 b.

Epicurus and Diodorus Cronus

2. εἰ μή τι ῥητέον κατὰ τοῦτον κεκινῆσθαι μέν τι, κινεῖσθαι δὲ μηδὲ ἕνα (48).
3. Chapter 8, pp. 112-113.
4. 240 b 26.
5. Sextus *Against the Mathematicians* 10 113: διττῆς δὲ οὔσης κινήσεως, μιᾶς μὲν τῆς κατ' ἐπικράτειαν, δευτέρας δὲ τῆς κατ' εἰλικρίνειαν. . . .
6. Zeller (1921-22) [Part II, vol. 1], p. 266.
7. Diodorus may have been criticizing the idea of κινεῖσθαι κατὰ τὸ ἐπικρατοῦν in Aristotle's *De Caelo* A2, 269 ᵃ 2. Compounds of the simple bodies, says Aristotle, move "according to the predominant element."

CHAPTER 10

EPICURUS AND DAVID HUME

THERE are some interesting similarities between the Epicurean theory of indivisibles and Hume's theory of space and time. I hope it may sharpen up the details of our picture of the Epicurean theory if we compare it at various points with Hume's.

Hume's theory is set out in his *Treatise of Human Nature*, Part II: I quote from the edition of Green and Grose (London, 1886).

> 'Tis universally allow'd, that the capacity of the mind is limited, and can never attain a full and adequate conception of infinity: And tho' it were not allow'd, 'twould be sufficiently evident from the plainest observation and experience. 'Tis also obvious, that whatever is capable of being divided *in infinitum*, must consist of an infinite number of parts, and that 'tis impossible to set any bounds to the number of parts, without setting bounds at the same time to the division. It requires scarce any induction to conclude from hence, that the *idea*, which we form of any finite quality, is not infinitely divisible, but that by proper distinctions and separations we may run up this idea to inferior ones, which will be perfectly simple and indivisible. In rejecting the infinite capacity of the mind, we suppose it may arrive at an end in the division of its ideas; nor are there any possible means of evading the evidence of this conclusion.
>
> (*Treatise of Human Nature* II, 1, pp. 334-335)

Hume's argument here plainly requires the assumption of one proposition which is not expressed—namely that to "attain a full and adequate conception" of a thing entails the comprehension of each and every one of its parts. The same unexpressed assumption is made by Epicurus in section C 2 of the passage examined in chapter 1. For the argument there depends on the notion that to have an idea of something which has infinite parts entails "arriving at infinity in thought"; and this is clearly supposed to be self-evidently absurd.*[1]

---

* Please see end of chapter for numbered references.

Epicurus and David Hume

The assumption, which is clearly false, is a more plausible one for these two philosophers than it might be for others, because they share the belief that to comprehend a thing, or to have an idea of it (in Hume's terminology), is to have a mental picture of it. It would be interesting to make a detailed comparison between Epicurus' "sensations" and "preconceptions" on the one hand, and Hume's "impressions" and "ideas" on the other; but this would take us too far from the present subject. In Greek thought, the word νοῦς and its derivatives from the earliest times were most commonly used in situations where we naturally use the word "see" in English (as in "I see the point," "I see what you mean").[2] But even the English "see" does not always denote having a mental picture (we can say "I see your argument"). The Greek νοῦς and νοεῖν were very commonly used in this more limited sense, particularly in the Homeric poems, but in later literature too. (It is fascinating to observe how William Golding has used this idea, whether in conscious imitation of the Greeks or not, in his brilliant novel about primitive men, *The Inheritors*. Thoughts are "pictures." "The pictures went out of his head for a while. . . . There were so many things to be said. He wished he could ask Mal what it was that joined a picture to a picture so that the last of many came out of the first.")

It is always helpful in understanding Greek philosophical theories of νοῦς to remember its natural connection with mental picturing. The connection is particularly close in Epicurus. His theory was that the atoms of *eidola* perceived by the senses printed their pattern in some way on the soul atoms, and this pattern was retained in such a way that it could be recalled on future occasions. Thinking, for him, was an operation with these retained patterns. If any such pattern could be shown to contain an infinite number of elements, this would involve the theory in the apparently insuperable difficulty mentioned by both Epicurus and Hume: the mind, which is certainly finite, would need to have an infinite capacity, if it was ever to comprehend such an object.

Hume continues:

> 'Tis therefore certain, that the imagination reaches a *minimum*, and may raise up to itself an idea, of which it cannot conceive any sub-division, and which cannot be diminished without a total

Indivisible Magnitudes

> annihilation. When you tell me of the thousandth and ten thousandth part of a grain of sand, I have a distinct idea of these numbers and of their different proportions; but the images, which I form in my mind to represent the things themselves, are nothing different from each other, nor inferior to that image, by which I represent the grain of sand itself, which is suppos'd so vastly to exceed them. What consists of parts is distinguishable into them, and what is distinguishable is separable. But whatever we may imagine of the thing, the idea of a grain of sand is not distinguishable, nor separable into twenty, much less into a thousand, ten thousand, or an infinite number of different ideas.
>
> (*Ibid.* 335)

When Hume speaks of "an idea, of which [the imagination] cannot conceive any subdivision, and which cannot be diminished *without a total annihilation*," we are reminded of Epicurus' statement that if we accept infinite divisibility we may "in our conceptions of the totals be compelled to grind away things that exist and let them go to waste *into the non-existent*" (B 1). Moreover, Hume appears to be saying that our idea of a fraction of a grain of sand will not differ from our idea of a whole grain, just as Epicurus insists that when we think we *can* make distinctions in the minimum, what we distinguish must be *equal* to the minimum (D 2).[3]

Hume continues, as Epicurus did, with an analogy between the imagination and the senses:

> 'Tis the same case with the impressions of the senses as with the ideas of the imagination. Put a spot of ink upon paper, fix your eye upon that spot, and retire to such a distance, that at last you lose sight of it; 'tis plain, that the moment before it vanish'd the image or impression was perfectly indivisible.
>
> (*Ibid.* 335)

Hume goes on to insist that the indivisible minimum of the imagination really is a minimum: the incapacity of the mind to conceive anything smaller is therefore not a limitation at all, since "nothing can be more minute than some ideas which we form in the fancy." The analogy with sense perception may give a wrong impression. We sometimes *see* as a minimum what we *know* to be actually composed of a great number of parts; but we must not conclude from this that our *idea* of a minimum is similarly temporary and unstable.

Epicurus and David Hume

So far Hume's argument moves on the level of "ideas"; he continues with an inference from the nature of ideas to the nature of things:

> Wherever ideas are adequate representations of objects, the relations, contradictions and agreements of the ideas are all applicable to the objects; and this we may in general observe to be the foundation of all human knowledge. But our ideas are adequate representations of the most minute parts of extension; and thro' whatever divisions and subdivisions we may suppose these parts to be arriv'd at, they can never become inferior to some ideas which we form. The plain consequence is, that whatever *appears* impossible and contradictory upon the comparison of these ideas, must be *really* impossible and contradictory, without any farther excuse or evasion.
>
> Everything capable of being infinitely divided contains an infinite number of parts; otherwise the division would be stopt short by the indivisible parts, which we should immediately arrive at. If therefore any finite extension be infinitely divisible, it can be no contradiction to suppose, that a finite extension contains an infinite number of parts; And *vice versa*, if it be a contradiction to suppose, that a finite extension contains an infinite number of parts, no finite extension can be infinitely divisible. But that this latter supposition is absurd, I easily convince myself by the consideration of my clear ideas. I first take the least idea I can form of a part of extension, and being certain that there is nothing more minute than this idea, I conclude, that whatever I discover by its means must be a real quality of extension. I then repeat this idea once, twice, thrice, &c., and find the compound idea of extension, arising from its repetition, always to augment, and become double, triple, quadruple, &c., till at last it swells up to a considerable bulk, greater or smaller, in proportion as I repeat more or less the same idea. When I stop in the addition of parts, the idea of extension ceases to augment; and were I to carry on the addition *in infinitum*, I clearly perceive, that the idea of extension must also become infinite. Upon the whole I conclude, that the idea of an infinite number of parts is individually the same idea with that of an infinite extension; that no finite extension is capable of containing an infinite number of parts; and consequently that no finite extension is infinitely divisible.
>
> (*Ibid.* II, 2, 336-337)

Hume's doctrine of "ideas" in this context produces an argument virtually identical with that of Epicurus. He tries to establish

Indivisible Magnitudes

first that, since infinite divisibility entails possessing an infinite number of parts, our *idea* of a finite extension cannot be infinitely divisible; for if it were, the idea would contain infinite parts, and the mind, being finite, could not have such an idea. We do have an idea of a finite extension; so there must be a *minimum* idea, than which nothing smaller can be conceived. Moreover, he argues (rather obscurely), nothing smaller than this minimum can *exist*, and in this sense our ideas "are adequate representations of the most minute parts of extension." Therefore, from the fact that an *idea* consisting of an infinite number of parts is shown by Hume's argument to be infinite, it follows that an extended *object* consisting of an infinite number of parts is also infinite.

Epicurus' inference from ideas to external objects is less explicit, but it is there. In C 2 he asserts in effect that there is a minimum idea, and that to comprehend something consisting of an infinite number of parts is "to reach infinity in thought." In F he asserts, like Hume, that such minima arranged in succession provide the means of measuring larger and smaller objects in the imagination. Epicurus assumes here that our thoughts, suitably tested and proved, tell the truth about the nature of imperceptible things, just as our senses tell us the truth about perceptible things.

Hume adds "another argument proposed by a noted author (Mons. Malezieu), which seems to me very strong and beautiful":

> 'Tis evident, that existence in itself belongs only to unity, and is never applicable to number, but on account of the unites, of which the number is compos'd. Twenty men may be said to exist; but 'tis only because one, two, three, four, &c. are existent, and if you deny the existence of the latter, that of the former falls of course. 'Tis therefore utterly absurd to suppose any number to exist, and yet deny the existence of unites; and as extension is always a number, according to the common sentiment of metaphysicians, and never resolves itself into any unite or indivisible quantity, it follows that extension can never at all exist. 'Tis in vain to reply, that any determinate quantity of extension is an unite; but such-a-one as admits of an infinite number of fractions, and is inexhaustible in its sub-divisions. For by the same rule these twenty men *may be consider'd as an unite*. The whole globe of earth, nay the whole universe, *may be consider'd as an unite*. That term of unity is merely a fictitious denomination, which the mind

> may apply to any quantity of objects it collects together; nor can such an unity any more exist alone than number can, as being in reality a true number. But the unity, which can exist alone, and whose existence is necessary to that of all number, is of another kind, and must be perfectly indivisible, and incapable of being resolved into any lesser unity.
>
> (*Ibid.* 337-338)

This is nothing but the Eleatic argument which we have studied in chapters 5 and 6, and which we have seen to be an important element in the construction of the ancient atomic theory.[4] I have quoted it in full here, because it gives a very clear illustration of Epicurus' difference from Aristotle, on the subject of unity and extension (see section D 3 in the passage of Epicurus studied in chapter 1, with my commentary).

So far, Hume and Epicurus seem to be pretty well in agreement. But now Hume begins to refer to his own theory as "the doctrine of indivisible *points.*" Epicurus referred to his indivisibles as "extremities" (ἄκρα) and as "limits" (πέρατα). But he never called them *points*; they were *minima*, not objects without magnitude. The question is: did Hume agree with this doctrine or differ from it? At first sight, it certainly appears that he differed from it.

> It has often been maintained in the schools, that extension must be divisible, *in infinitum*, because the system of mathematical points is absurd; and that system is absurd, because a mathematical point is a non-entity, and consequently can never by its conjunction with others form a real existence. This wou'd be perfectly decisive, were there no medium betwixt the infinite divisibility of matter, and the non-entity of mathematical points. But there is evidently a medium, *viz.* the bestowing a colour or solidity on these points; and the absurdity of both the extremes is a demonstration of the truth and reality of this medium. The system of *physical* points, which is another medium, is too absurd to need a refutation. A real extension, such as a physical point is suppos'd to be, can never exist without parts, different from each other; and wherever objects are different, they are distinguishable and separable by the imagination.
>
> (*Ibid.* II, 4, 346)

So it appears that Hume's points have no "real extension," since real extension entails having parts. Nevertheless, they have color and solidity, and they are not "non-entities." This is a baffling doctrine.

Indivisible Magnitudes

Hume's points are not limits, like mathematical points, since a number of them put together makes an extended magnitude. They are not infinitesimals, since an infinite number of them makes an infinite magnitude, not a finite one. But they are not extended magnitudes themselves, so we are told.

We might extract Hume from this maze by supposing that his "extension" is to be construed like "plurality" rather than like the Greek μέγεθος; there cannot be a plurality consisting of one unit, but there can be a μέγεθος of one unit, according to the Atomists. There is some evidence that this is in fact what Hume meant. He observes that "the idea of space or extension is nothing but the idea of visible or tangible points distributed in a certain order" (p. 340): thus he appears to *define* extension as a *plurality* of his points. As two or more arithmetical units make a plurality, so two or more "points" make an extension; but the unit itself has no plurality, and the point has no extension. Two arithmetical units added together, *without any third member*, make a pair; so two of Hume's points added together, *without any third thing*, make an extended magnitude.

The passage just quoted is mysterious in that it distinguishes mathematical points with color and solidity from physical points. It is particularly interesting that the expression "physical points," rejected contemptuously here, is restored to favor in the later *Enquiry Concerning Human Understanding*, in a footnote:

> Whatever disputes there may be about mathematical points, we must allow that there are physical points; that is, parts of extension, which cannot be divided or lessened, either by the eye or imagination.
>
> (*Enquiry*, XII, part 2, note 1)

I take this to confirm that there is a difference between Hume's points and mathematical points, and that Hume came to realize it. His points, having color and solidity, and being *parts* of extension (as he often calls them), cannot differ from physical points.

It must be admitted, however, that it is hard work to maintain that whenever Hume uses the word "points" in this context, he means "minima." For instance here:

> A surface is *defin'd* to be length and breadth without depth: A line to be length without breadth or depth: A point to be what

Epicurus and David Hume

has neither length, breadth nor depth. 'Tis evident that all this is perfectly unintelligible upon any other supposition than that of the composition of extension by indivisible points or atoms. How else cou'd anything exist without length, without breadth, or without depth?

(*Treatise* II, 4, 348)

We can save Hume from trouble here only by supposing that he is imposing the same limit on the use of "length," "breadth," and "depth" that he has already imposed on "extension"—that is, that they always refer to objects containing at least *two* units of dimension.

Hume runs into the same trouble as Epicurus on the subject of extremities. Both philosophers are convinced that the extremity of a thing must be a part of it and must be of the same order of being. Epicurus said that "the finite body has an extremity which is distinguishable, even though it cannot be thought of in isolation" (C 2); the fact that it is distinguishable implies for Epicurus that it is a *part* of the whole, similarly to other parts. Hume writes:

A surface terminates a solid; a line terminates a surface; a point terminates a line; but I assert, that if the *ideas* of a point, line or surface were not indivisible, 'tis impossible we should ever conceive these terminations: for let these ideas be suppos'd infinitely divisible; and then let the fancy endeavour to fix itself on the idea of the last surface, line or point: it immediately finds this idea to break into parts; and upon its seizing the last of these parts, it loses its hold by a new division, and so on *in infinitum*, without any possibility of its arriving at a concluding idea. The number of fractions bring it no nearer the last division, than the first idea it form'd. Every particle eludes the grasp by a new fraction; like quicksilver, when we endeavour to seize it. But as in fact there must be something, which terminates the idea of every finite quantity; and as this terminating idea cannot itself consist of parts or inferior ideas; otherwise it wou'd be the last of its parts, which finish'd the idea, and so on; this is a clear proof, that the ideas of surfaces, lines and points admit not of any division; those of surfaces in depth; of lines in breadth and depth; and of points in any dimension.

(*Ibid.* 349-350)

Since we have *ideas* of surfaces, etc., which are indivisible, it follows from Hume's doctrine of Ideas that the corresponding objects may

Indivisible Magnitudes

exist. In this argument he clearly identifies the indivisible *minimum* with the *extremity*.

I have already observed that this identification left Epicurus without any vocabulary for describing juxtaposition of the minima with each other (see chapter 8, p. 116). The same calamity can be seen in Hume's theory, and much more clearly. In the following passage he considers a possible objection to his theory:

> The second objection is deriv'd from the necessity there wou'd be of *penetration*, if extension consisted of mathematical points. A simple and indivisible atom, that touches another, must necessarily penetrate it; for 'tis impossible it can touch it by its external parts, from the very supposition of its perfect simplicity, which excludes all parts. It must therefore touch it intimately, and in its whole essence, *secundum se, tota, & totaliter*; which is the very definition of penetration. But penetration is impossible: Mathematical points are of consequence equally impossible.
>
> I answer this objection by substituting a juster idea of penetration. Suppose two bodies containing no void within their circumference, to approach each other, and to unite in such a manner that the body, which results from their union, is no more extended than either of them; 'tis this we must mean when we talk of penetration. But 'tis evident this penetration is nothing but the annihilation of one of these bodies, and the preservation of the other, without our being able to distinguish particularly which is preserv'd and which annihilated. Before the approach we have the idea of two bodies. After it we have the idea of only one. 'Tis impossible for the mind to preserve any notion of difference betwixt two bodies of the same nature existing in the same place at the same time.
>
> Taking then penetration in this sense, for the annihilation of one body upon its approach to another, I ask anyone, if he sees a necessity, that a colour'd or tangible point should be annihilated upon the approach of another colour'd or tangible point? On the contrary, does he not evidently perceive, that from the union of these points there results an object, which is compounded and divisible, and may be distinguish'd into two parts, of which each preserves its existence distinct and separate, notwithstanding its contiguity to the other? Let him aid his fancy by conceiving these points to be of different colours, the better to prevent their coalition and confusion. A blue and a red point may surely lie contiguous without any penetration or annihilation. For if they cannot, what possibly can become of them? Whether shall the red

or the blue be annihilated? Or if these colours unite into one, what new colour will they produce by their union?

(*Ibid.* 346-347)

Here Hume has given away too much in the first paragraph, by speaking of external *parts*. Of course an indivisible cannot have parts. But his idea of two "points" lying contiguous, without penetration or annihilation, requires the concept of extremities or edges of points which are not parts of them.

This comparison of Hume and Epicurus has led me to think that Hume's theory, in spite of being called a theory of indivisible *points*, probably did not differ from Epicurus' theory of indivisible *magnitudes*. So I have arrived at a rather different appreciation of his doctrine from that given by Professor C. D. Broad in a lecture to the British Academy in 1961. Hume speaks of his indivisibles both as minima and as points; but they cannot literally be both, and so we must choose to discount one or the other as being an imprecise expression. It seems to me that the important thing for Hume is that his indivisibles are minima, and that he could jettison the expression "points" without serious damage to his theory (though it would need a good deal of rewriting, as we have seen). Professor Broad takes the opposite view; his severest criticisms are connected with the doctrine of indivisible *points*. Thus he examines Hume's notion of the contiguity of points, and concludes that the only way to make sense of the notion of contiguity, in the case of two points, is to suppose that there is *an intrinsic minimum distance*, such that two points cannot be nearer together than this. Naturally enough, he finds this theory so full of paradoxes that it "can be fairly safely dismissed as rubbish".[5] If we interpret Hume's "points" as minima, most of Professor Broad's criticisms of them are irrelevant.

But that is not to say, of course, that the doctrine cannot be criticized on other grounds. There are two questions: was the doctrine of indivisible minima a reasonable theory in itself for a philosopher of Hume's day to hold? and do Hume's arguments in support of the doctrine *merely* require rewriting more precisely, or do some of them *depend* on the identification of the minimum and the mathematical point? I do not feel capable of answering the first question, since I am too ignorant of eighteenth-century geometry; but I will

Indivisible Magnitudes

try at the end of this chapter to assess the *Epicurean* theory in its historical context. As to the second, the arguments for the existence of minima which I have quoted do not appear to depend on the identification of the minimum and the point, though there is one place where this is doubtful. It is essential for Hume that the minimum idea really *is* a minimum; and he sometimes appears to regard this as established because it is "perfectly simple and indivisible." He again uses the expression "perfect simplicity, which excludes all parts," when speaking of mathematical points as conceived by the mathematicians (346-47). Now of course nothing can be smaller than a true mathematical point, since it is defined as having no magnitude at all. But this premise should not be used by Hume, if his "points" are consistently regarded as minima. So far as I can see, he has no other argument for this proposition. But I am not sure that he needs one. At least his argument for the existence of a minimum *idea* is independent of this proposition. It is only in the inference from ideas to objects that the proposition is needed.

But this inference is no doubt liable to more fundamental criticisms than that it makes use of this one dubious proposition. Professor Broad observes:[6] "I have no doubt that Hume's general account of what is involved in having an idea of so-and-so is, and can be shown to be, rubbish." I shall not attempt to criticize this theory now, except to the extent of observing that the concepts required for explaining the juxtaposition of indivisible minima would be difficult to accommodate in Hume's theory of ideas.

Notes to Chapter 10

1. See also *On Indivisible Lines* 968 a 22*ff.*, and chapter 5, p. 70 above.
2. See further my article "The early History of the Concept of Soul," *Bulletin of the Institute of Classical Studies*, University of London, 3 (1956), pp. 1-18, and the works quoted there.
3. It may be objected that Hume has already fallen into a contradiction. He states that the idea of a grain of sand is not distinguishable into twenty or a thousand different ideas; but he also admits that "I have a distinct idea of these numbers and their proportions." It might seem to follow, even for Hume, that one could distinguish the idea of 1/1000 of a grain of sand from that of 1/10,000 of a grain of

Epicurus and David Hume

sand, at least to the extent of saying that the former is 10 times as large as the latter.

But I think Hume is consistent here. He admits that we can distinguish "these *numbers* and their proportions." We can operate successfully with the fractions 1/1000 and 1/10,000. He might agree to the conditional statement: "*If* we could distinguish between the ideas of 1/1000 and 1/10,000 of a grain of sand, the former would be 10 times as large as the latter." It is still open to him, however, to say that as a matter of fact we *cannot* distinguish them; concepts are not distinguished simply by naming them, even if the names we give them entail some mutual relations. Because we can see what proportional relation would exist between a thousandth and a ten-thousandth of a molecule of salt, for example, it does not follow that we could make any *other* sensible statements about them.

This example may help to clarify Hume's argument. If we are prepared to accept that a thousandth of a molecule of salt is "inconceivable" in a sense, this is because we know that one molecule is the *minimum quantity* of salt. When Hume asserts that the ideas of a thousandth and of a ten-thousandth of a grain of sand are indistinguishable, this is because he is satisfied that they are less than the minimum quantity of *extension*. His mistake is in supposing that there *is* a minimum quantity of extension. But because we can *speak* of 1/1000 of an inch and 1/10,000 of an inch, it does not follow that an inch *is divisible* into such fractions; that conclusion depends on what an inch is, not on the numerical relations between these fractions.

4. Zeno A 21. See chapter 5, p. 67; chapter 6, pp. 82-83.
5. Broad (1961), p. 171.
6. *Ibid.* p. 165.

CHAPTER 11

CONCLUSION

I HAVE tried in the preceding chapters to establish the facts about the Epicurean theory of minimal parts and about its origins and purpose. The final task is to make an attempt to evaluate it in its historical context. Did it offer a better or worse solution of the problem of divisibility than others available at the time? In other words, was it better or worse than Aristotle's solution? It would be wrong to shirk these questions altogether, but I shall not attempt to do more than suggest some lines of thought; I am well aware that a full appraisal would need a better knowledge of the philosophy and mathematics of the continuum than I have.

To understand Aristotle's theory, it is essential to be clear about the sense of *potentiality* as it appears there, since it entails some odd consequences which are not always observed. We have studied in some detail Aristotle's critique of the Atomists' theory in *De Generatione et Corruptione* (see ch. 6); there he puts forward his own idea that spatial magnitude is potentially divisible to infinity as the solution of the dilemma which seemed to lead to indivisible magnitudes. But this potentiality is more fully explained in the *Physics*:

> That infinite magnitude does not exist in actuality has already been said; but it does exist by division (for it is not difficult to demolish "indivisible lines"); so it remains that the infinite exists potentially. But this potential being must not be taken to mean that, just as this is potentially a statue because it *will be* a statue, so there is an infinite which *will be* in actuality. On the contrary, being has many senses, and the being of the infinite is like that of a day or a festival of games, by a succession of different things always happening (for in these cases too there is potentiality and actuality: "the Olympic games exist" means both that the contest *can* happen and that it *does* happen). The infinite is manifested in one way in the case of time and the generations of men, and

Conclusion

in another way in the division of magnitudes. For in general the infinite exists in this way, by one thing always being taken after another, that which is taken always being finite itself, but always different from the last; but in the division of magnitudes that which is taken remains, whereas in the case of time and men the members perish, though in such a way that the series does not fail.[a]

In its most usual sense in Aristotle, potential being is secondary to actual being. In *Metaphysics* Θ 8, he explains in detail that actuality is prior to potentiality in substance or being, as well as in knowledge and definition. That should entail—and Aristotle clearly means it to entail—that we cannot have knowledge of or define a potential being in any class without reference to an actual member of the same class; and, more fundamentally, that the existence of a potential being in any class has as its essential condition the existence of an actual being in the same class. One of his favorite examples is the one used in the passage just quoted—the bronze which is potentially a statue. The name "statue" refers primarily to actual statues: it would have no use if there had never been actual statues. To call a lump of bronze a potential statue is to think of a future in which it will be an actual statue. The form of the statue must be actual in our minds if we call the bronze a potential statue.

But a spatial magnitude has the potentiality of infinite divisibility in a different sense. In this case there is *no* possibility that it will ever actually be divided to infinity, and we can never think of it as having been divided to infinity. The potentiality is all there is.

Is this merely juggling with words? If we remove the technical word "potentiality" (δύναμις) and substitute "can" (δύνασθαι), are we saying merely that a magnitude can be divided to infinity but

---

[a] τὸ δὲ μέγεθος ὅτι μὲν κατ' ἐνέργειαν οὐκ ἔστιν ἄπειρον, εἴρηται, διαιρέσει δ' ἐστίν· οὐ γὰρ χαλεπὸν ἀνελεῖν τὰς ἀτόμους γραμμάς· λείπεται οὖν δυνάμει εἶναι τὸ ἄπειρον. οὐ δεῖ δὲ τὸ δυνάμει ὂν λαμβάνειν, ὥσπερ εἰ δυνατὸν τοῦτ' ἀνδριάντα εἶναι, ὡς καὶ ἔσται τοῦτ' ἀνδριάς, οὕτω καὶ ἄπειρον ὃ ἔσται ἐνεργείᾳ· ἀλλ' ἐπεὶ πολλαχῶς τὸ εἶναι, ὥσπερ ἡ ἡμέρα ἔστι καὶ ὁ ἀγὼν τῷ ἀεὶ ἄλλο καὶ ἄλλο γίγνεσθαι, οὕτω καὶ τὸ ἄπειρον (καὶ γὰρ ἐπὶ τούτων ἔστι καὶ δυνάμει καὶ ἐνεργείᾳ· Ὀλύμπια γὰρ ἔστι καὶ τῷ δύνασθαι τὸν ἀγῶνα γίγνεσθαι καὶ τῷ γίγνεσθαι)· ἄλλως δ' ἔν τε τῷ χρόνῳ δῆλον [τὸ ἄπειρον] καὶ ἐπὶ τῶν ἀνθρώπων, καὶ ἐπὶ τῆς διαιρέσεως τῶν μεγεθῶν. ὅλως μὲν γὰρ οὕτως ἔστιν τὸ ἄπειρον, τῷ ἀεὶ ἄλλο καὶ ἄλλο λαμβάνεσθαι, καὶ τὸ λαμβανόμενον μὲν ἀεὶ εἶναι πεπερασμένον, ἀλλ' ἀεί γε ἕτερον καὶ ἕτερον· ἀλλ' ἐν τοῖς μεγέθεσιν ὑπομένοντος τοῦ ληφθέντος [τοῦτο συμβαίνει], ἐπὶ δὲ τοῦ χρόνου καὶ τῶν ἀνθρώπων φθειρομένων οὕτως ὥστε μὴ ἐπιλείπειν. (Physics Γ 6, 206 a 16–b 3.)

Indivisible Magnitudes

also cannot? Diodorus Cronus would have said so, since he defined the possible (τὸ δυνατόν) as "that which either is or will be true" (perhaps indeed he did say so, and Epicurus followed him; but that can never be more than a guess).*[1] But Aristotle provided illustrations to clarify his meaning: the mode of existence of the infinite is similar to that of a day or of the games, which have actual existence but by virtue of a succession of events, not all at once. These examples are not free from ambiguity. Presumably he was not thinking of the day and the games as being *infinitely* divisible, as every period of time is, in his view. In that case they would hardly serve as clarifications of the mode of existence of the infinite: they would merely be *cases* of the phenomenon that is to be explained. Moreover, both the day and the games differ from the infinite in that they are at some time completed. Probably the point of the illustrations is this: we can truly say "it is Wednesday" or "the games are on," even though the *whole* of Wednesday and the *whole* of the games are never in actual being at one time. Their mode of being is a succession of happenings; and this is also true of the infinite. Aristotle adds that there is a difference between magnitudes and days or games, in that in the former case the succession does not mean that each part in turn disappears or passes away, whereas in the latter case it does.

The examples of the day and the games do not solve the problem, however, because both are at some time completed. Aristotle's doctrine of the infinite is that it can never be completed: it means precisely that. "The infinite is not where there is nothing further, but where there is always something further."[2] The question still arises, therefore, whether this is a legitimate form of potentiality in Aristotle's philosophy.

Much light has been shed on this question by the excellent discussion in Professor Wolfgang Wieland's recent book, *Die aristotelische Physik*.[3] He points out the essential connection between the infinite and *motion* in Aristotle's theory. Infinite divisibility is a process in time: as Aristotle puts it himself, "infinity does not stay but is always in progress."[4] To say that a magnitude is infinitely divisible is to say that the *process* of dividing it is an endless one. The

* Please see end of chapter for numbered references.

Conclusion

important thing about this is not so much its positive content as what it excludes: it implies that finite spatial magnitudes, though infinitely divisible, *do not consist of an infinite number of parts*.

This is a point that is often missed. Modern mathematicians can work with infinite sets, and the process of integration in the calculus is sometimes regarded as finding the aggregate of an infinite number of parts (rather than the limit of an infinite series). Aristotle's theory of infinite divisibility has been found sufficiently similar to modern theories to suggest that he held this view as well. That would mean that the difference between Aristotle and Epicurus lay precisely in this, that Aristotle denied what Epicurus asserted in C 1 of the passage we studied in chapter 1: "When someone once says that there are infinite parts in something, however small they may be, it is impossible to see how this can still be finite in size; for obviously the infinite parts must be of *some* size, and whatever size they may happen to be, the size of the total would be infinite." But in fact *Aristotle could agree with Epicurus about it*. Since this statement may appear paradoxical, I shall produce some support for it before considering how it affects our estimate of Aristotle's theory.

At times, Aristotle may seem to contradict Epicurus' assertion. In a passage of the *Physics* he argues that "the infinite by addition" corresponds with "the infinite by division"; that is to say, if we divide a length A to give A' and a remainder, and then divide the remainder so as to give A'' and a remainder, and so on, then since division goes on *ad infinitum*, we are at the same time establishing that there is a series $A' + A'' + \ldots$ which goes on *ad infinitum*. He writes:

> In a finite magnitude, if one takes a definite part and adds to it *in the same ratio*, not taking *the same part* of the whole magnitude, then one will not traverse the finite magnitude: but if one so increases the ratio that one always takes the same magnitude—any one—then one will traverse it, since every finite magnitude is exhausted by any finite magnitude.[b]

Aristotle here agrees with Epicurus in the second sentence that by taking a sufficiently large number of parts, if the parts are all of the

---

[b] ἐν γὰρ τῷ πεπερασμένῳ μεγέθει ἂν λαβών τις ὡρισμένον προσλαμβάνῃ τῷ αὐτῷ λόγῳ, μὴ τὸ αὐτό τι τοῦ ὅλου μέγεθος περιλαμβάνων, οὐ διέξεισι τὸ πεπερασμένον· ἐὰν δ' οὕτως αὔξῃ τὸν λόγον ὥστε ἀεί τι τὸ αὐτὸ περιλαμβάνειν μέγεθος, διέξεισι, διὰ τὸ πᾶν πεπερασμένον ἀναιρεῖσθαι ὁτῳοῦν ὡρισμένῳ. (Physics Γ 6, 206 b 7-12.)

Indivisible Magnitudes

same size, however small, one can exhaust any finite magnitude; so that an infinite number of *equal* parts, however small, would make an infinite magnitude; but at first sight he seems to *differ* from Epicurus in his first sentence by observing that if the parts diminish each time in a fixed proportion, then an infinite number of them will not make an infinite magnitude. However, that is not exactly what Aristotle says. What he does say is that if you take one part A' of the magnitude A, and then another part A'' such that $A:A'::A':A''$, and so on, you will never traverse A. However far you go, there is still further to go. One might indeed be tempted to say that the magnitude A is therefore the sum of an infinite series of parts $A', A'', \ldots$ But *Aristotle* does not say so, and it would be truer to his view to say that however long one continued to find parts like A', A'', there would still be something left of A; hence A does not consist of parts like A', A''.

This point can be confirmed from a later section of the *Physics*, where Aristotle asserts that any one of the infinite number of points in a continuum at which it is potentially divisible is actualized only if and when the continuum is divided there. So a point is not actualized if something in continuous motion merely passes through it, but only if a pause is made there—i.e. if the motion is no longer continuous.

> So we must say to the man who asks if it is possible to traverse an infinite ⟨number of stages⟩ either in time or in distance, that in a sense it is possible, but in another sense not. It is not possible to traverse them in a state of actuality, but in potentiality it is possible. That which moves continuously has traversed an infinite ⟨number of stages⟩ *per accidens*, but not in an unqualified sense. For *incidentally* the line has an infinite number of "halves," but its essence and being are different from that.[c]

This is the nearest Aristotle comes to saying that a finite magnitude may be considered as having an infinite number of parts.[5]

Aristotle's discussion of the continuum, in *Physics* Z and elsewhere, is considered by some to be his best work. There can be no

[c] ὥστε λεκτέον πρὸς τὸν ἐρωτῶντα εἰ ἐνδέχεται ἄπειρα διεξελθεῖν ἢ ἐν χρόνῳ ἢ ἐν μήκει, ὅτι ἔστιν ὡς, ἔστιν δ᾽ ὡς οὔ. ἐντελεχείᾳ μὲν γὰρ ὄντα οὐκ ἐνδέχεται, δυνάμει δὲ ἐνδέχεται· ὁ γὰρ συνεχῶς κινούμενος κατὰ συμβεβηκὸς ἄπειρα διελήλυθεν, ἁπλῶς δ᾽ οὔ· συμβέβηκε γὰρ τῇ γραμμῇ ἄπειρα ἡμίσεα εἶναι, ἡ δ᾽ οὐσία ἐστὶν ἑτέρα καὶ τὸ εἶναι. (*Physics* Θ 8, 263 b 3-9.)

Conclusion

doubt that his analysis of the concepts of *edges, surfaces, contact, succession*, and so on, is astonishingly advanced. His solution of the divisibility problem was successful in that it stopped philosophers, except the determined Atomists, from concerning themselves with indivisible magnitudes. It made possible a much better understanding of the nature of continuous motion (though as a matter of fact very little progress was made in that field in the centuries after Aristotle's death). It is a natural supposition that it must have proved useful to mathematicians: Euclidian geometry used the principle of infinite divisibility, and one supposes that geometers would be grateful to Aristotle for laying the ghost of indivisible magnitudes. But the situation is not as clear as that. As we have seen, Aristotle's theory did not admit the concept of the sum of an infinite series. The ancient geometrical method of "exhaustion" assumes that by adding continuously to a finite magnitude one will equal the assigned magnitude; and this is precisely what is denied by the Aristotelian theory. The celebrated theorems in Archimedes' *Method*, which come very close to using integrations, are sometimes said[6] to use the assumption that an area is made up of an infinite number of lines. But I can find no statement that the number is supposed to be infinite; it is quite possible that Archimedes thought of them as mathematical atoms, as Boyer remarks in his *History of the Calculus* (p. 50). In any case, even if Archimedes did believe that the area can be regarded as containing an infinite number of lines, this would not be an application of Aristotle's theory: for Archimedes uses the expression "the triangle *is composed of* all the lines . . .," and this is not an Aristotelian concept, as we have seen.[7] It is not clear, therefore, that Aristotle's theory of the continuum was used by ancient mathematicians, or could have been used by them.[8]

But we have not yet answered the question whether Aristotle's theory is ultimately consistent with the rest of his philosophy, and it is still a hard question to answer. As we saw above (p. 148), in his discussion of the potentiality of the infinite, Aristotle speaks first of the potential as opposed to actual *being*, as if he were using the terms just as he normally does. If this were so, then he would have admitted a potential being, "the infinite," to which no actual being corresponds, and this would indeed be inconsistent with the very

Indivisible Magnitudes

important and fundamental proposition that actual being is prior to potential being. However, Wieland is clearly right to draw attention to Aristotle's theory of motion in this connection. Motion is defined as the actualization of an *incomplete* potentiality;[9] there is no reason why Aristotle should insist on the existence of a completed motion as a prior condition. The potentiality of the infinite seems to be as legitimate as the potentiality of motion.

Whatever may be the status of this concept within the framework of Aristotle's system, it was not likely to recommend itself to the Atomists, who had no room in their system for potentiality in any form. Aristotle's answer to the problem of divisibility dispensed altogether with *ultimate* parts. This was reasonable enough, since in his metaphysics it is the specific form or essence that is the most real thing, and as such is the primary object of knowledge. Constituent parts are secondary: knowledge of the parts comes from understanding their relation to the whole. Matter, as opposed to form, is the indefinable element in a thing. Epicurus' total divergence from this way of thought is plain enough, and it can be seen clearly in the passage studied in chapter 1. There he argues that a finite magnitude cannot be infinitely divisible, since if it were it would have to be possible to "reach infinity in thought." He implies that to think of a thing is to get a view of all its parts; so a thing cannot be composed of an infinite number of parts, if it is to be comprehensible. If things are infinitely divisible, then they "crumble away into non-being," and there is no stability or firmness in our conceptions of them (B 1). This insistence on the necessity for irreducible parts on the theoretical level corresponds closely, as we have already seen in chapter 1, with the argument for the existence of indivisible physical parts—i.e. atoms: if they did not exist, everything would be in danger of "perishing into non-being" (*Letter to Herodotus* §41). It is true, of course, that for Epicurus the basis of our knowledge of things is sense perception, and sense perception deals with wholes, not directly with ultimate parts. But the data of sense perception are explained by reference to the ultimate parts; sensible qualities are reducible to non-sensible properties of *atoms*. At the theoretical level, these properties of atoms are themselves reducible to the numbers and arrangement of their ultimate parts.

Conclusion

These are the fundamental units of the Epicurean world.

Thus Epicurus was bound to reject the idea of a division which dispensed altogether with ultimate parts. It would seem to him contradictory to say that a finite magnitude is *potentially* divisible to infinity, and yet to deny that it consists of an infinitely large number of parts; to divide is to divide into parts, and a thing consists of those things into which it is divided. He would be impatient with the idea of a potentiality which never can be actualized.[10]

Epicurus had some reason, then, for rejecting Aristotle's theory. But he is certainly open to criticism for not making clear how far he was prepared to take his atomism, and what was the relation between his own atomistic view of matter and space and the infinitely divisible magnitude of contemporary geometry. We must examine this relation more closely. Was Epicurus committed to *rejecting* geometry? Did he wish to substitute another geometry? Was he simply indifferent to geometry?

Before considering the position of Epicurus directly, we must look at some earlier figures. It is sometimes said by historians of Greek philosophy and mathematics that Zeno of Elea *proved* the infinite divisibility of extended magnitude, that the existence of incommensurables, discovered in the fifth century, *entailed* infinite divisibility and was proved to entail it, and consequently that anyone in the fourth century who denied infinite divisibility was either ignorant or incompetent. I have tried to show, in chapter 7, that such a picture as this is not a true representation of the facts. At least in Plato's Academy there were men who were not novices in mathematics who asserted the existence of indivisible magnitudes. We have Aristotle's explicit statement[11] that Plato himself wished to substitute "indivisible lines" for the points of the geometricians, and I do not think we can avoid construing this as a denial of the infinite divisibility of extended magnitude.

How did the Academy attempt to reconcile "indivisible lines" with the rest of geometry? I cannot work out any satisfactory answer to this question. It seemed that there was a dilemma. The discovery of the incommensurables, followed by the *proof* of the irrationality of $\sqrt{2}$ etc., followed by Eudoxus' method of bringing the irrationals into a general theory of proportion, seemed to prove

Indivisible Magnitudes

the infinite divisibility of all extended magnitude. On the other hand, infinite divisibility seemed to entail an infinite number of parts, each having magnitude; and Zeno's arguments seemed to show that there could not be an infinite number of such parts in a *finite* magnitude. Since Berkeley and Hume were puzzled by this same dilemma, it does not seem to me surprising that Plato's Academy, two millennia earlier, found it difficult. So far as I can understand it, part of Plato's solution of the dilemma was to include certain irrational dimensions in his elementary and irreducible triangles: thus his stock of basic units, as it were, *includes* irrationals, and does not have to create them. But I do not understand how this idea is related to "indivisible lines," or to the rest of the geometry of which he was a passionate advocate.

With Epicurus, the position may have been much simpler. His view was that the real world of atoms and void was composed of minima. Any account of the basic structure of the world therefore must consist of *counting* the minima: there is nothing more to it. What we should expect, therefore, *a priori*, is that Epicurus would regard geometry as irrelevant to the study of nature, because one of its essential principles (that of infinite divisibility) was contrary to the facts of nature.

There is little evidence for Epicurus' views about geometry, but such as it is it exactly confirms this expectation. Sextus, at the beginning of his *Adversus Mathematicos*, reports that the Epicureans regarded the *mathemata* (a class of subjects to be learnt which included geometry) as "contributing nothing to the perfection of wisdom." Proclus, in his *Commentary on Euclid* (Friedlein, p. 199), divides the critics of geometry into two classes: those who object to its principles, and those who complain that its theorems do not follow from the principles as given. The former class is divided into those who criticize the principles of knowledge in general (the Sceptics), and those who criticize the principles of geometry alone (the Epicureans).

The Epicurean theory of minimal parts, if it has been correctly described in this essay, was a typical piece of Epicurean philosophy. We might say that Epicurus was confronted with a choice—between infinite divisibility and minimal parts. He thought he saw that the former alternative would lead him into positions inconsistent with

Conclusion

experience: for instance, it would be necessary for a man to be able to "reach infinity in thought," and this was contrary to experience. There was no counter-evidence against the existence of minimal parts in nature; the analogy of the senses suggested that there was a minimum; so he opted for this alternative, and doggedly worked out the details, in so far as he thought it necessary. But he made no attempt, apparently, to work out a fully systematic mathematical theory to support his physics. On his own premises, there was no reason why he should. His purpose was to teach peace of mind. However deplorable his rejection of philosophical enquiry may be, we may accept it as explaining why we can find no trace of a New Geometry.

Notes to Chapter 11

1. Diodorus quoted by Arrian, *Epict. Diss.* 2.19.1. See Oskar Becker (1956).
2. 207 a 1-2.
3. Wieland (1962), pp. 278-316.
4. 207 b 14: οὐδὲ μένει ἡ ἀπειρία ἀλλὰ γίγνεται.
5. Simplicius actually goes further than Aristotle in agreeing with Epicurus. See his *Physics* 142.10-15 and 459.22-26. He goes further in that he puts the point more positively than Aristotle: "that which is made of infinitely numerous magnitudes must be infinite in magnitude." (τὸ ἐξ ἀπείρων τῷ πλήθει μεγεθῶν ἄπειρον ἂν εἴη τῷ μεγέθει (142.12).)
6. E.g. by Heath (1912).
7. *Archimedes*, II, 436.23: ἐκ τῶν ἐν τῷ ΓΖΑ τριγώνῳ [sc. γραμμῶν] τὸ ΓΖΑ τρίγωνον συνέστηκεν.
8. Wieland (1962), p. 289, opposes Ross's contention that Aristotle's theory of the continuum showed him to have a good mathematical mind: "Mir scheint dagegen, dass kaum etwas so deutlich wie die Kontinuitätslehre beweist, dass Aristoteles kein Mathematiker war, sondern ein Physiker, der die Grundstrukturen der phänomenalen, anschaulichen Welt analysiert. Im Sinne einer mathematischen Strukturtheorie sind Zenons Überlegungen oder Platons Theorie der unteilbaren Linien Beispiele für eine schon höher entwickelte abstrakte Mathematik, wenn man sie mit der aristotelischen Kontinuitätslehre vergleicht."
9. *Physics* Γ 2, 201 b 31-33.
10. He is not alone. Cf. Sir David Ross, *Aristotle's Physics*, Introduction, p. 53: "It seems impossible to accept [Aristotle's] view that the points in a line are brought into existence either by our act of dividing it or by our counting points in it, or by a body's coming to rest at them. All these processes alike must be held to imply the pre-existence of the points, and thus the existence of an actual infinity of points

Indivisible Magnitudes

in a line." So also, of course, David Hume: "'Tis obvious, that whatever is capable of being divided *in infinitum*, must consist of an infinity of parts" (*Treatise* II, 1, quoted in chapter 10).

It is perhaps worth noting that Kant shared Aristotle's view: see *The Critique of Pure Reason*, p. 459 (ed. Kemp Smith): "We are not entitled to say of a whole which is divisible to infinity, that *it is made up of infinitely many parts*. For although all parts are contained in the intuition of the whole, *the whole division* is not so contained, but consists only in the decomposition, that is, in the regress itself, whereby the series first becomes actual. Since this regress is infinite, all the members or parts at which it arrives are contained in the given whole, viewed as an *aggregate*. But the whole *series of the division* is not so contained, for it is a successive infinite and never *whole*, and cannot, therefore, exhibit an infinite multiplicity, or any combination of an infinite multiplicity in a whole."

11. *Metaphysics* A 9, 992 a 22*ff*. quoted in chapter 7, note a.

Study II

ARISTOTLE AND EPICURUS ON VOLUNTARY ACTION

INTRODUCTION

THE subject of this study is often referred to as the Epicurean "theory of free will." It is a convenient name, but it has its dangers. The Greeks up to the time of Epicurus managed to discuss and theorize about human behavior without using the concept of will at all; consequently any attempt to make their theories conform to a system which does use this concept is apt to generate confusion. Lucretius' expression *libera voluntas* does indeed look like a Latin version of "free will"; but it does not correspond closely with any single Greek expression. Since I am trying to understand the original Epicurean theory, I shall try to avoid talking about "free will," or at any rate to put the phrase in quotation marks to show that it is being used only as a handy abbreviation.

It might be said that the problem which Epicurus' theory tried to solve arose out of the context of *excuses*. When the philosophers discussed the subject of moral judgment, they found they had to separate human misdemeanors into two classes: those for which the alleged culprit had an adequate excuse and for which he could not therefore reasonably be blamed, and those for which he had no excuse and for which he was therefore responsible. They had to draw up a list of criteria for placing any given action into one class or the other. Difficulties arose when certain criteria were proposed which seemed to imply that *all* actions were excused from blame, and were correspondingly exempt from praise also. Epicurus' philosophical system led to a difficulty of this kind. One of the obvious criteria for classifying actions as culpable or not was the question of whether or not they were the result of merely physical or corporeal interactions. Thus a man cannot reasonably be blamed for being over six feet tall, or for getting his clothes dirty if he is beaten up by thugs. But the Epicurean system was one which allowed *only* physical interactions: the one possible interaction was the collision of atoms with each other. This applied to the human *psyche* as much

Aristotle and Epicurus on Voluntary Action

as to any other compound in the world. Epicurus was therefore required to show that morality was not meaningless in such a system: he had to find criteria for distinguishing actions which are, and actions which are not, liable to praise and blame.

It is generally agreed now among interpreters of Epicurus that in some way he used the concept of a swerve of atoms (*clinamen*, παρέγκλισις) for this purpose. There have been attempts in the past (for example by A. Brieger, in his *Die Urbewegung der Atome und die Weltentstehung bei Leukipp und Demokrit*, 1884) to argue that the connection between human morality and the random swerve of atoms was made not by Epicurus himself but by his blundering disciples. But it is unlikely that anyone will now want to maintain that the connection is not orthodox, although there is no statement of it in the surviving works of Epicurus. The question now is not *whether* Epicurus used the swerve in his explanation of human action, but *how* he used it.

There is an interpretation of Epicurus' theory which is commonly put forward now, based largely on the work of C. Giussani (*Studi lucreziani* in his edition of Lucretius, 1896) and C. Bailey (*The Greek Atomists and Epicurus*, 1928, and *Lucretius*, 1947). In outline it is as follows. The human *psyche* consists of atoms, which like the atoms of all compounds in Epicurean theory are in motion. By the mechanism of sense perception, atomic *eidola* are received from the environment into the sense organs, and by collisions the atoms of these *eidola* transmit an impulse to the atoms of the *psyche* so as to alter *their* motions. These alterations constitute both a *phantasia*, that is, an impression of the nature of the object which caused them, and a *pathos*, that is, a reaction of pleasure or pain to this object. The reaction stimulates in response a movement to *take* or to *avoid* the object. But somewhere in this sequence of events there is a break in continuity. If there were no break in continuity, the responsive movement would be *necessitated* by the conjunction of the original motions of the soul atoms with the motions of the atoms of the *eidola* received from outside. The required break in continuity is supplied by the atomic swerve, which is something new, something that was not present in the initial conditions.

Giussani puts it in this way: "The motives, that is to say the idea

Introduction

or perceived image of the object and the consequent desire to pursue or avoid it, are reducible in substance to internal motions of atoms, and the act of volition too consists solely of internal atomic motions; but the passage from the former to the latter is not a mechanical connection or a mechanical transformation of the former into the latter—that would mean the rule of necessity—but the latter is determined (or not determined) spontaneously, just as the atomic swerve is spontaneous" (*Studi lucreziani*, p. 126).

According to this account Epicurus posited an atomic swerve for every instance of free action. Between the stimulus and the response, if the response is to be a free one, it must happen that an atom in the agent's soul swerves from its path. But the swerve's occurring at just this place and time, after the receipt of a stimulus which requires action, can only be a matter of coincidence. There can be no causal connection between the stimulus and the swerve, since it was certainly part of Epicurus' theory that no cause could be assigned for a swerve. The occurrence of a swerve was an event completely isolated from all preceding events.

Hence Epicurus' theory as described by Giussani and Bailey contains a startling paradox. The reason for insisting on human freedom (in this sense) is that we want to distinguish between actions which are subject to moral appraisal and those which are not. But the atomic swerve seems to be well adapted to produce unexplained, random, sudden, motiveless actions, but totally unsuitable to produce the deliberate actions which are typically liable to moral appraisal. The stage is all set for someone to produce a rational, normal, decent action: he sees a friend in distress, his character predisposes him to help—then the swerve takes place, and instead he catches a No. 27 bus to Kew. And that—catching the bus—is a typically free action.

Of course, Giussani and Bailey both observed the implausibility of this. They both tried to evade it by introducing the concept of a *concilium* into the story. It is not the motion of a single atom that produces the volition, but the motion of a *concilium* of soul atoms; and this, they think, somehow makes it a more plausible hypothesis. The random swerve of single atoms in the *concilium* which constitutes the soul somehow causes the *concilium* to move in such a way

Aristotle and Epicurus on Voluntary Action

that the resultant action is not random but appropriate. Bailey writes (*Lucretius*, note on 4.877-887): "What in the individual atom is a matter of chance, in the conscious complex of the 'animus' is 'conscious chance', which was to Epicurus the equivalent of will."

The more I studied this account of Epicurean doctrine, the more incomprehensible I found it. I could make nothing of the idea of "conscious chance," either as an interpretation of the Epicurean texts or indeed as a usable concept in any psychological theory. Moreover, the introduction of a random element into every deliberate human action seemed to me strange in itself, and not explained by anything in the history of philosophy before Epicurus. I went back to the texts, therefore, to see if they did in fact force us to believe that this was what Epicurus meant.

The most important text, indeed the only one which positively expounds the subject, is Lucretius 2.251-293. The conclusion of my study of this text, which is presented in chapter 1, was that Lucretius did not appear to say that there is a swerve of atoms between the stimulus and the response in the case of every deliberate action. It seemed to me that he introduced the swerve at another point in the biography of the agent.

In order to confirm this impression, and to explain it if it turned out to be correct, the obvious move was to study the previous attempts which had been made by Greek philosophers to tackle the problem. It is always possible of course that a theory is completely new. But I believe it is a useful heuristic principle to assume that completely new ideas are rare in the history of philosophy—and in any case Epicurus is plainly not the most original of philosophers.

It was not necessary to look further than Aristotle for the confirmation and the explanation. Cyril Bailey, whose books on Epicureanism have been most influential on students of the subject during the last three or four decades, rather overlooked the importance of Aristotle in the development of Epicureanism. It was forced on the attention of the learned world, with an almost operatic flourish, by Ettore Bignone, in a number of articles and a very large book (*L' Aristotele perduto e la formazione filosofica di Epicuro*, 1936). It was perhaps unfortunate that Bignone complicated his account of the history of the relation between Aristotle and Epicurus with

Introduction

the theory that Epicurus knew *only* the "published" works, and particularly the dialogues, of Aristotle. It is an implausible thesis, and it was not supported with sufficient arguments. Moreover, some of Bignone's connections between Aristotle and Epicurus, particularly those taken from Aristotle's *Protrepticus*, were excessively fine-drawn. However, weaknesses of this kind in Bignone's case should not persuade anyone to overlook the formative influence of Aristotle's work on Epicurus.

I have not made a systematic attempt to prove that Epicurus could have read or did read Aristotle's "school treatises." It would in fact be impossible to prove that he did read them, against Bignone's thesis, since Bignone barricades himself against attack behind the unfalsifiable proposition that *any* doctrine from the school treatises which was known to Epicurus must have been repeated in the "published" and now lost works of Aristotle. In the other essay in this book I found that Epicurus' doctrine could coherently be explained on the assumption that he read and attempted to answer *Physics* Z. It seems to me more economical to assume that he used this book, and not another, unknown, book with the same contents. In this second study my hypothesis is that he used Aristotle's *Nicomachean Ethics*, *De Motu Animalium* and perhaps *De Anima*; it is possible that he found the same doctrines in some other text unknown to us, but I have not yet seen any evidence that makes this the more likely alternative. I have no proof that he knew anything about these Aristotelian doctrines, other than the similarity of his own doctrines, which I try to demonstrate in this essay.*¹

Aristotle shows, in Book III of the *Nicomachean Ethics*, that the moral philosopher must distinguish between voluntary and involuntary actions. If the Giussani–Bailey exposition of Epicurus were correct, it would be reasonable to look in Aristotle as well as Epicurus for a theory which allowed for a "free" or "spontaneous" choice—that is, for a choice which could not be explained by antecedent or external causes. There are plenty of passages in Aristotle which say that a moral action must be the result of an ὄρεξις, but none which says that the ὄρεξις itself, to be free, must be uncaused and spontaneous, like the swerve of an Epicurean atom. On the

---
* Please see end of chapter for numbered references.

Aristotle and Epicurus on Voluntary Action

contrary, Aristotle explains that even individual actions which are deliberately chosen *can* be explained by the combination of an external stimulus and an established disposition. Aristotle's own theory of human action would be wrecked by any discontinuity between stimulus and response such as Giussani thought necessary for Epicurus.

If Aristotle accepts that an established disposition together with the receipt of a stimulus may be sufficient cause of an action, how does he rescue the action from being called "involuntary" and so dismissed from the arena of morality? He does so by insisting that our *dispositions* are not made by anything or anybody but ourselves. Our dispositions are our own affair, and if our actions proceed from those dispositions then the actions are our own affair too.

Thus it seemed to me that Aristotle's theory was totally unlike the Epicurean theory as expounded by Giussani and Bailey. But my examination of the Epicurean texts, on the contrary, showed striking similarities to Aristotle, and I came to the conclusion that Epicurus' theory was basically the same as Aristotle's. Neither of them sought for the criterion of a voluntary action in any discontinuity between stimulus and response: it is not at this point that Epicurus' atomic swerve is required or attested. Both philosophers sought for this criterion in habits of mind which are our own affair, not given to us by nature; and this is where the atomic swerve might well be thought to be required, and is attested.

In this essay, I have begun with a study of the relevant text of Lucretius, pointing out some difficulties in the interpretations of Bailey and Giussani, and drawing attention to the *two* kinds of "necessity" from which Lucretius aims to save human actions. Next comes an examination of some passages of the *Nicomachean Ethics*, in which the same two kinds of necessity can be found, and I explain Aristotle's method of dealing with them. The rest of the essay is an attempt to argue that Epicurus' method of dealing with them was similar to Aristotle's. In chapter 3 I discuss some concepts used by Epicurus in his psychology; the chief purpose of this chapter is the negative one of showing that Epicurus' use of these concepts offers no support to those who attribute to him the doctrine of uncaused volitions. In chapter 4 I compare Aristotle's psychology of action

Introduction

with Epicurus', so far as the latter can be reconstructed. The intention is again partly the negative one of showing that neither Aristotle nor Epicurus inserted a spontaneous break in the causation between stimulus and response. In chapter 5 I return to the passage of Lucretius examined in chapter 1, and attempt to work out its implications in the light of the similarities to Aristotle analyzed in the intervening chapters. This chapter is very tentative, because there is practically no further textual evidence on the subject. The result is a new interpretation of the Epicurean theory—a highly speculative one, but no more so than the interpretation it is designed to replace.

NOTE TO INTRODUCTION

1. See further Philip Merlan's review of Bignone's book in *Gnomon* 1941, and his *Studies in Epicurus and Aristotle*, 1960 (though this latter book does not attempt to show what works of Aristotle Epicurus read nor how he reacted to them). Also Friedrich Solmsen "Epicurus and Cosmological Heresies" in *American Journal of Philology*, 1951.

Perhaps the most important contribution on Epicurus' relation to Aristotle is made by C. Diano in a long series of articles, "La psicologia d' Epicuro e la teoria delle passioni" in *Giornale critico della Filosofia italiana*, 1939–1942. These articles examine Epicurus' debt to Aristotle over a much wider field than their title suggests, and I have learned much from them. On the subject of this essay, Diano has the outstanding merit of taking seriously the detail of our one surviving Epicurean text (see my chapter 1, n. 8), and this leads him very close to the right explanation of Epicurus' theory, as I believe. He sees that the swerve should have no place in the account of normal deliberate action. But he still retains the idea, which I think is unjustified, that the swerve is needed to break "the necessity of the first and immediate *orexis*" in the case of individual actions. He concludes that if external conditions are such that by following purely natural motions a man gets what he wants (namely peace of mind), then there is no need of a swerve; but if external conditions are not right (i.e. if the immediate pain ought to be endured for the sake of some further good), then the inner necessity of the immediate *orexis* must be broken by a swerve.

The difficulty about this is of course that we still have to assume the coincidence of a swerve at just the right moment.

However, I am not quite sure if I have understood Diano correctly. He writes that the mind in Epicurean theory learns by experiencing choices and avoidances, and the habits thus acquired by the mind produce the reactions to particular situations. Thus the final *orexis* comes into being with respect to all the past experiences which determine it. When the mind is full of experience, *its future is determined by its present*, and the will assumes the form of a syllogism. But in the beginning? A reaction to pain which may equally lead to pleasure or to pain; a swerve which can only be random and therefore cannot occur at will; and instead of the liberty which consists in logical necessity, the servitude which consists in casual necessity.

This suggests that Diano's view of the swerve is much the same as my own; but I do not quite understand how this is to be reconciled with his earlier account of the swerve as connected with ἐπιβολὴ τῆς διανοίας and as being *guided* by intellect.

Another who argues that Epicurus was acquainted with some of Aristotle's "school treatises" is Jürgen Mau, in his article in *Philologus* 99 (1955), especially pp. 103-111.

CHAPTER I

LUCRETIUS 2.251-293

THE Epicurean notion of the swerve of atoms attracted a great deal of criticism in antiquity. There are many hostile witnesses. The only friendly witness of any importance is Lucretius; and there is only one passage of Lucretius that treats the matter in detail. The whole theory has to be reconstructed almost entirely on the evidence of half a dozen lines. So it is of crucial importance to be quite sure of the meaning of these lines.

Their position in Lucretius' structure must first be settled, since some strange things have been said about it. The passage on the subject of *libera voluntas* is the second of two arguments designed to prove the existence of *clinamen* as a kind of atomic motion. It comes near the end of the section on the motion of atoms. The plan can be summarized as follows:

                    Motion of Atoms: 2.62-332.
- (a) 62-79   Introduction: we can *see* that motion exists.
- (b) 80-141 Atoms move perpetually through the infinite void, because of their own weight and collisions with each other, with shorter or longer intervals between collisions.
- (c) 142-166 Speed of motion of atoms.
- (d) 167-183 Digression: no need for gods as causes of creation.
- (e) 184-215 Upward motion is not natural; weight causes everything to move downward unless it is prevented.
- (f) 216-293 The swerve of atoms.
  - (i) 216-250 If there were no swerve, all atoms would still be falling downward parallel to each other, and there would never have been a collision, since lighter and

heavier atoms fall with the same speed if there is no resistance.

(ii) 251-293 Moreover, atoms must swerve if living creatures are to have *fatis avulsa voluntas*.

(g) 294-307 The atoms have always had and always will have the same motions as now, since nothing can increase or decrease the density of atoms in the void.

(h) 308-332 Atomic motion lies below the level of sense perception.

The crucial passage appears in this summary as (f ii). But before looking more closely at it, I should draw attention to a few points in my summary, and particularly to a difference between it and that offered by Bailey.

In his interpretation of the vital lines 287-293, Bailey advances the view*[1] that they are "the conclusion of the whole section on motion from 62 onwards, and Lucr. goes back in thought, as Giussani pointed out, to the original opposition to the views of Democritus." I shall criticize this view in detail later on, but I wish to observe now that it gains plausibility from the fact that the sections which *follow* this alleged conclusion (g and h in my summary) are described as *appendices* by Bailey. The unprejudiced reader will see, I think, that the organization of the whole book is not so tight and orderly that these sections can properly be described as appendices. They seem to be as relevant to the subject of motion as any of the other sections, and to show a typically Lucretian sequence of thought.

The careful reader of Lucretius may also be surprised by Bailey's mention of Democritus in connection with section (b) (80-140). "The form which the argument takes," he writes,[2] "is best understood if it is realised that Lucr., following Epicurus, is correcting two mistaken or insufficient views in the traditional atomism of Democritus. Democritus had held (1) that the 'free' atoms were 'naturally' always in motion in all directions in the void, and (2) that in a compound body, the component atoms being interlocked with one another suspended their own 'natural' motions and adopted that of the whole compound body."

---

* Please see end of chapter for numbered references.

Lucretius 2.251-293

As a matter of fact, as Bailey observes in a footnote, neither of these two views can be attributed to Democritus with certainty. But that need not concern us now. What matters is that even if they were certainly Democritus' own views, the present passage of Lucretius would not be the Epicurean correction of them. For it is not the idea that *retention in a compound* stops the motion of atoms which Lucretius first attacks, but that there is a boundary to the universe (89-94). He never mentions or even hints at an idea that atoms in a compound might be *at rest*; he merely explains that atoms rebounding with short intervals make hard things like stone, those rebounding with long intervals make rare things like air, and others wander *magnum per inane* without forming compounds at all.

But of course it was not *Democritus* who suggested that there is a boundary to the universe at which matter might come to rest, but *Aristotle*. And the opening lines of this section show clearly enough that it is directed against the Aristotelian theory of motion:

if you think the atoms can come to rest,
and by coming to rest can give rise to new elementary motions,[3]
then you are wandering far away from the path of true reason.[a]

According to the Aristotelian theory, the four elements each had a "proper place" in the universe: fire at the outside, next to the innermost etherial sphere, earth at the center, and the other two in between. Each element, if out of its proper place, had a natural motion towards it, and came to rest when it reached it. But having reached its proper place it was liable to change into another element (through the action of the sun), and so to move in another direction. This, or something like it, is clearly what Lucretius is attacking. That is also why he devotes a whole section (e) to refuting the theory that there is a natural motion *upward*.

Section (b) thus contains no polemic against a Democritean theory that atoms in compounds are at rest. Nor does it have anything to say about the other of the two Democritean ideas mentioned by Bailey—that "free" atoms move naturally in all directions in the void. As regards this idea, Bailey says[4] "Epicurus did not

---

[a] Si cessare putas rerum primordia posse
cessandoque novos rerum progignere motus,
avius a vera longe ratione vagaris.

(2.80-82)

Aristotle and Epicurus on Voluntary Action

deny it—he fully agreed with it—but he endeavoured to get behind it to the causes of this ceaseless motion in all directions." The proof of this endeavor, Bailey finds in lines 83-87, which he translates in his commentary as follows: "the reason why the atoms move in all directions (*vagantur*) in the void is either their weight which is carrying them downwards or the blows which are moving them in other directions; for when they meet they dash apart in varying directions." It is only necessary to read the lines of Lucretius to see the distortion of emphasis achieved here by Bailey's transposition of the subordinate clause and the main clause of the first sentence:

> For since they wander through the void, it must come about
> that all the atoms move either through their own weight,
> or perhaps through collision with another. For whenever, as they move,
> they meet and crash together, at once with opposite motion
> they spring apart; which is not to be wondered at, since they are very hard,
> and of compact mass, and nothing is in their way behind them.[b]

In fact there is no emphasis on the *direction* of motion, but only on the *fact* and the *causes* of motion. The word *vagantur* by itself does not stress that the motions are in different directions: it is used without any such stress twice in the later lines of this section (105 and 109). Nor is any stress laid on this point in *diversa dissiliant*; the stress is on the fact that they *do* rebound, not in the direction of the rebound, as the following sentence (omitted by Bailey) shows. In any case, if this is really an attempt to explain differences of direction, only collisions need be mentioned; the introduction of weight is redundant.

No; the main stress is clearly on the fact that all things move *in a void*. Since they move *in a void*, all things must move either through their weight or through collisions—through collisions, because atoms are hard and do not "give," and there is only *void* behind them and so there is nothing to stop their rebound. I doubt

[b] nam quoniam per inane vagantur, cuncta necessest
aut gravitate sua ferri primordia rerum
aut ictu forte alterius. nam ⟨cum⟩ cita saepe
obvia conflixere, fit ut diversa repente
dissiliant; neque enim mirum, durissima quae sint
ponderibus solidis neque quicquam a tergo ibus obstet.

(2.83-88)

Lucretius 2.251-293

whether this is directed against any theory of motion in particular.

It was necessary to demolish Bailey's hypothesis that this section is directed against Democritus, because of the use he makes of it in explaining lines 287-293. I shall refer to this later. We may now look directly at the section on *clinamen*.

The cosmological argument for the existence of a swerve need not detain us. It is clear (within limits), and well known. Epicurus asserted that weight carries all atoms downward at a constant speed, and that the universe is infinite. (It has always been a problem to know what "downward" means, if the universe is infinite, but it is fortunately a problem which can on this occasion be left on one side.) Some explanation is therefore demanded of those collisions of atoms which feature in Epicurean accounts of all the events in the cosmos. The explanation offered is that atoms swerve from the straight downward path, "at an undetermined time and in undetermined places."

That the swerve is minimal is proved by the fact that we never *see* things falling in anything but straight lines; but no perceptible evidence can refute the hypothesis that atoms swerve an imperceptible amount. No explanation is given for the swerve and no hint as to whether all atoms swerve, and how often—except that the plural *corpora* in line 217 seems to rule out one possibility, that a *single* swerve began the whole process of collision and rebound; this could not have been ruled out *a priori*.

I now come to (f ii), the crucial text. It can be discussed in three parts, of which the third will be most important.

> Finally, if every motion is always joined up
> and the new arises out of the old motion in fixed order
> and the elements by swerving do not make of motion
> a new beginning to burst the bonds of fate,
> so that cause may not follow cause from infinity,   255
> then whence to living creatures comes this free will,
> whence comes, I say, this will torn from the fates,
> through which we move where each man's pleasure leads him,
> and change our motions neither at any fixed time
> nor at any fixed place, but however our mind has taken us?c

---

c Denique si semper motus conectitur omnis
   et vetere exoritur ⟨motu⟩ novus ordine certo

Aristotle and Epicurus on Voluntary Action

Neither of the two textual problems in this passage offers much trouble. The supplement *motu* in 252 seems likely enough; but no reasonable supplement to fill the gap will change the meaning much. In 257-258 all the MSS have *voluptas . . . voluntas*. But *fatis avulsa voluptas* is a most improbable expression, as Bailey observes, and all editors agree in rejecting it. Whether one follows Lachmann or Lambinus does not matter much.

One point in the translation should be explained. The word *ubi* may mean either "when" or "where"; I imagine that Lucretius exploits this ambiguity in line 260, and so I translate "however" rather than "whenever" or "wherever."

"Fate" is of course a concept particularly associated with the Stoics. There were Stoic etymologies of the equivalent Greek word "εἱμαρμένη" which are reminiscent of Lucretius' words here. They derived it from the verb "εἴρειν," meaning "to string together" like a necklace of beads: εἱμαρμένη is defined by the Stoics as a "linked-up cause of things that exist" (αἰτία τῶν ὄντων εἰρομένη), according to Diogenes Laertius.[5] According to Servius' commentary on the *Aeneid*,[6] Cicero used the words "fatum est conexio rerum per aeternitatem se invicem tenens." The idea of fate as a chain of causes is certainly Stoic, but may well not be confined to a particular school.

In any case, it is most unlikely that Epicurus' own attack on the concept of fate was directed against the Stoics. There are reports that he wrote a book on the subject, but that is lost, and we have only one, famous, sentence about it in the *Letter to Menoeceus*:

It was better to follow the myth about the gods than to be a slave of the "fate" of the physicists: for the former suggests a hope of

> nec declinando faciunt primordia motus
> principium quoddam quod fati foedera rumpat,
> ex infinito ne causam causa sequatur, 255
> libera per terras unde haec animantibus exstat,
> unde est haec, inquam, fatis avulsa voluntas
> per quam progredimur quo ducit quemque voluptas,
> declinamus item motus nec tempore certo
> nec regione loci certa, sed ubi ipsa tulit mens?
>
> (2.251-260)
>
> 252 semper *add. L.:* motus *Bockemüller:* motu *Bailey*
> 257, 258 voluntas... voluptas *Lambinus*: uoluptas... uoluntas *OQ*: potestas... voluntas *Lachmann*

Lucretius 2.251-293

forgiveness, in return for honor, but the latter has an ineluctable necessity.[d]

It is commonly said that this polemic of Epicurus' is directed against Democritus, who "accepted in its fulness" the conception of irresistible destiny or necessity (Bailey, *Greek Atomists and Epicurus* p. 318). There is obviously a good deal to be said for this idea, particularly if we can accept the testimony of Pseudo-Plutarch *Stromateis* (DK 68 A 39): "Democritus maintained ... that the causes of what is coming into being now had no beginning, but all that has come into being and is and will be, without qualification, was controlled by necessity from infinite time in the past." The Epicurean Diogenes of Oenoanda (33.2) deliberately contrasts Epicurus' theory of the swerve with the theory of Democritus, who said that "all things apparently move through necessity" and thus denied the existence of a "free" movement of the atoms. There is good ancient authority, therefore, for reading a criticism of Democritus into Epicurus' words.

Nevertheless, I am not quite convinced. At least I doubt if Democritus was really a "fatalist" in any recognizable sense: his ethical views do not seem to me consistent with a belief in fatalism. Epicurus may, however, have thought that fatalism followed from Democritus' physical theories. But it is possible that he had others in mind when he spoke of "the destiny of the natural philosophers": for example, Nausiphanes, who may have had some special claim to the name "φυσικός," to judge from the remarks about him in Philodemus' *Volumina Rhetorica* (see Sudhaus' index, s.v. Nausiphanes).

For the interpretation of our passage of Lucretius the identification of the opponent is not yet particularly important, because Lucretius explains unmistakably what aspect of the concept of fate he has in mind. It is that every event in the world has its sufficient causes in preceding events and that this chain of causes stretches back to infinity. If this were true, he implies, then the time and place of all our actions would be predetermined—that is to say, fixed without

[d] κρεῖττον ἦν τῷ περὶ θεῶν μύθῳ κατακολουθεῖν ἢ τῇ τῶν φυσικῶν εἱμαρμένῃ δουλεύειν· ὁ μὲν γὰρ ἐλπίδα παραιτήσεως ὑπογράφει θεῶν διὰ τιμῆς, ἡ δὲ ἀπαραίτητον ἔχει τὴν ἀνάγκην. (*Letter to Menoeceus* §134.)

reference to us. We must return to this section later. For the moment I stress only one point: Lucretius does not say that our voluntary actions must be *uncaused*, but only that the chain of causation must not stretch infinitely far back. The only suggestion that our actions are themselves uncaused lies in his use of the word "declinamus" in line 259—the same word which he uses to refer to the uncaused swerve of an atom. But it will be seen later that this suggestion cannot be maintained.

> For doubtless in these matters each man's will
> makes a beginning, and from this the motions flow through the limbs.
> Do you not see, indeed, that when at an instant of time
> the gates are opened the horses' eager power
> cannot burst out as quickly as their mind desires? 265
> For over the whole of their body the whole store of matter
> must be stirred, so that when it is stirred in every limb
> it may exert itself and follow the mind's desire.
> So you may see that the beginning of motion is made in the heart
> and proceeds first from the mind's will, 270
> and thence is spread further, through all the body and all the limbs.
> And it is different when we move under the impulse of a blow,
> when another man uses great strength and compulsion upon us.
> For then all the matter of our whole body
> plainly moves and is pushed along with ourselves unwilling, 275
> until our will has reined it back through the limbs.
> So now do you see that although external force
> drives many and forces them at times to move unwillingly
> and to be rushed headlong, yet there is in our breast
> something which can fight and resist? 280
> At its bidding, too, the store of matter
> is at times forced to move through all the limbs
> and when thrust forward is checked and subsides again.[e]

> [e] nam dubio procul his rebus sua cuique voluntas
> principium dat et hinc motus per membra rigantur.
> nonne vides etiam patefactis tempore puncto
> carceribus non posse tamen prorumpere equorum
> vim cupidam tam de subito quam mens avet ipsa? 265
> omnis enim totum per corpus materiai
> copia conciri debet, concita per artus
> omnis ut studium mentis conixa sequatur;
> ut videas initum motus a corde creari
> ex animique voluntate id procedere primum, 270
> inde dari porro per totum corpus et artus.

Lucretius 2.251-293

This is best considered, I think, as a single argument. Its point is to show that there is such a thing as *voluntary* action as opposed to *forced* action, and it does so by appealing to experience, in orthodox Epicurean fashion. In the case of voluntary action, the argument asserts, the perceptible behavior which we call the action is the last thing that happens; there is an interval between the observed stimulus (the opening of the gates) and the bodily movement of the horses. When the action is forced, the opposite (as it were) is true. The bodily action comes first, and is gradually countered by the will.

I want to stress this contrast, because it is misleading to consider the positive instance (the horses' voluntary motion) independently. When Lucretius says (in lines 261-262) that each man's will makes a beginning, he does not mean a beginning totally detached from *all* causation (which is what he *does* mean when he speaks in line 253 of the atoms making a beginning of motion by swerving), but a beginning not wholly due to *external* causation. This may seem hard to believe, in view of the close parallel between the language of lines 253 and 262. It is sometimes implied that the delay in the horses' reaction to the stimulus is to allow time for an uncaused act of *willing* on the horses' part—an act which consists of or contains an atomic swerve and which is a necessary constituent of a piece of "free" and moral behavior. But this cannot be the case. For if it were, the "act of will" would have to intervene between the reception of the stimulus and the formation in the mind of the determination to respond to it. Yet Lucretius stresses that the horses cannot react *as immediately as their mind wishes to act*. The implication is that the *mental* reaction is virtually simultaneous. The whole point

> nec similest ut cum impulsi procedimus ictu
> viribus alterius magnis magnoque coactu.
> nam tum materiem totius corporis omnem
> perspicuumst nobis invitis ire rapique, 275
> donec eam refrenavit per membra voluntas.
> iamne vides igitur, quamquam vis extera multos
> pellat et invitos cogat procedere saepe
> praecipitesque rapi, tamen esse in pectore nostro
> quiddam quod contra pugnare obstareque possit? 280
> cuius ad arbitrium quoque copia materiai
> cogitur interdum flecti per membra per artus
> et proiecta refrenatur retroque residit.
>
> (2.261-283)

Aristotle and Epicurus on Voluntary Action

of mentioning the delay is to contrast action to which the mind assents, with action (if it can be called action) which is the result of physical force *from outside*, applied directly to the body.

This is a very crude distinction indeed. It is in fact the simplest possible instance of the distinction made by Aristotle in *Nicomachean Ethics* between voluntary actions (ἑκούσια) and forced actions (βίαια). Aristotle, of course, worked it out with much more subtlety.

We must now look at the last, exceptionally difficult, section of Lucretius' argument.

> Hence you must acknowledge the same thing in the atoms too,
> that as well as blows and weight there is another cause   285
> of motions, from which we have this inborn power,
> since we see that nothing can come from nothing.
> For weight forbids that all things come about by blows
> as if by external force. But that the mind itself
> has no internal necessity in performing all its acts   290
> and is not overpowered and forced, as it were, to suffer and endure,
> that is the work of a tiny swerve of atoms
> at no fixed place and at no fixed time.[†]

Certain things must be observed and borne in mind all the time when we try to interpret this crucial passage:

(1) *Quare* in the first line links it to the preceding lines, which have established that there is *in us* something which can be opposed to external force.

(2) *Enim* in line 288 shows that lines 288*ff.* give an argument for what has just been asserted, namely that there must be a third cause of motion to account for the distinction between voluntary and forced action.

[†] quare in seminibus quoque idem fateare necessest,
esse aliam praeter plagas et pondera causam   285
motibus, unde haec est nobis innata potestas,
de nilo quoniam fieri nil posse videmus.
pondus enim prohibet ne plagis omnia fiant
externa quasi vi. sed ne mens ipsa necessum
intestinum habeat cunctis in rebus agendis   290
et devicta quasi cogatur ferre patique,
id facit exiguum clinamen principiorum
nec regione loci certa nec tempore certo.
(2.284-293)

289 mens *Lambinus:* res *OQ*

Lucretius 2.251–293

(3) *Externa* in line 289 is contrasted with *intestinum* in the following line; hence, unless this is a dishonest verbal trick, both words must have the same point of reference.

We must begin, I think, with the question of the text of line 289. The manuscripts all have *res*. It was emended by Lambinus (in 1563) to *mens*, and Lambinus' emendation has been accepted by all the subsequent editors I have consulted, except Martin. The point is of the utmost importance, in view of the third observation above. For if *mens* is right, not only the "internal necessity" of line 290 but also the "external force" of line 289 must be so named with reference to the mind. And this point will radically affect the interpretation of these lines.[7] Why then did Lambinus propose the change, and why have modern editors accepted it?

Of the modern editors, Lachmann and Giussani accept the emendation without comment. Bailey observes that "*res* might mean either 'the actual facts of the case' or 'the compound body itself', but with either of these meanings 290 and 291 are unintelligible." So he accepts *mens*, remarking that *mens* may have been written *mēs*. Martin retains the MS reading, but without an adequate explanation.

Before accepting the emendation, we have a duty to make the best possible sense of the received text. The only possible thing that *res ipsa* could mean in the context is "the atom itself." For the opening line asserts that *in the atoms* we find "the same thing" as we have just found in living creatures—namely that there is a kind of action which can be distinguished from forced action. So it is only of the atom (if not of the mind) that it would now make sense to deny that its motions are forced. First, then, if this is the meaning, it is denied that the atom's movements are all caused by the external force of other atoms in collision with it; this is denied because there is also weight, which resists the force of collisions. Secondly it is denied that the atom's movements are all caused by a necessity internal to it; and this is denied because the swerve prevents it.

Up to a point this makes very good sense, and I cannot be wholly sure that it is wrong. There are, however, some objections. One is the oddity of the phrase *res ipsa* as an expression for the atom; though it seems a possible expression, I have not been able to find a parallel. Another is the fact that this *res*, in the nominative, would

Aristotle and Epicurus on Voluntary Action

be one of the *principia*, in the genitive plural, mentioned in line 292: "that the atom itself has no internal necessity . . . is the work of a tiny swerve of the atoms." A third is that *cunctis in rebus agendis* is a queer phrase to use in talking of an atom, but much less queer to use in talking of the mind. A fourth and more powerful objection is that it would not be quite "the same thing" that we have now found in the atom as that which was found in living creatures. For they have been shown to exhibit only freedom from *external* force, but the atom is now said to be free both from external force and from internal necessity. And a fifth objection is that it is perhaps odd to suppose that an atom without the swerve is the victim of "an inner necessity," "overpowered and forced, as it were, to suffer and endure." The atom certainly does not *will* its swerve, so that its swerving appears to be as much a matter of necessity as a motion due to weight or collision.

I cannot feel sure, however, that these objections are wholly convincing, either individually or collectively. The whole question really turns on whether we require from Lucretius an *explanation* of how the swerve is related to the mind's actions or not. If we retain *res*, we have no explanation at all; these last lines merely *assert* that the distinction between voluntary and forced action requires a swerve as well as weight and collision in the atoms. If we are persuaded by the objections, and change *res* to *mens*, then we have an explanation, of a kind.

But it is certainly not the explanation it has been taken to be. I have observed that if the "internal necessity" of line 290 is internal to the mind, then the "external force" of line 289 must be external *to the mind*. If so, then lines 288-289 say that what saves the mind from external force (obviously the force of some external stimulus, the *eidola* of a sensible object—we shall return to this point) is *weight*; and it is only the internal necessity of the mind which is obviated by the swerve. Since this directly contradicts the common account of the Epicurean theory the editors have had recourse to some complex devices to explain away this uncomfortable sentence.

Giussani seems to have been the first to notice the difficulty. He attempted to explain it in this way. These lines 288-293 form the conclusion, not of section (f ii), but of the larger unit formed by (e)

Lucretius 2.251–293

and (f) (i.e. not of 251-293, but of 184-293). In this longer section, Giussani thinks, there appear two modifications in the atomic theory of *Democritus*—motion because of weight, and motion because of the swerve. So Lucretius can sum up the whole argument by saying, '*Weight* prevents all things from happening because of blows, and we also have *clinamen*, proved by free will."

But there is no merit in this solution. As we have seen, the structure of Lucretius' examination of motion is not to be explained by referring to the atomism of Democritus; hence there is no call for a summing-up of arguments against Democritus. Secondly, if this is really a summing-up, there should be a mention of the cosmological argument for the swerve as well as the psychological argument. But there are two more fatal objections. In Giussani's reading of these lines, the "external force" of line 289 is external to the *atom*, while the "internal necessity" of line 290 is internal to the *mind*; and this destroys the point of the contrast. And the word *enim* in line 288 now has no point at all; it must introduce an argument for what has preceded, not a summary of it. Giussani indeed perceived this:[8] "Come conclusione, per altro, questi versi non s' attaccano bene ai precedenti, e l' *enim* salta fuori un po strano." He adds that if we are unwilling to admit a short lacuna between lines 287 and 288, the expression must at least be regarded as elliptical. The argument in full would run like this: It is therefore proved that besides *plagae* there is *pondus* and *clinamen*; and that is required by the *recta naturai ratio*; *pondus enim* etc. But the part of this which is truly a conclusion or summing-up, beginning with the proper particle "therefore," is totally absent from the Latin. I do not believe it can reasonably be supplied by the reader's imagination, and the hypothesis of a lacuna must not be adopted if there is any other solution.

Bailey follows Giussani, with one unimportant variation. Lines 288-293, he writes,[9] "are the conclusion of the whole section on motion from 62 onwards, and Lucretius goes back in thought ... to the original opposition to the views of Democritus." I have already said that Democritus is *not* the target either of the whole section from 62 onwards or of the smaller section from 184 onwards. This slight change in Giussani's explanation does not improve it at all. And in all other respects Bailey's note is open to the same objections as Giussani's; it is indeed still less convincing, because Bailey totally ignores the difficulty of *enim*.

If *mens* is what Lucretius wrote in line 289, then his argument may be paraphrased as follows. If *every* motion has its causes in preceding motions and this chain of causes can be traced back to infinity (which would be the case if weight and collisions were the only causes of motion), then there would be no *libera voluntas*. But experience shows that there *is* a distinction between actions which result from *voluntas* and those which result from external force (261-283). Hence there must be the same distinction in the atoms, since everything has a cause: weight is sufficient to save the mind from the external force of collisions, but the swerve saves the mind from the constraint of an inner necessity (284-293). How the weight and the swerve of atoms are supposed to perform this service will be discussed in chapter 5.

It should be noted that the last ten lines, if *mens* is the right reading, *add* to our knowledge of the relation between *clinamen* and *voluntas*: the addition is simply that *clinamen* is to save the mind not from external force but from internal necessity. This addition is withdrawn *but not contradicted* if the reading is *res*. In the rest of this study I shall try to present other evidence on this question which will serve, I hope, as a substitute for the evidence of Lucretius if that is ruled to be inadmissible. But in referring back to this passage I shall use the reading *mens*, without attempting to provide an alternative solution each time.

NOTES TO CHAPTER 1

1. Bailey (1947), p. 850.
2. *Ibid.*, p. 813.
3. *Novos rerum motus*: if my interpretation of this as anti-Aristotelian is right, it gives a better sense to this phrase, which the commentators have often found puzzling: "new motions belonging to (different) elements." Of course, the only aspect of Aristotelianism considered here is the theory of natural places and the interchange of elements: the atoms are not Aristotelian.
4. Bailey (1947), p. 813.

Lucretius 2.251–293

5. 7.149: *SVF* 2.915.
6. Servius *Aeneid* 3.376: *SVF* 2.919.
7. Only C. Diano, so far as I have noticed, has seen this point (1942, 18*ff.*).
8. Giussani (1896), I, 144, n. 2.
9. Bailey (1947), p. 850.

CHAPTER 2

THE VOLUNTARY AND THE COMPULSIVE, IN ARISTOTLE'S ETHICS AND EPICURUS

It is time now to look at the background of discussion against which Epicurus worked out his theories. From an analysis of the text of Lucretius, we have not yet arrived at a complete description of the function of the atomic swerve in saving the human mind from fate. However, we can reasonably hope that the historical context will provide clues from which we can solve the puzzle.

Epicurus believed that he had to save the human mind from fate in order to give meaning to the concepts of morality. "That which is in our power is free," he says, "and blame and its opposite are applicable to this."[a] The same point is made and elaborated in the first five chapters of Aristotle's *Nicomachean Ethics*:

> Virtue, then, is a matter of feelings and actions. Since praise and blame are attached to what is voluntary, while what is involuntary receives forgiveness, or sometimes even pity, those who study virtue must obviously establish the distinction between the voluntary and the involuntary.*[1b]

There is no need here to repeat the details of Aristotle's distinction. He treats the involuntary first, and thus arrives at a definition of the voluntary.[2] Things are involuntary if they are brought about through external force, or through ignorance. Hence, the voluntary must be "that of which the source is in the agent himself, provided

---

* Please see end of chapter for numbered references.

[a] τὸ δὲ παρ' ἡμᾶς ἀδέσποτον, ᾧ καὶ τὸ μεμπτὸν καὶ τὸ ἐναντίον παρακολουθεῖν πέφυκεν. (*Letter to Menoeceus* §133.)

[b] Τῆς ἀρετῆς δὴ περὶ πάθη τε καὶ πράξεις οὔσης, καὶ ἐπὶ μὲν τοῖς ἑκουσίοις ἐπαίνων καὶ ψόγων γινομένων, ἐπὶ δὲ τοῖς ἀκουσίοις συγγνώμης, ἐνίοτε δὲ καὶ ἐλέου, τὸ ἑκούσιον καὶ τὸ ἀκούσιον ἀναγκαῖον ἴσως διορίσαι τοῖς περὶ ἀρετῆς ἐπισκοποῦσι. (*Nicomachean Ethics* Γ 1, 1109 b 30-34.)

The Voluntary and the Compulsive

that he knows the particular circumstances in which the action takes place." [c]

Now Epicurus, as we know, thought he had to refute a theory according to which there would be no place at all for voluntary action. Aristotle, too, mentions one such theory, and rejects it, in the course of his discussions of the involuntary:

> Suppose someone says that pleasant and good objects are compulsive, since they exercise force upon us and are external to us. Then (1) everything would be compulsive on such a theory, since these are the objects for which everyone does everything. Moreover (2) people who act because they are forced, involuntarily, do so with pain, whereas those who act because of anything pleasant and good do so with pleasure. But (3) it is absurd to blame external objects, rather than oneself as being too easily caught by such attractions, and to take the credit oneself for one's good behavior but blame pleasant objects for one's bad behavior.[d]

It is important to observe both the nature of the suggestion here rejected by Aristotle and the means by which he demolishes it. The suggestion follows a discussion of some borderline cases, which cannot be placed at once in the category of the voluntary or the involuntary. Some actions may be in themselves involuntary, because they are in some way disadvantageous to the agent, and yet in certain circumstances they may be preferable to all other possible courses of action, and therefore voluntary. It is hard, Aristotle says, to lay down general principles, because circumstances alter cases; but it may *not* be held that actions can be involuntary simply because they are stimulated by pleasant objects which are external to us. Such is the context of the passage we are considering.

Aristotle gives three reasons for rejecting this suggestion (or so I think; by punctuating differently it is possible to set out the argument differently). The first is simply to point out that it would destroy altogether the distinction between the voluntary and the involuntary; so in this context at least Aristotle assumes what Epicurus had to prove. The second again fails to answer the question

[c] οὗ ἡ ἀρχὴ ἐν αὐτῷ εἰδότι τὰ καθ' ἕκαστα ἐν οἷς ἡ πρᾶξις. (Ibid. 1111 a 23.)

[d] εἰ δέ τις τὰ ἡδέα καὶ τὰ καλὰ φαίη βίαια εἶναι (ἀναγκάζειν γὰρ ἔξω ὄντα), πάντα ἂν εἴη αὐτῷ βίαια· τούτων γὰρ χάριν πάντες πάντα πράττουσιν. καὶ οἱ μὲν βίᾳ καὶ ἄκοντες λυπηρῶς, οἱ δὲ διὰ τὸ ἡδὺ καὶ καλὸν μεθ' ἡδονῆς· γελοῖον δὲ τὸ αἰτιᾶσθαι τὰ ἐκτός, ἀλλὰ μὴ αὑτὸν εὐθήρατον ὄντα ὑπὸ τῶν τοιούτων, καὶ τῶν μὲν καλῶν ἑαυτόν, τῶν δ' αἰσχρῶν τὰ ἡδέα. (Ibid. 1110 b 9–15.)

Aristotle and Epicurus on Voluntary Action

which Epicurus put to himself, since a pleasant action *may* be forced. The third is a more interesting one. It asserts (without proof) that the proper target for blame is the deficiency of one's own character, not the external object which stimulates the action. If the suggestion is pressed in spite of Aristotle's insistence that there *is* a distinction between the voluntary and the involuntary, the third reason is the only one which will bear any weight.

Aristotle was not much troubled by the idea that the attraction of external objects might be a form of compulsion, so that all actions performed with such an end in view would be exempt from moral appraisal. But for Epicurus the case was more acute. For Epicurus was a hedonist. He held that as a matter of fact men seek what is pleasant and avoid what is painful, and that to obtain pleasure is the whole end of all actions. Moreover, he held that pleasure or pain is the *inevitable* accompaniment of every experience. The implication of this might appear to be that a pleasant object *necessarily* arouses feeling, and feeling *necessarily* provokes action. He had to find an answer, therefore, to this damaging suggestion.

We may now go back to the main text for the Epicurean doctrine of *voluntas*. We found evidence in Lucretius that *two* kinds of necessity were thought to endanger the freedom of the will—a necessity external to the mind and a necessity internal to it (assuming, that is, that *mens* is the correct reading in line 289). The first of these may now be identified. For what else can it be but the compulsion allegedly exercised by "pleasant objects which are external to us," as Aristotle puts it? In the crude, mechanical theory of sense perception adopted by Epicurus, the atomic *eidola* given off from the surface of perceptible objects impinge upon the soul atoms of the perceiver, and cause not only an impression of what the object is, but also a feeling about the object. When Epicurus describes the operation of these *eidola* in the *Letter to Herodotus* (§49), he says "We see and get an idea of the forms of things when something *enters from things external to us* ... when certain images *enter* us from the objects."[e]

The identification of this external necessity is made quite certain

---

[e] ἐπεισιόντος τινὸς ἀπὸ τῶν ἔξωθεν τὰς μορφὰς ὁρᾶν ἡμᾶς καὶ διανοεῖσθαι ... τύπων τινων ἐπεισιόντων ἡμῖν ἀπὸ τῶν πραγμάτων. (*Letter to Herodotus* §49.)

The Voluntary and the Compulsive

by a fragment of Epicurus' book *On Nature*. Very luckily, we have a few lines which can be read with some confidence and which contrast, as clearly as could be wished, "having the cause in themselves" with two kinds of necessity:

> ... admonishing and combating and reforming each other, as having the cause in themselves, and not just in their initial constitution and in the automatic necessity of that which surrounds and enters.[1]

In view of this passage, it seems to me that there can be no doubt about three points of the utmost importance for understanding the Epicurean theory. First, the connection between moral appraisal and "having the cause in oneself" shows an affinity with Aristotle's distinction between the voluntary and the involuntary. Second, the "external force" mentioned by Lucretius is to be explained as compulsion exercised by external objects through the medium of sense perception, and the idea of such compulsion is probably taken from the same passage of Aristotle. The third point of course concerns the existence and identity of a second kind of necessity; but this must be postponed a little.

We must first go back to the *Nicomachean Ethics*. We have seen that Aristotle's only good reason for rejecting the suggestion that all actions are necessitated by external objects was that the blame really belongs to weakness of character. But it may be suggested, by someone determined to break down the distinction between the voluntary and the involuntary, that character after all may be "out of our power," in the sense that it is given by nature. Aristotle considers such a suggestion, in a passage that may be worth quoting at length.

He has already established the distinction between the voluntary and the involuntary, and analyzed the concepts of choice (προαίρεσις), deliberation (βούλευσις) and wish (βούλησις). It follows from this analysis, he says, that virtue and vice are "in our power"; for

---

[1] ... [τῶι ν]ουθε[τ]εῖν τε ἀλλήλους καὶ [μ]άχε[σ]θαι καὶ μεταρυθμίζειν ὡς ἔχοντας καὶ ἐν ἑα[υ]τοῖς τὴν αἰτίαν καὶ οὐχὶ ἐν τῆι ἐξ ἀρχῆς μόνον συστάσει καὶ ἐν τῆι τοῦ περιέχοντος καὶ ἐπεισιόντος κατὰ τὸ αὐτόματον [ἀ]νάγκη[ι]. (Epicurus *On Nature* 31.27.3–9 Arrighetti.)

I have bracketed those letters which are missing in *both* papyri (P697 and P1056) according to C. Diano, *Epicuri Ethica*, pp. 40–41.

virtue and vice are simply enduring dispositions which are produced by performing actions of the voluntary kind. So to say, with Socrates, that no one is voluntarily wicked, or unwillingly good, is partly true and partly false; it is true that no one is unwillingly good, but wickedness is a voluntary thing.

> Or else we must dispute what has just been said, and deny that a man is the source and originator of his actions as he is of his children. But if we approve what has been said and cannot go back to sources beyond those which are in us, then those actions will be in our power, and voluntary, whose sources are in us. This seems to be confirmed both in the sphere of private life and in public legislation too. People impose punishment and retribution on those who do wicked things (provided that they do not do them either through force or through ignorance for which they are not themselves responsible), and they give honor to those who do good, with the purpose of encouraging the latter and restraining the former. On the other hand, no one is encouraged to do the kind of thing that is not in our power or voluntary, since there is no point in being persuaded (for example) not to get hot or suffer pain or hunger, etc. etc.; we shall not thereby suffer any less.[g]

The similarity between this argument and the fragment of Epicurus' *On Nature* (see p. 187) is unmistakable and far-reaching. Both insist on the criterion of "having the cause in ourselves," and work out the distinction in the context of moral discourse; and both relate moral discourse to the possibility of changing people's behavior.

Aristotle continues with the defense of his thesis that virtue and vice are "in our power."

> Punishment is imposed for ignorance itself, too, if the man seems to be responsible for his ignorance; for example, penalties are

---

[g] ἢ τοῖς γε νῦν εἰρημένοις ἀμφισβητητέον, καὶ τὸν ἄνθρωπον οὐ φατέον ἀρχὴν εἶναι οὐδὲ γεννητὴν τῶν πράξεων ὥσπερ καὶ τέκνων. εἰ δὲ ταῦτα φαίνεται καὶ μὴ ἔχομεν εἰς ἄλλας ἀρχὰς ἀναγαγεῖν παρὰ τὰς ἐν ἡμῖν, ὧν καὶ αἱ ἀρχαὶ ἐν ἡμῖν, καὶ αὐτὰ ἐφ' ἡμῖν καὶ ἑκούσια. τούτοις δ' ἔοικε μαρτυρεῖσθαι καὶ ἰδίᾳ ὑφ' ἑκάστων καὶ ὑπ' αὐτῶν τῶν νομοθετῶν· κολάζουσι γὰρ καὶ τιμωροῦνται τοὺς δρῶντας μοχθηρά, ὅσοι μὴ βίᾳ ἢ δι' ἄγνοιαν ἧς μὴ αὐτοὶ αἴτιοι. τοὺς δὲ τὰ καλὰ πράττοντας τιμῶσιν, ὡς τοὺς μὲν προτρέψοντες τοὺς δὲ κωλύσοντες. καίτοι ὅσα μήτ' ἐφ' ἡμῖν ἐστι μήθ' ἑκούσια, οὐδεὶς προτρέπεται πράττειν, ὡς οὐδὲν πρὸ ἔργου ὂν τὸ πεισθῆναι μὴ θερμαίνεσθαι ἢ ἀλγεῖν ἢ πεινῆν ἢ ἄλλ' ὁτιοῦν τῶν τοιούτων· οὐθὲν γὰρ ἧττον πεισόμεθα αὐτά. (*Nicomachean Ethics* Γ 5, 1113 b 17 ff.)

The Voluntary and the Compulsive

doubled in cases of drunkenness, since the source of action is in the man himself—for he was in a position *not* to get drunk, and his getting drunk was the cause of his ignorance. Punishments are imposed, too, on those who are ignorant of anything in the law which it is their duty to know and which is not difficult to learn. Similarly in other cases, people are punished for ignorance which seems to result from lack of care, on the ground that this ignorance is in their power, since they were in a position to take care.[h]

It is from this part of his argument that Aristotle develops a line of thought which is of great importance for understanding both his own and Epicurus' theories.

But perhaps he is the kind of man *not* to take care. No; people are themselves responsible for having become men of this kind, by living in a slack way. They are responsible for being unjust or overindulgent, by cheating, or by spending their lives drinking and so on. In every field of action, actions of a certain kind make a corresponding kind of man. This is clear from the case of people who practice for any sort of contest or similar activity—they practice by continually repeating the action.[1]

The reader will see that the suggestion considered here by Aristotle, that "perhaps he is the kind of man not to take care," follows on, in a sense, from the suggestion he considered and rejected in the first chapter of *Nicomachean Ethics* (see pp. 185*ff*.). There he rejected the suggestion that actions are compelled by external attractions, by insisting that the blame belongs to *character*. Here he takes up the possibility that character itself is something given, something out of our power. He rejects this by insisting that character is not given, but grows from our actions.

We seem to have a distinction between two periods of a man's life, in Aristotle's theory—before and after the formation of his

[h] καὶ γὰρ ἐπ' αὐτῷ τῷ ἀγνοεῖν κολάζουσιν, ἐὰν αἴτιος εἶναι δοκῇ τῆς ἀγνοίας, οἷον τοῖς μεθύουσι διπλᾶ τὰ ἐπιτίμια· ἡ γὰρ ἀρχὴ ἐν αὐτῷ· κύριος γὰρ τοῦ μὴ μεθυσθῆναι, τοῦτο δ' αἴτιον τῆς ἀγνοίας. καὶ τοὺς ἀγνοοῦντάς τι τῶν ἐν τοῖς νόμοις, ἃ δεῖ ἐπίστασθαι καὶ μὴ χαλεπά ἐστι, κολάζουσιν, ὁμοίως δὲ καὶ ἐν τοῖς ἄλλοις, ὅσα δι' ἀμέλειαν ἀγνοεῖν δοκοῦσιν, ὡς ἐπ' αὐτοῖς ὂν τὸ μὴ ἀγνοεῖν· τοῦ γὰρ ἐπιμεληθῆναι κύριοι. (*Ibid.* 1113 b 30*ff*.)

[1] ἀλλ' ἴσως τοιοῦτός ἐστιν ὥστε μὴ ἐπιμεληθῆναι. ἀλλὰ τοῦ τοιούτους γενέσθαι αὐτοὶ αἴτιοι ζῶντες ἀνειμένως, καὶ τοῦ ἀδίκους ἢ ἀκολάστους εἶναι, οἱ μὲν κακουργοῦντες, οἱ δὲ ἐν πότοις καὶ τοῖς τοιούτοις διάγοντες· αἱ γὰρ περὶ ἕκαστα ἐνέργειαι τοιούτους ποιοῦσιν. τοῦτο δὲ δῆλον ἐκ τῶν μελετώντων πρὸς ἡντινοῦν ἀγωνίαν ἢ πρᾶξιν· διατελοῦσι γὰρ ἐνεργοῦντες. (*Ibid.* 1114 a 3*ff*.)

Aristotle and Epicurus on Voluntary Action

character. Or rather, before and after the formation of each particular disposition (ἕξις); for character (I am assuming) is simply the sum of a man's dispositions, and some dispositions (those connected with food and drink, some physical skills, etc.) may develop before others (skill in driving a car, attitudes to bringing up children). Before a man's disposition is formed, he is apparently "in a position" (κύριος) to act in different ways. Once it is formed, however, this is no longer true. But nothing is said about the first stage. Aristotle continues his exposition with some notes on the second stage, after first ruling out one particular plea of ignorance: one cannot plead ignorance of the fact that actions do establish corresponding dispositions. He goes on:

> If a man does the things that will make him unjust, and is not ignorant of this, then he must be *voluntarily* unjust. But nevertheless he will not cease to be unjust and become just, whenever he wishes. For the sick man does not return to health whenever he wishes, although (it may be) he is *voluntarily* sick through living an undisciplined life and disobeying the doctors. *Then* it was possible for him not to fall sick, but once he has let things go it is no longer possible; just as a man who has thrown a stone cannot get it back again, in spite of the fact that the throwing of it was in his power, since the source of the action was in himself. It is the same with the unjust man and the overindulgent man: in the beginning it was possible for them not to become men of this kind, and so they are *voluntarily* men of this kind; but once they have become so, it is no longer possible for them not to be so.¹

I am not sure whether Aristotle would stand by the letter of this pessimistic passage, if pressed. It implies, if taken literally, that men become, after a certain degree of development, incorrigible. Evidently, however, he did not think that many men become incorrigible soon, since the *Ethics* is explicitly designed to make men better, and is not directed at the young.³ On the other hand, he does repeat the same point in another context, when he is making a dis-

---

¹ εἰ δὲ μὴ ἀγνοῶν τις πράττει ἐξ ὧν ἔσται ἄδικος, ἑκὼν ἄδικος ἂν εἴη, οὐ μὴν ἐάν γε βούληται, ἄδικος ὢν παύσεται καὶ ἔσται δίκαιος. οὐδὲ γὰρ ὁ νοσῶν ὑγιής. καὶ εἰ οὕτως ἔτυχεν, ἑκὼν νοσεῖ, ἀκρατῶς βιοτεύων καὶ ἀπειθῶν τοῖς ἰατροῖς. τότε μὲν οὖν ἐξῆν αὐτῷ μὴ νοσεῖν, προεμένῳ δ' οὐκέτι, ὥσπερ οὐδ' ἀφέντι λίθον ἔτ' αὐτὸν δυνατὸν ἀναλαβεῖν· ἀλλ' ὅμως ἐπ' αὐτῷ τὸ βαλεῖν [καὶ ῥῖψαι]· ἡ γὰρ ἀρχὴ ἐν αὐτῷ. οὕτω δὲ καὶ τῷ ἀδίκῳ καὶ τῷ ἀκολάστῳ ἐξ ἀρχῆς μὲν ἐξῆν τοιούτοις μὴ γενέσθαι, διὸ ἑκόντες εἰσίν· γενομένοις δ' οὐκέτι ἔστι μὴ εἶναι. (*Ibid.* 1114 a 12ff.)

The Voluntary and the Compulsive

tinction between "intemperance" (ἀκολασία) and "incontinence" (ἀκρασία). The man who is merely incontinent is one who knows what is right (the precise sense of "know" here is discussed at length by Aristotle), but is led by passion to do the opposite. The man who is viciously intemperate, on the other hand, does *not* know what is right. He chooses, deliberately, and with full consciousness, a bad course of action, believing it to be right. Hence, Aristotle adds, he is incurable (ἀνίατος). "If we make the comparison with diseases, vice is like dropsy or consumption, whereas incontinence is like epilepsy, since the former is uninterrupted wickedness, whereas the latter is not."[4] It seems that he seriously believed in the incorrigible wickedness of those who had grown up, through bad habits, into bad dispositions.

The significant thing is that Aristotle does not seek a criterion of what is voluntary or involuntary in whether or not a man may act otherwise *now*, or in whether or not his behavior can be accurately predicted. He does not say or imply that an act is voluntary only because it is "freely chosen," or because it is preceded by "a free act of will." If we imagine his unjust man confronted with a temptation to gain something for himself by cheating, we can predict his response to this temptation; in a sense he may be on this occasion "unable to do otherwise" than cheat—for what else does it mean to say "he will not cease to be unjust and become just, whenever he wishes"? In fact, Aristotle might not wish to go so far as to say that he was *unable* to do otherwise; he might not wish to say that a certain disposition *necessarily* brings about actions of a certain type. But this point does not seem to be relevant to his doctrine of the voluntary and the involuntary. From the moral point of view, an act is voluntary if it proceeds from a disposition which is voluntary.

I shall return to this point in chapter 4, and consider whether my statement of it needs to be modified in view of certain passages of Aristotle which we have not yet considered. Meanwhile we must continue our study of the text of *Nicomachean Ethics* Γ 5.

Aristotle observes that, as well as states of the *psyche*, some physical conditions fall into the category of what can be morally appraised, for some physical conditions are the result, not of nature,

Aristotle and Epicurus on Voluntary Action

but of behavior. He continues then to raise and answer another objection that may be brought against his belief in the voluntariness of virtue and vice:

> Suppose someone were to say that everybody desires what *appears* good; but we are not masters of what appears to us—the goal appears to each man in accordance with the kind of man he is. But (against this) if each of us *is* somehow responsible for his disposition, he will be somehow responsible for this appearance; otherwise no one is himself responsible for acting badly, but does these things through ignorance of the goal, believing that he will achieve what is best for himself by these means. And the desire for the goal is not a matter of choice, but it is necessary to be born with a natural faculty of sight, as it were, by which one will judge well and choose what is really and truly good; in that case, to be well born will be to have a good natural faculty of this kind. For it will be the greatest and best thing, and one which a man cannot get or learn from someone else but will possess or not according to his nature at birth; so to have such a good and fine nature would be the perfect and genuine "good birth."
>
> Well,[5] if this is true, how will virtue be any more voluntary than vice? To both alike, the good man and the bad man, the goal is presented and established by nature or however else it may be; and they both act in whatever way they do act by referring all the rest to this. So, whether the goal is presented to each man in whatever form it may be presented not by nature but with some dependence on the man himself, or the goal is natural but virtue is voluntary because the good man performs the actions leading to the good voluntarily, in either case vice must be no less voluntary than virtue. For the bad man also has this property of doing something by himself, in his actions even if not in his goal. So if the virtues are voluntary, as we say (because we are somehow responsible in part for our dispositions, and we establish such and such a goal for ourselves by being people of such and such a kind), then the vice must be voluntary too, since the cases are similar.[k]

[k] εἰ δέ τις λέγοι ὅτι πάντες ἐφίενται τοῦ φαινομένου ἀγαθοῦ, τῆς δὲ φαντασίας οὐ κύριοι, ἀλλ' ὁποῖός ποθ' ἕκαστός ἐστι, τοιοῦτο καὶ τὸ τέλος φαίνεται αὐτῷ· εἰ μὲν οὖν ἕκαστος ἑαυτῷ τῆς ἕξεώς ἐστί πως αἴτιος, καὶ τῆς φαντασίας ἔσται πως αὐτὸς αἴτιος· εἰ δὲ μή, οὐθεὶς αὑτῷ αἴτιος τοῦ κακοποιεῖν, ἀλλὰ δι' ἄγνοιαν τοῦ τέλους ταῦτα πράττει, διὰ τούτων οἰόμενος αὑτῷ τὸ ἄριστον ἔσεσθαι, ἡ δὲ τοῦ τέλους ἔφεσις οὐκ αὐθαίρετος, ἀλλὰ φῦναι δεῖ ὥσπερ ὄψιν ἔχοντα, ᾗ κρινεῖ καλῶς καὶ τὸ κατ' ἀλήθειαν ἀγαθὸν αἱρήσεται, καὶ ἔστιν εὐφυὴς ᾧ τοῦτο καλῶς πέφυκεν· τὸ γὰρ μέγιστον καὶ κάλλιστον, καὶ ὃ παρ' ἑτέρου μὴ οἷόν τε λαβεῖν μηδὲ μαθεῖν, ἀλλ'

The Voluntary and the Compulsive

Here we have a suggestion that moral character is determined at birth. It may be regarded as a development of the suggestion already considered at 1114 a 3 (see p. 189) that "perhaps he is the kind of man not to take care." In both passages, the essence of the suggestion is that behavior is the outcome of character—i.e. of a man's fixed dispositions—and that character is "out of our power." In the later passage Aristotle makes more precise the sense in which character may be out of our power. It is because character may be just a matter of one's constitution at birth; the causes of his genetic constitution cannot be "in the man himself," and therefore character must be involuntary, according to the definition laid down at the beginning of the book.

In the later passage, just quoted, it will be obvious that Aristotle gives an unsatisfactory answer. He merely points out that if character is a matter of genetic constitution, then virtue is out of our power, as well as vice. The reason for this is that the whole passage —and no doubt the whole of Aristotle's thinking on the subject— starts from the famous Socratic paradox "no one is voluntarily wicked" (1113 b 14). By this Socrates meant—or, what is more significant, Plato said that he meant—that men only stray from the right course through some kind of ignorance. That is why Aristotle is more concerned with defining the relations between *ignorance* and voluntary action than those between *compulsion* and voluntary action.

The fact that Aristotle's argument is to a great extent *ad hominem* (a fact excellently brought out by Gauthier and Jolif, 1959) accounts for some differences between himself and Epicurus. It was enough for Aristotle to show that the Socratic paradox, unqualified, would

---

οἷον ἔφυ τοιοῦτον ἕξει, καὶ τὸ εὖ καὶ τὸ καλῶς τοῦτο πεφυκέναι ἡ τελεία καὶ ἀληθινὴ ἂν εἴη εὐφυΐα.

εἰ δὴ ταῦτ' ἐστὶν ἀληθῆ, τί μᾶλλον ἡ ἀρετὴ τῆς κακίας ἔσται ἑκούσιον; ἀμφοῖν γὰρ ὁμοίως, τῷ ἀγαθῷ καὶ τῷ κακῷ, τὸ τέλος φύσει ἢ ὁπωσδήποτε φαίνεται καὶ κεῖται, τὰ δὲ λοιπὰ πρὸς τοῦτο ἀναφέροντες πράττουσιν ὁπωσδήποτε. εἴτε δὴ τὸ τέλος μὴ φύσει ἑκάστῳ φαίνεται οἱονδήποτε, ἀλλά τι καὶ παρ' αὐτόν ἐστιν, εἴτε τὸ μὲν τέλος φυσικόν, τῷ δὲ τὰ λοιπὰ πράττειν ἑκουσίως τὸν σπουδαῖον ἡ ἀρετὴ ἑκούσιόν ἐστιν, οὐθὲν ἧττον καὶ κακία ἑκούσιον ἂν εἴη· ὁμοίως γὰρ καὶ τῷ κακῷ ὑπάρχει τὸ δι' αὐτὸν ἐν ταῖς πράξεσι καὶ εἰ μὴ ἐν τῷ τέλει. εἰ οὖν, ὥσπερ λέγεται, ἑκούσιοί εἰσιν αἱ ἀρεταί (καὶ γὰρ τῶν ἕξεων συναίτιοί πως αὐτοί ἐσμεν, καὶ τῷ ποιοί τινες εἶναι τὸ τέλος τοιόνδε τιθέμεθα), καὶ αἱ κακίαι ἑκούσιοι ἂν εἶεν· ὁμοίως γάρ. (*Ibid.* 1114 a 31–b 25.)

Aristotle and Epicurus on Voluntary Action

exempt *good* behavior, as well as bad, from moral appraisal; for this would be fatal to the teaching of Socrates and Plato. But it was not enough for Epicurus, who had to defend himself against arguments which would remove all actions from the realm of moral appraisal.

However, although it is true that Aristotle is largely content to reply *ad hominem*, we can find in the text the outline of a more general reply. It lies of course in his insistence that a man's dispositions are established by nothing but his own actions, the source of which is certainly "in himself" and cannot be traced back any further. It is odd that Aristotle never (to my knowledge) asks himself why the discipline of parents and teachers is not to be taken as an external cause of a man's dispositions. Our own experience of "juvenile delinquency," and the generally held belief that young people's crimes may be due not to wickedness but to faulty environment, raise this question at once. But Aristotle seems never to have considered this point.

We are now in a position to see the point of the second kind of necessity—internal necessity—from which the Epicurean theory had to save men's *voluntas*. The danger was that moral character might be something given by nature, a part of a man's constitution at birth. A man would be *born* virtuous or vicious, and in this sense his behavior would be traced back to causes which were not "in himself." This is in fact clearly indicated in the fragment of Epicurus *On Nature* quoted on p. 187:[6] ". . . having the cause in themselves, and not just *in their initial constitution* and in the automatic necessity of that which surrounds and enters."

The position the argument has reached may now be summed up as follows. In the first chapter it was shown that the Epicurean theory took into account two kinds of "necessity" and maintained that *voluntas* was not constrained by either of them. In Epicurus' *On Nature* we have found a valuable confirmation of this, and some indications that we ought to look at Aristotle's theory of the Voluntary for the historical context of the Epicurean theory. In Aristotle's discussion we have found an examination of two propositions which might endanger the existence of the Voluntary; and these two propositions bear enough resemblance to the two kinds of necessity

The Voluntary and the Compulsive

which feature in the Epicurean theory for us to be sure that the former are the direct forerunners of the latter.

The next task is to look more closely at Epicurean psychology.

Notes to Chapter 2

1. I am of course aware of the difficulties which arise from this or any other English translation of ἑκούσιον and ἀκούσιον. See Gauthier and Jolif (1959), II, 1, 169-170. I hope this translation will not be misleading.
2. A significant point incidentally. Cf. J. L. Austin, "A Plea for Excuses," *Aristotelian Society Proceedings* 1956-57, p. 6.
3. *Nicomachean Ethics* A 3, 1095 a 2-11.
4. *Ibid.* H 8, 1150 b 32-35.
5. For this translation of δή see Denniston (1954), pp. 238-239.
6. Arrighetti, 31.27.2ff.

CHAPTER 3

OUTLINE OF EPICUREAN PSYCHOLOGY

THE purpose of this chapter is mainly negative. I believe that the swerve of atoms played a very small part in Epicurean psychology. On the other hand, in the version of it currently accepted and taught it plays a rather large part. I think it is necessary to examine the psychological concepts used by Epicurus, chiefly with a view to showing that there is certainly no direct evidence of a major role for the swerve, and that some of the allegations made about it are not plausible. But in addition I hope to throw a little light on Epicurean psychology in general.

THE COMPOSITION OF THE PSYCHE

The *psyche* in Epicurean theory is made of atoms, of three or four kinds only:

> The *psyche* is corporeal, of fine texture, distributed over the whole frame, most similar to *pneuma* with an admixture of heat, being like the former in one way and the latter in another; in addition there is the part greatly exceeding even these in fineness of texture and by virtue of this being the more closely associated in feeling with the rest of the frame.[a]

This carefully qualified summary mentions only three constituents—something like *pneuma*, heat, and something finer than these. Later doxographers,[*1] and Epicurus' own disciple Lucretius, raise the number to four. According to Lucretius (3.231*ff*.), there is *aura* (*pneuma*), *vapor* (which seems to mean something hot), and *aer*, as

---

[a] ἡ ψυχὴ σῶμά ἐστι λεπτομερές, παρ' ὅλον τὸ ἄθροισμα παρεσπαρμένον, προσεμφερέστατον δὲ πνεύματι, θερμοῦ τινα κρᾶσιν ἔχοντι καὶ πῇ μὲν τούτῳ προσεμφερές, πῇ δὲ τούτῳ· ἔστι δὲ τὸ μέρος πολλὴν παραλλαγὴν εἰληφὸς τῇ λεπτομερείᾳ καὶ αὐτῶν τούτων, συμπαθὲς δὲ τούτῳ μᾶλλον καὶ τῷ λοιπῷ ἀθροίσματι. (*Letter to Herodotus* §63. Bailey's text.)

* Please see end of chapter for numbered references.

Outline of Epicurean Psychology

well as the fourth and finest element, which has no name.

Both *psyche* as a whole and mind, which is a part of it, consist of these elements and no others. It must be remembered that Epicurean atoms themselves possess no qualities, apart from shape, size, and weight, and cannot change in quality. It follows that all changes in the *psyche* must be accounted for by rearrangements of the existing stock of atoms or else by the addition or subtraction of atoms *of one or another of these four types*. This is fatal, or so it seems to me, to any account of Epicurean epistemology which asserts that the perceptible *eidola* are incorporated in the *psyche* of the perceiver. For the *eidola* of (say) an object made of iron consist of iron atoms, not of soul atoms; and the iron cannot enter into the Epicurean soul.

The proportions of at least three of the four kinds may vary from one *psyche* to another; we have the authority of Lucretius for this:

> There is more of the hot element in those whose bitter heart
> and wrathful mind easily explodes in anger.
> In this class above all is the forceful, violent lion,
> who bursts his breast with noise when he roars
> and can't contain the waves of anger in his breast.
> The chilly mind of deer is more full of breath
> and wafts cool breezes through their bodies,
> which impart a trembling movement to their limbs.
> The species of cattle lives more on air, which is placid;
> anger's firebrand is never much charged to stir them
> smokily, filling them with the darkness of blind fog,
> nor do they cower transfixed by the chilly arrows of fear;
> they are betwixt and between the deer and the fierce lions.
> So it is with the race of men.[b]

[b] sed calidi plus est illis quibus acria corda
iracundaque mens facile effervescit in ira.
quo genere in primis vis est violenta leonum,
pectora qui fremitu rumpunt plerumque gementes
nec capere irarum fluctus in pectore possunt.
at ventosa magis cervorum frigida mens est
et gelidas citius per viscera concitat auras
quae tremulum faciunt membris exsistere motum.
at natura boum placido magis aere vivit,
nec nimis irai fax umquam subdita percit
fumida, suffundens caecae caliginis umbra,
nec gelidis torpet telis perfixa pavoris:
interutrasque sitast, cervos saevosque leones.
sic hominum genus est.
(3.294–307)

Aristotle and Epicurus on Voluntary Action

It will be seen at once that this is a perilous doctrine for an Epicurean to hold. For it seems to entail that a man's character and his reactions to the world will be determined at his birth by the proportions of *pneuma*, heat, and air in his soul. If this is the case, there is no hope of success in the ultimate aim of the Epicurean philosophy —to teach men tranquillity. We are tranquil, if it is our nature to be; if not, not. Lucretius therefore goes on at once to reassure the reader:

> Although learning makes some men
> all equally well-mannered, it still leaves
> the basic remnants of each man's natural mind.
> It mustn't be thought that faults can totally be rooted out,   310
> so that no longer does this man relapse too fast into bitter anger,
> and that man yield a little too fast to fear, and the third
> accept some things more calmly than he should.
> And in many other things it must be true
> that men's natures differ, and the habits their natures entail;   315
> I cannot now expound the hidden causes of these,
> nor find enough names for the numerous figures
> of the atoms which give rise to this variety of things.
> This much can certainly be said on these matters,
> that only such *small* remnants of our natures are left,   320
> beyond the power of reason to drive out of us,
> that nothing prevents us living a life worthy of the gods.[c]

We must pause for a while over this, since the argument has sometimes been obscured by the commentators. Learning (*doctrina*,

---

[c]
> quamvis doctrina politos
> constituat pariter quosdam, tamen illa relinquit
> naturae cuiusque animi vestigia prima.
> nec radicitus evelli mala posse putandumst,   310
> quin proclivius hic iras decurrat ad acris,
> ille metu citius paulo temptetur, at ille
> tertius accipiat quaedam clementius aequo.
> inque aliis rebus multis differre necessest
> naturas hominum varias moresque sequaces;   315
> quorum ego nunc nequeo caecas exponere causas
> nec reperire figurarum tot nomina quot sunt
> principiis, unde haec oritur variantia rerum.
> illud in his rebus video firmare potesse,
> usque adeo naturarum vestigia linqui   320
> parvula quae nequeat ratio depellere nobis,
> ut nil impediat dignam dis degere vitam.
> (3.307–322)

Outline of Epicurean Psychology

307), says Lucretius, makes certain people equally refined or well-mannered, but it cannot wholly eradicate natural differences. Only such tiny traces of these natural differences are left untouched by reason (*ratio*, 321) that nothing prevents one from living a life worthy of the gods. Bailey, perhaps following up a hint dropped by Giussani,[2] distinguishes sharply between *doctrina* and *ratio*: *doctrina* translates "παιδεία," which Epicurus disliked; *ratio* is the Epicurean philosophy. "Education can do something to bring men to the same level of culture, but it cannot eradicate the natural tendencies, and they will from time to time burst forth. Yet *ratio*, the Epicurean philosophy, can enable men in spite of these innate tendencies to live a life worthy of the gods."[3] It will be seen that Bailey's distinction rests on nothing but the use of two words instead of one. For Lucretius makes no distinction between the *effects* of *doctrina* and *ratio*; he says of both that they can eliminate natural differences to a sufficient extent but not completely. Between the opening statement about *doctrina* and the closing statement about *ratio* he observes that there are very many differences of character besides the three most obvious ones which have already been identified. The pattern of the section from lines 307 to 322 is therefore "statement—amplification—summing-up"; a very usual Lucretian structure. Without convincing evidence that *doctrina* always or usually means something different from *ratio* in Lucretius, Bailey's distinction cannot be maintained.

It is vital for our enquiry into the nature of voluntary action to understand how training (for we can now drop the attempt to distinguish between *doctrina* and *ratio*) can control the natural tendencies which result from a lack of balance in the composition of the *psyche*. Unfortunately, Lucretius does not develop this point. One can perhaps squeeze a drop of information from the word *figurarum* in line 317. "In many other things," says Lucretius—meaning "other than anger, fear, and placidity"—"there must be differences in the natures of men and in the habits which follow" (sc. from these differences). He adds that he cannot now expound the hidden causes of these differences, nor find "as many names of formations (?) as the atoms have, from which so much variety of things arises." The *rerum* of this last line are presumably in the same category as the *rebus* of line 314—dispositions or characteristics of the *psyche*.

Aristotle and Epicurus on Voluntary Action

Lucretius cannot be talking *in general* about the differences of shape exhibited by atoms; only atoms of four kinds exist in the *psyche*. And each kind is characterized by its shape and size alone, so that there cannot be much differentiation of shape *within* each kind. However, from what Lucretius says in 2.333ff., where he discusses the different shapes of atoms, it seems to follow that there are *some* differences of shapes of atoms which make up a single substance. For instance, he observes that not all grains of corn are exactly alike, and deduces from this that there are differences in the shapes of their component atoms. The atoms must, it seems, be sufficiently *alike* to make each of these compounds into a grain of corn, yet sufficiently *different* to make the compounds different. Since we are told that soul atoms are especially smooth and fine, there cannot be much scope for variation in their shape; but there may be enough to account for what Lucretius says. Alternatively, we may suppose that the *figurae* of which he speaks are not the shapes of atoms but the shapes or structures of *groups* of atoms; this is Bailey's view, and I think it is more likely to be correct.

If we assume, as we must, that learning cannot add to or subtract from the stock of atoms which compose an individual *psyche*, the only possible effect it can have is to rearrange the atoms into new patterns. Learning cannot diminish the sum of "hot" atoms in a passionate man's *psyche*, but perhaps it can push them away into less effective regions (or something like that). These patterns, it should be added, are not to be thought of as stationary, like a mosaic or a *pointilliste* picture, because in Epicurean theory atoms are always in motion. There is room in the theory, however, for more or less durable patterns of motion among the atoms.

Mental Images

The normal way in which a man learns about the external world is of course by sense perception. It is perhaps worth quoting at length the definitive statement about perception from Epicurus' *Letter to Herodotus*:

> We must believe, too, that it is through the entrance of something from external objects that we see their shapes and appre-

hend them. For external objects would not stamp upon us their nature in respect of color and shape, through the air which lies between them and us, either by rays or by any other kind of effluence proceeding from us to them, so well as by means of τυποί of the same color and shape as the objects, which enter into us from the objects, either into our faculty of sight or into our mind, according to size; moving very quickly and for that reason bringing about a mental image of the single, continuous object; and preserving their affinity with the parent object through the uniform pressure exerted by the object because of the oscillation of the atoms in the depth of its solid body. And whatever mental image of shape or of properties we get by apprehension of the mind or the sense organs, this is the shape of the solid object, and it comes about because of the successive repetition of the εἴδωλον, or because of what is left behind.[d]

The τύπος or εἴδωλον, which consists of a thin skin of atoms emitted from the surface of all objects (emitted by the force of the atoms vibrating inside the object), "enters into us." It may enter through one of the sense organs, or directly into the mind; this depends on its size—that is, on the fineness of its texture. It is not one such εἴδωλον that gives us a mental image or perception; either a constant succession of similar ones, by the speed with which they succeed one another, gives the impression of a single, continuous object (like the successive frames of a piece of motion picture film); or it is "what is left behind" which produces the continuous image. I suppose this means that though the earlier εἴδωλα may themselves have become dissipated by the time later ones arrive, nevertheless something is left behind by the earlier ones which in some way chimes or connects with the later ones.

This is a tantalizing text, because we want very badly to know

[d] Δεῖ δὲ καὶ νομίζειν ἐπεισιόντος τινὸς ἀπὸ τῶν ἔξωθεν τὰς μορφὰς ὁρᾶν ἡμᾶς καὶ διανοεῖσθαι· οὐ γὰρ ἂν ἐναποσφραγίσαιτο τὰ ἔξω τὴν ἑαυτῶν φύσιν τοῦ τε χρώματος καὶ τῆς μορφῆς διὰ τοῦ ἀέρος τοῦ μεταξὺ ἡμῶν τε κἀκείνων, οὐδὲ διὰ τῶν ἀκτίνων ἢ ὧν δήποτε ῥευμάτων ἀφ' ἡμῶν πρὸς ἐκεῖνα παραγινομένων, οὕτως ὡς τύπων τινῶν ἐπεισιόντων ἡμῖν ἀπὸ τῶν πραγμάτων ὁμοχρόων τε καὶ ὁμοιομόρφων κατὰ τὸ ἐναρμόττον μέγεθος εἰς τὴν ὄψιν ἢ τὴν διάνοιαν, ὠκέως ταῖς φοραῖς χρωμένων εἶτα διὰ ταύτην τὴν αἰτίαν τοῦ ἑνὸς καὶ συνεχοῦς τὴν φαντασίαν ἀποδιδόντων καὶ τὴν συμπάθειαν ἀπὸ τοῦ ὑποκειμένου σῳζόντων κατὰ τὸν ἐκεῖθεν σύμμετρον ἐπερεισμὸν ἐκ τῆς κατὰ βάθος ἐν τῷ στερεμνίῳ τῶν ἀτόμων πάλσεως. καὶ ἣν ἂν λάβωμεν φαντασίαν ἐπιβλητικῶς τῇ διανοίᾳ ἢ τοῖς αἰσθητηρίοις εἴτε μορφῆς εἴτε συμβεβηκότων, μορφή ἐστιν αὕτη τοῦ στερεμνίου, γινομένη κατὰ τὸ ἑξῆς πύκνωμα ἢ ἐγκατάλειμμα τοῦ εἰδώλου. (*Letter to Herodotus* §§49–50.)

Aristotle and Epicurus on Voluntary Action

what exactly is left behind; and nothing further is said about it. Since nothing more is said, we may go on with the hypothesis already suggested—that the *eidola* impose a new pattern upon the soul atoms. This is "what is left"; and if other similar *eidola* confirm the new pattern, a mental image results. That is to say, the mental image *is* the new pattern. It is not the case that the new pattern *causes* some other event in the mind, which is the mental image; for such an event could not be anything but another change of motion in the soul atoms, and nothing is gained by the assumption of another change of motion.

After the image produced by the act of perception has disappeared for the moment, it can be recalled again as a memory. This implies (though there is no explicit confirmation in the texts) that the pattern of motion of the soul atoms which constitutes the image does not disintegrate after the supply of *eidola* has ceased, but may be retained, more or less intact, somewhere in the mind.

Πρόληψις, ἐπιβολή, δόξα

A brief review of these concepts seems to be necessary, if we are to understand the Epicurean psychology of action.

According to Diogenes Laertius (10.31), Epicurus said in his book called *The Canon* that there are three criteria of truth: "sensations and προλήψεις, and feelings" (my punctuation is intended to point to Diogenes' omission of the definite article with "προλήψεις"; the first two are grouped together). When we turn to the writings of Epicurus himself and Lucretius to look for confirmation, we find no evidence for any such precise doctrine. In the epistemological sections of the *Letter to Herodotus* (§§38, 63, 68, and 82), where Epicurus stresses the supreme importance of sense perception and feeling, there is no mention of πρόληψις. The word is used once (§72) in a discussion of time, but the context offers little help toward establishing its meaning. There are, however, three other instances of its use in the extant works of Epicurus. In the *Letter to Menoeceus* (§124) he says of the popular statements about the gods that they are not προλήψεις but false suppositions (ὑπολήψεις ψευδεῖς). This makes it clear that the word could mean an idea or conception, and that without further qualification it implies that the idea is a true or valid one. The other two instances are to all intents and purposes identical. Epicurus explains in *Principal Doctrines* that justice is a derivative concept and depends upon its utility to society:

> 37. Of the things supposed to be just, when there is evidence to confirm that one is suited to the needs of society, then this must have a place in the field of justice, whether all people get the same or not. [I take the last clause to be a reference to discussions about the relation between justice and equality, such as are found in Aristotle *Nicomachean Ethics* E3.] But if someone sets up a law and it turns out not to be beneficial to society, then this no longer has the nature of the Just. And if what is beneficial in the field of justice changes, but for a time it still fits our πρόληψις, it is[4] nevertheless just, during this time, for those who do not confuse themselves with empty words but consider the facts.
>
> 38. When circumstances do not change, if what is supposed to be just is shown *not* to fit our πρόληψις in relation to the facts, then it is not just. If in changed circumstances the same things laid down as being just are no longer beneficial, then they *were* just, when they were beneficial to the society of citizens, but later they are no longer just, when they are not beneficial.[e]

This throws some light on the meaning of "πρόληψις." The main part of the word (λῆψις) certainly means "conception" or "comprehension" or something like that. Morphologically it could mean either a process or the result of a process; either the act or process of conceiving, or a conception or concept. The phrase "ἐναρμόττειν εἰς τὴν πρόληψιν" points clearly enough to the latter meaning. The sense of the prefix "προ-" has caused some bafflement, since some of our second-hand evidence suggests that πρόληψις

---

[e] XXXVII Τὸ μὲν ἐπιμαρτυρούμενον ὅτι συμφέρει ἐν ταῖς χρείαις τῆς πρὸς ἀλλήλους κοινωνίας τῶν νομισθέντων εἶναι δικαίων ἔχειν τοῦ δικαίου χώραν ⟨δ⟩εῖ, ἐάν τε τὸ αὐτὸ πᾶσι γένηται ἐάν τε μὴ τὸ αὐτό· ἐὰν δὲ νόμον θῆταί τις, μὴ ἀποβαίνῃ δὲ κατὰ τὸ συμφέρον τῆς πρὸς ἀλλήλους κοινωνίας, οὐκέτι τοῦτο τὴν τοῦ δικαίου φύσιν ἔχει· κἂν μεταπίπτῃ τὸ κατὰ τὸ δίκαιον συμφέρον, χρόνον δέ τινα εἰς τὴν πρόληψιν ἐναρμόττῃ, οὐδὲν ἧττον ἐκεῖνον τὸν χρόνον ἦν δίκαιον τοῖς μὴ φωναῖς κεναῖς ἑαυτοὺς συνταράττουσιν ἀλλ' εἰς τὰ πράγματα βλέπουσιν.

XXXVIII Ἔνθα μὴ καινῶν γενομένων τῶν περιεστώτων πραγμάτων ἀνεφάνη μὴ ἁρμόττοντα εἰς τὴν πρόληψιν τὰ νομισθέντα δίκαια ἐπ' αὐτῶν τῶν ἔργων, οὐκ ἦν ταῦτα δίκαια· ἔνθα δὲ καινῶν γενομένων τῶν πραγμάτων οὐκέτι συνέφερε τὰ αὐτὰ δίκαια κείμενα, ἐνταῦθα δὴ τότε μὲν ἦν δίκαια ὅτε συνέφερεν εἰς τὴν πρὸς ἀλλήλους κοινωνίαν τῶν συμπολιτευομένων, ὕστερον δ' οὐκ ἦν ἔτι δίκαια ὅτε μὴ συνέφερεν. (*Principal Doctrines* 37-38.)

comes at the end of a process rather than at the beginning. Here, however, the sense seems clear enough: we have a conception of what is just *before* we consider the particular instance under discussion.

We can perhaps extract a little more information from the end of §37. It is said there that, if circumstances change, something that was formerly beneficial and therefore just, but is so no longer, may continue for a while to fit our preconception; and in that case it remains just for us, until our preconception is changed—otherwise, Epicurus implies, we shall be confusing ourselves with empty words. It appears from this, then, that the word "just" will be an empty one for us if it is used in a way which does not conform with our preconception of justice.

This reference to "empty words" suggests that we might look for further information on πρόληψις at the sections of the *Letter to Herodotus* in which Epicurus propounds rules for the use of words:

> First, then, Herodotus, we must keep in our grasp the things which are assigned to words, so that we may be able to test our opinions and problems and difficulties by reference to them, and everything may not be untestable, involving us in a demonstrative argument that goes back to infinity, and we may not use empty words. For the first thing that comes to mind must be considered, in respect of each word, and it must need no demonstrative argument in addition, if we are to have something to which we can refer our problems and difficulties and opinions.[f]

And he continues with a statement of the importance of sense perception.

This has not much connection with Epicurus' theory of the *origin* of language, as some have thought. That theory (described in the *Letter to Herodotus* §§75-76, and in Lucretius 5, 1028-90) was part of the Epicurean defense of natural causes against the teleologists; it had to do with how the human species as a whole learned its language. This paragraph on the other hand is epistemological, and

---

[f] Πρῶτον μὲν οὖν τὰ ὑποτεταγμένα τοῖς φθόγγοις, ὦ Ἡρόδοτε, δεῖ εἰληφέναι, ὅπως ἂν τὰ δοξαζόμενα ἢ ζητούμενα ἢ ἀπορούμενα ἔχωμεν εἰς ταῦτα ἀναγαγόντες ἐπικρίνειν, καὶ μὴ ἄκριτα πάντα ἡμῖν ⟨ᾖ⟩ εἰς ἄπειρον ἀποδεικνύουσιν ἢ κενοὺς φθόγγους ἔχωμεν· ἀνάγκη γὰρ τὸ πρῶτον ἐννόημα καθ' ἕκαστον φθόγγον βλέπεσθαι καὶ μηθὲν ἀποδείξεως προσδεῖσθαι, εἴπερ ἕξομεν τὸ ζητούμενον ἢ ἀπορούμενον καὶ δοξαζόμενον ἐφ' ὃ ἀνάξομεν. (*Letter to Herodotus* §§37-38.)

Outline of Epicurean Psychology

it has to do with the learning of individual men. There may well be some connection: the notion that a word has a single meaning given to it (as it were) by nature is common to both topics. But Epicurus can hardly have wished to say that we all individually learn to use words in the same way as the human species learned to use them.[5] It seems to me that this paragraph corresponds with the last chapter of Aristotle's *Posterior Analytics*, in that both play a similar part in their author's theory of knowledge. All teaching and all learning, Aristotle says, must start from pre-existing knowledge. How then can learning ever get started? Demonstrative argument ($ἀπόδειξις$) cannot start by itself, since it presupposes premises that are already known. The basic premises must be known by sense perception. All animals have sense perception, but only some of them have the capacity to retain the percept, and of these only some (viz. men) develop the power of using the retained percepts in more highly organized ways.

Like Aristotle, Epicurus insists that demonstrative argument cannot go back to infinity. We must have a starting point. And the starting point, as he insists over and over again, is sense perception. We learn to attach words to our perceptions; and thus when the word is mentioned we have a "preconception" of what the word refers to. But there is a danger that we may forget that this is the use of words, and try to give them an independent life. So he insists that we must keep in mind the things which are assigned to our words ($τὰ\ ὑποτεταγμένα\ τοῖς\ φθόγγοις$), and so avoid using *empty* words. We must use words in a way which corresponds with our $προλήψεις$ because if we cut them adrift they will be aimless and uncontrollable.

Although this argument is based on a theory of knowledge such as Aristotle put forward in the *Posterior Analytics*, it is also to some extent a polemic against Aristotle, and others. It is part of a positivistic attack on metaphysics. However, the details of that attack can be omitted; the important question now is: what can be said about Epicurus' use of "$πρόληψις$"? It seems certain that the word retains the sense of "*preconception*"; it emphasizes that this comes *before* a particular instance. Some have suggested that $προλήψεις$ were innate ideas. If so they were independent of sense perception and should therefore have been listed by Epicurus along with sensation and feeling as "criteria of truth" (but there are other sufficient reasons for rejecting this suggestion). It is certain that προλήψεις are derivatives of sense perception. The probable conclusion is that the elevation of πρόληψις to the position of a third criterion along with sensation and feeling is the work of the doxographers, who liked to make systematic lists of terms. Epicurus himself used the word simply to refer to the function of the retained sense image in comparisons with new sense perceptions.[6]

This concept, then, adds very little to our knowledge of Epicurean psychology. Epicurus clearly had some idea of what happened to the mind atoms to bring about the retention of a sense image; there was no need for him to add anything to this to account for πρόληψις.

The second of the three concepts, ἐπιβολή, might be expected to have a more direct relevance to the problem of voluntary action. According to Bailey's interpretation of the texts,[7] ἐπιβολή usually implies something active on the part of the observer, as opposed to the mere passive reception of mental images, either directly or through the medium of sense perception. As with πρόληψις, it seems to me a mistake to try to construct a consistent technical use for this word in the Epicurean system; and Bailey's treatment of the evidence is extremely questionable.[8] However, the lengthy demolition of others' theories is tedious both for the writer and the reader; perhaps a brief review of a few of the texts will suffice for present purposes. Since the third concept, δόξα, is intimately connected in the texts with ἐπιβολή, both may be examined together.

The most revealing text is §§50-51 of the *Letter to Herodotus*, the earlier part of which was translated above (p. 201):

And whatever mental image, of shape or of properties, we get by apprehension of the mind or the sense organs, this is the shape of the solid object, and it comes about because of the successive repetition of the εἴδωλον, or because of what is left behind, but falsehood and error always lie in the addition made by judgment (δόξα).... For there would have been no similarity between, on the one hand, the appearances seen as if in a picture or occurring in dreams or in any of the other apprehensions (ἐπιβολαί) of the mind or of the other criteria, and, on the other hand, things that

Outline of Epicurean Psychology

really exist and are called "true," unless these things which we apprehend really existed. But the *error* would not have happened, if we did not have a second motion, in ourselves, connected with the apprehension of the image but different from it. From this motion, if there is no confirmatory evidence or there is counter-evidence, error arises, or if there is confirmatory evidence or no counterevidence, truth. This judgment (δόξα) must be very firmly kept in check, so that the criteria derived from clear observations (κατὰ τὰς ἐναργείας) may not be destroyed, and error may not be similarly established and thus throw everything into confusion.[g]

In the second sentence, there is a clear distinction between illusion and reality: only thus does the sentence hang together logically. So "τῶν φαντασμῶν οἱονεὶ ἐν εἰκόνι λαμβανομένων" are certainly *illusory* appearances, not (as Bailey says) "the images perceived as a kind of likeness (i.e. the normal images of sensation)." I am not quite sure what "εἰκών" implies here, but since Plato it usually carried the implication of a *mere* copy or representation, as opposed to the real thing. Lucretius (4, 722-776) speaks first of imaginary creatures like Centaurs, and then of images perceived in sleep; so perhaps Epicurus deals with things in the same order. He insists, then, that imaginary visions and dream images, because of their similarity to real things, must have a real origin; that is, they are caused by real εἴδωλα. But error arises (that is, we confuse these imaginary visions with reality) because of the addition of δόξα. A real object stamps its image on our mind by sending a constant stream of εἴδωλα to our sense organs. Imaginary visions are the product of random images which, as Lucretius says, "wander in large

[g] καὶ ἣν ἂν λάβωμεν φαντασίαν ἐπιβλητικῶς τῇ διανοίᾳ ἢ τοῖς αἰσθητηρίοις εἴτε μορφῆς εἴτε συμβεβηκότων, μορφή ἐστιν αὕτη τοῦ στερεμνίου, γινομένη κατὰ τὸ ἑξῆς πύκνωμα ἢ ἐγκατάλειμμα τοῦ εἰδώλου. τὸ δὲ ψεῦδος καὶ τὸ διημαρτημένον ἐν τῷ προσδοξαζομένῳ ἀεί ἐστιν. . . . ἥ τε γὰρ ὁμοιότης τῶν φαντασμῶν οἱονεὶ ἐν εἰκόνι λαμβανομένων ἢ καθ' ὕπνους γινομένων ἢ κατ' ἄλλας τινὰς ἐπιβολὰς τῆς διανοίας ἢ τῶν λοιπῶν κριτηρίων οὐκ ἄν ποτε ὑπῆρχε τοῖς οὖσί τε καὶ ἀληθέσι προσαγορευομένοις, εἰ μὴ ἦν τινα καὶ ταῦτα πρὸς ἃ ⟨ἐπι⟩βάλλομεν· τὸ δὲ διημαρτημένον οὐκ ἂν ὑπῆρχεν, εἰ μὴ ἐλαμβάνομεν καὶ ἄλλην τινὰ κίνησιν ἐν ἡμῖν αὐτοῖς συνημμένην μὲν ⟨τῇ φανταστικῇ ἐπιβολῇ⟩, διάληψιν δὲ ἔχουσαν· κατὰ δὲ ταύτην ἐὰν μὲν μὴ ἐπιμαρτυρηθῇ ἢ ἀντιμαρτυρηθῇ, τὸ ψεῦδος γίνεται· ἐὰν δὲ ἐπιμαρτυρηθῇ ἢ μὴ ἀντιμαρτυρηθῇ, τὸ ἀληθές. καὶ ταύτην οὖν σφόδρα γε δεῖ τὴν δόξαν κατέχειν, ἵνα μήτε τὰ κριτήρια ἀναιρῆται τὰ κατὰ τὰς ἐναργείας μήτε τὸ διημαρτημένον ὁμοίως βεβαιούμενον πάντα συνταράττῃ. (*Letter to Herodotus* §§50-52.)

numbers in many ways in all directions everywhere." It is the business of δόξα to pronounce whether a particular mental image is the result of a constant stream of εἴδωλα or a random one or two.

In this passage, then, the ἐπιβολαὶ τῆς διανοίας ἢ τῶν λοιπῶν κριτηρίων are apprehensions of *illusory* images. Both waking visions and dream images are included in the category of ἐπιβολαί, if the word ἄλλας has any meaning. We have therefore incontrovertible evidence that ἐπιβολή is *not* necessarily an act of concentration or deliberate attention. An examination of other instances of its use would show, I think, that it adds nothing of importance to Epicurus' theory of knowledge and psychology.

On the other hand, δόξα is important. We are told that it is a *motion*, and that it is *in us*. It must of course be a motion of soul atoms; and it is *in us*, presumably, because it is not caused wholly by the εἴδωλα coming from outside. It is said to be connected with the apprehension of the mental image (συνημμένη τῇ φανταστικῇ ἐπιβολῇ), but distinct from it.[9] The apprehension of the image is a passive business, caused entirely by the entrance of the εἴδωλα. But δόξα is not wholly the result of external causes.

Is δόξα, then, a swerve of the *psyche* atoms, or is it caused by such a swerve? I do not believe for a moment that this is what Epicurus meant. We have been told that δόξα is *connected* with the apprehension of the image in sense perception, and that the swerve which gives us free will is "at no fixed place and at no fixed time"; these seem to be incompatible predicates. Neither Epicurus nor Lucretius mentions δόξα and the swerve together. Moreover, as I hope to show in the remaining chapters, this is not where the swerve is required in Epicurean psychology.

NOTES TO CHAPTER 3

1. Aëtius 4.3.11; Plutarch *Adversus Coloten* 1118 d (=Usener 315 and 314).
2. Giussani (1896), on 3, 307.
3. Bailey (1947), p. 1035.
4. My translation of the tenses here and in 38 follows Bailey.
5. Nor is this implied by Lucretius 5.1030-1032.

Outline of Epicurean Psychology

6. This may be overstated. There are some propositions (those of science, for instance) which cannot be tested against perceptions immediately, but only against προλήψεις. In this sense πρόληψις may be described as one of the criteria. But of course it is still a derivative of sense perception.
7. Bailey (1928), appendix III.
8. Note for instance that the quotation at the top of p. 565 is not "extracted" but rewritten.
9. The MS text is corrupt at this point, but there is little doubt that Usener's restoration, which I have printed, is correct. For full details, see the *apparatus criticus* in Bailey, Arrighetti or Long.

CHAPTER 4

PSYCHOLOGY OF ACTION, EPICUREAN AND ARISTOTELIAN

For the Epicurean theory we are dependent on two passages of Lucretius; the text of Epicurus to which they correspond has been lost. Like others which have been analyzed in this book, they have sometimes been misrepresented by being detached from their context in the poem. We can understand what is the emphasis, and why such and such points are emphasized, only if we appreciate the general intention of the part of the poem to which they belong.

The first passage (4.777-822) is important because it suggests that we are able to choose certain *simulacra* and reject others, and if this can be maintained it is obviously relevant to the theme of voluntary action. It forms part of a larger section (lines 722-822) which is said by Giussani and Bailey to be on the subject of "thought." So it is, in a sense; but only in a limited sense. A careful study of the whole passage shows that the object is to give an account of a certain class of mental images which might be thought incompatible with the theory that all such images are the result of *simulacra* coming from outside.

There are two lines of introduction (722-723) which do admittedly suggest that the subject is "thought" as a whole. But at once Lucretius turns to the subject of visions of imaginary creatures such as Centaurs. The *whole* of this section (724-745) deals with this subject. (Bailey asserts that it also contains in 722-731 and 745-748 a treatment of "the ordinary process of visual thought," but this is obviously wrong, and is in any case contradicted by his note on 726.) Epicurean theory had to explain Centaurs because it asserted both that all visions occur because of *simulacra*, and that there are no Centaurs.

Next, Lucretius adds an argument to show that mental images

Psychology of Action, Epicurean and Aristotelian

must have similar causes to visual images, since they look the same. Thus (*nec ratione alia*, line 757) dream images are explained: the mind picks up a *simulacrum* of someone now dead, and since the senses are not available to test the impression, one dreams that one is in the presence of the dead man. Again, the problem was to show that such an image has no other source than *simulacra* picked up from the external world. Once it is seen that this is the intention, the next lines follow quite logically. Dream images sometimes appear *to dance*, even though there is no moving object to account for their changing shape, because there are very many such *simulacra* abroad, of differing shapes, and when one succeeds another rapidly, the image appears to move.

Lucretius then develops the notion of the speed with which *simulacra* may enter the mind, and uses it to explain not only the fact that dream images dance, but also the fact that one can call to mind an image whenever one wishes. For this too might be thought to require a special explanation ("or do the *simulacra* wait upon our will...?"). The explanation is that there is an extraordinary number of *simulacra*. Within a measurable period of time there are many smaller units, the existence of which cannot be perceived but can be deduced: we have already studied this theory in Study I, chapter 8. It is suggested, then, that in each of these indivisible and imperceptible units of time a different *simulacrum* enters our mind. It must then be explained how it is that we "see" one but not others; and the explanation is interesting:

And because they are tenuous, except what the mind strains to see
it cannot observe sharply; and so all the rest
perish, apart from those for which it has prepared itself.
It prepares itself, then, and hopes   805
to see what follows each thing; so it happens.
You can see how our eyes, too, when they set about seeing
objects that are fine, strain and prepare themselves,
and without this effort we cannot observe things sharply.   810
But even in things open to view, you may notice
that if you do not apply your mind to them, it is then as if the thing
were all the time separated and far removed from you.
Why is it surprising, then, if the mind loses everything
except what it has devoted itself to?   815

Aristotle and Epicurus on Voluntary Action

And then we make great judgments from small evidence
and lead ourselves into the trap of deceit.[a]

The mind can prepare itself to receive some images and not others. The sense in which it can prepare itself is defined more closely: "it hopes it will see what follows each thing: so this happens." It is like focusing your eyes.

There is admittedly in these lines an assertion that the mind can concentrate on some *simulacra* and reject others. I wish to stress, however, the very limited use which Lucretius makes of this assertion. It is used to explain how dream images can dance (!), and how we can visualize anything we like at any time. Its purpose is essentially defensive: it refutes the suggestion that these phenomena cannot be explained by the theory of *simulacra*. All the time Lucretius is thinking of imaginary and particularly of illusory appearances. So he concludes by remarking that when we pick up these stray images we are apt to conclude with a judgment about them and so *lead ourselves astray*. This is surely fatal to any interpretation of these lines which finds in them a reference to ἐπιβολὴ τῆς διανοίας as an essential feature of Epicurus' theory of knowledge. The apprehension of these stray *simulacra* might well be ascribed as an ἐπιβολὴ τῆς διανοίας; but there is no justification for generalizing Lucretius' statements here beyond their defensive context.

[a] et quia tenvia sunt, nisi quae contendit, acute
cernere non potis est animus; proinde omnia quae sunt
praeterea pereunt, nisi ⟨si ad⟩ quae se ipse paravit.
ipse parat sese porro speratque futurum   805
ut videat quod consequitur rem quamque; fit ergo.
nonne vides oculos etiam, cum tenvia quae sunt
cernere coeperunt, contendere se atque parare,   809
nec sine eo fieri posse ut cernamus acute?   810
et tamen in rebus quoque apertis noscere possis,
si non advertas animum, proinde esse quasi omni
tempore semotum fuerit longeque remotum.
cur igitur mirumst, animus si cetera perdit
praeterquam quibus est in rebus deditus ipse?   815
deinde adopinamur de signis maxima parvis
ac nos in fraudem induimus frustraminis ipsi.

(4.802-817)

804, ⟨si ad⟩ quae *Brieger*: que ex OQ

Psychology of Action, Epicurean and Aristotelian

THE second passage is lines 877-906. Again we must study the context. The sequence of the text as the manuscripts have it is as follows:

A 823-857 A polemic against teleology.
B 858-876 An account of the physical origins of hunger.
C 877-906 The explanation of voluntary movement.
D 907-961 Sleep.

After this the book becomes somewhat digressive. From 962 to 1036 there is a further explanation of dreams, finishing with erotic dreams; and this leads into a long study of sex relations.

Lachmann observed that it was hard to see the sequence of thought in this section: after dealing with sense perception and then with mental images, Lucretius could logically go on to the effects produced by the mind—walking, sleep, love; but *A* and *B* had no place here. He concluded that they were written at another time, before the poem as a whole was written. Various other attempts were made to rearrange the poem in order to improve the sequence of thought. Giussani, however, argued differently: up to line 822, Lucretius has dealt with sensation (rather, with sense perception and mental perception); from 858 onwards he deals with "certain vital functions," in which the mind plays a part but not an all-important part. Between the two, Lucretius interpolates a characteristic attack on teleology, to remind the reader once again of the moral purpose of the whole poem; the interpolation arises naturally out of the preceding mechanistic account of perception, and the following passage on hunger arises naturally enough out of it.

Bailey followed Giussani, but missed the essential point in Giussani's exposition. For section A was not explained by Giussani simply as an interpolation between two sections on different topics, but as the explanation of a general point *relevant* both to what precedes it and to what follows it. To call the preceding section "Thought" and the following section "Some Functions of the Body considered in connexion with Psychology," as Bailey does, is to miss the essential link. The whole passage from 722 to 961 might be entitled: "No need for any explanation other than *simulacra*." We have seen already that in the section to which Bailey gives the title "Thought," the subject is not Thought as a whole, but those aspects of the

213

Aristotle and Epicurus on Voluntary Action

imagination which might be supposed to need a special, non-mechanical explanation. In the section we are now considering the same limitation applies. Once this is seen (and I think Giussani did see it), section A has a perfectly natural place in the sequence, and B, C, and D follow quite logically.

But C is the section which interests us, and we can now examine it more closely, bearing in mind all the time its defensive, anti-teleological purpose.

> Now, how comes it that we can take steps forward
> when we wish, and that the power is given us to move in various ways?
> What thing has the task of shifting the heavy load
> of our bodies? This I will tell you; listen to my words.   880
> I tell you that images of walking first come
> to our minds and strike upon our minds, as I have told before.
> Thence comes will; for no one begins to do anything,
> before the mind has first foreseen what it wants to do.
> An image is formed of that which the mind foresees.   885
> Then, when the mind so stirs itself as to want to move
> and step forward, it puts pressure at once on that force of the soul
> which is spread over the limbs and members of the whole body.
> And this is easy, because it is all joined in association.
> Then this force puts pressure on the body. . . .[b]

It will be seen how Lucretius stresses the need for an *imago* in the mind before action can begin, and relates the occurrence of this *imago* to what has been said before. Presumably this reference is to lines 779-806 (above, p. 211). What we are told, then, is that before we walk, the following episodes must take place: (1) *Simulacra*

> [b] Nunc qui fiat uti passus proferre queamus,
> cum volumus, varieque datum sit membra movere,
> et quae res tantum hoc oneris protrudere nostri
> corporis insuerit, dicam: tu percipe dicta.   880
> dico animo nostro primum simulacra meandi
> accidere atque animum pulsare, ut diximus ante.
> inde voluntas fit; neque enim facere incipit ullam
> rem quisquam, ⟨quam⟩ mens providit quid velit ante.
> id quod providet, illius rei constat imago.   885
> ergo animus cum sese ita commovet ut velit ire
> inque gredi, ferit extemplo quae in corpore toto
> per membra atque artus animai dissita vis est.
> et facilest factu, quoniam coniuncta tenetur.
> inde ea proporro corpus ferit. . . .   890
> (4.877–890)

Psychology of Action, Epicurean and Aristotelian

meandi must strike our minds, among the innumerable other *simulacra* which are always abroad in the air (881-885). (2) The mind must be focused, as it were, on walking, so that these *simulacra* form an image while others do not (802-806). (3) *Voluntas fit;* . . . *animus sese ita commovet ut velit ire* (883, 886). (4) The mind transmits motion to the limbs, bit by bit (887-891).

This is Lucretius' account of the psychology of voluntary action, and voluntary action, we were told in Book 2, is possible only because of the atomic swerve. But the swerve is not mentioned at all here. The editors have sought for opportunities to insert a swerve somewhere in these four stages or between them. Perhaps stage 2 is a swerve? But this is highly unlikely, because Lucretius goes to great lengths to give a causal explanation of why the mind focuses on some things rather than others.*[1] Perhaps, then, stage 3 is a swerve? This is much more plausible. Editors have seen a hint in the words *animus sese ita commovet*. But the fact remains that Lucretius says nothing whatever about it. He certainly *could* have said it. Furthermore, it would have been very much to the point to mention it in this context, since it could have proved a useful weapon on the side of efficient causes against teleology. My conclusion is that the part played by the swerve in saving voluntary action from necessity is probably not covered by any of the four stages mentioned here.

However, that is by no means proved. I hope to make the case more convincing by studying the historical context in which Epicurus' theory was developed. To understand this last passage of Lucretius, and the theory described in it, we must again refer back to Aristotle. The relevant text is his *De Motu Animalium*, the last chapters of which have a clear similarity to this passage of Lucretius.[2]

THE point that I wish to emphasize is that Aristotle's discussion, though it is explicitly about *voluntary* movement, is as apparently "mechanistic" as the Lucretian text. I have already quoted Giussani on the Epicurean doctrine:[3] "The motives, that is to say the idea or perceived image of the object and the consequent desire to pursue

* Please see end of chapter for numbered references.

Aristotle and Epicurus on Voluntary Action

or avoid it, are reducible in substance to internal motions of atoms, and the act of volition too consists solely of internal atomic motions; but the passage from the former to the latter is not a mechanical connection or a mechanical transformation of the former into the latter—that would mean the rule of necessity—but the latter is determined (or not determined) spontaneously." We have just seen that this is an unsupported assertion, for which there is no real evidence in the text of Lucretius. I want to point out now that there is, similarly, no break in the chain of causation from stimulus to response in Aristotle's theory.

The things which move an animal, says Aristotle,[4] are thought, imagination, choice, wish, and appetite; but since imagination and sense perception can be classified as "mind," and wish and temper and appetite are all forms of desire (ὄρεξις), and choice is something which shares in both thought and desire, it follows that all the motives of animals can be attributed to two things alone—thought and desire. After further discussion of these two, Aristotle sums up:

> The animal moves and walks through desire or choice, because some change has been caused as a result of sense perception or imagination.[c]

The "change" or "alteration" mentioned here is described in more detail later on after some examples of the practical syllogism which do not seem to add much of importance to our subject. Aristotle compares the movement of animals with the movement of *automata*—that is, semi-automatic marionettes—and with the movement of a toy cart with wheels of unequal size. The point of comparison is a little obscure, but I think it is supposed to show that one small and simple movement can by purely automatic means bring about a complex series of *different* movements. A simple turning of a cylinder on which strings are wound causes the puppet to perform complex movements with its limbs, and the end of one movement brings about the beginning of another. A simple push on the cart drives it straight forward for a while; then it loses equilibrium, heels over on to a smaller wheel, and so begins to move in a circle. (I am not sure of the details of either of these illustrations,

---

[c] κινεῖται γὰρ καὶ πορεύεται τὸ ζῷον ὀρέξει ἢ προαιρέσει, ἀλλοιωθέντος τινὸς κατὰ τὴν αἴσθησιν ἢ τὴν φαντασίαν. (*De Motu Animalium* 701 a 4–6.)

Psychology of Action, Epicurean and Aristotelian

but this must be approximately right.) In marionettes and toy carts, Aristotle notes, no change of size takes place, though if it did the effect would be similar. But in animals there *is* change:

> In the animal the same part can become larger and smaller and change its shape, as the tissues become swollen with heat and contract again with cold and so change. The causes of change are acts of imagination and sense perception and thought. Sense perceptions are themselves changes of a kind, and imagination and thought have the same force as their objects have. For in a way, the mental image of what is hot or cold or pleasant or terrifying is the same sort of thing as its object. That is why people shiver and are afraid simply as a result of a thought.[d]

He continues:

> The cause of movement, then, as I have said, is the object of pursuit or avoidance in the sphere of what is practical. The thought or imagination of these objects is *necessarily* followed by heating or cooling. For anything painful is an object of avoidance and anything pleasant is an object of pursuit (though in small instances we don't notice this), and anything painful or pleasant is normally accompanied by some cooling or heating.[e]

Aristotle gives a few examples: confidence, fear, and lust have the sort of effect he has described, and the same effect is produced in some degree by memories and anticipations of these feelings. The human body, he says, is suitably arranged, in that the regions near the origin of motion in the limbs are able to change, from pliant to rigid, from soft to hard, and vice versa. He goes on:

> Since these parts are affected as described, and since, furthermore, there is that connection between the active and the passive which

---

[d] ἐν δὲ τῷ ζῴῳ δύναται τὸ αὐτὸ καὶ μεῖζον καὶ ἔλαττον γίνεσθαι καὶ τὰ σχήματα μεταβάλλειν, αὐξανομένων τῶν μορίων διὰ θερμότητα καὶ πάλιν συστελλομένων διὰ ψύξιν καὶ ἀλλοιουμένων. ἀλλοιοῦσι δ' αἱ φαντασίαι καὶ αἱ αἰσθήσεις καὶ αἱ ἔννοιαι. αἱ μὲν γὰρ αἰσθήσεις εὐθὺς ὑπάρχουσιν ἀλλοιώσεις τινὲς οὖσαι, ἡ δὲ φαντασία καὶ ἡ νόησις τὴν τῶν πραγμάτων ἔχουσι δύναμιν· τρόπον γάρ τινα τὸ εἶδος τὸ νοούμενον τὸ τοῦ θερμοῦ ἢ ψυχροῦ ἢ ἡδέος ἢ φοβεροῦ τοιοῦτον τυγχάνει ὂν οἷόν περ καὶ τῶν πραγμάτων ἕκαστον, διὸ καὶ φρίττουσι καὶ φοβοῦνται νοήσαντες μόνον. (Ibid. 701 b 13–22.)

[e] Ἀρχὴ μὲν οὖν, ὥσπερ εἴρηται, τῆς κινήσεως τὸ ἐν τῷ πρακτῷ διωκτὸν καὶ φευκτόν· ἐξ ἀνάγκης δ' ἀκολουθεῖ τῇ νοήσει καὶ τῇ φαντασίᾳ αὐτῶν θερμότης καὶ ψύξις. τὸ μὲν γὰρ λυπηρὸν φευκτόν, τὸ δ' ἡδὺ διωκτόν (ἀλλὰ λανθάνει περὶ τὰ μικρὰ τοῦτο συμβαῖνον), ἔστι δὲ τὰ λυπηρὰ καὶ ἡδέα πάντα σχεδὸν μετὰ ψύξεώς τινος καὶ θερμότητος. (Ibid. 701 b 33–702 a 1.)

Aristotle and Epicurus on Voluntary Action

we have often spoken of, whenever it happens that there *is* an active and a passive, both of them perfectly fulfilling the definition, then immediately the one acts and the other is acted on. That is why a man sees that he must walk, and pretty well instantly walks, so long as nothing prevents him. For the organic parts are brought into the right condition by the feelings, the feelings by desire, desire by the mental picture; and this last is produced either by thought or by sense perception. The immediacy and speed of the reaction is due to the natural connection between the active and the passive.[f]

It will be seen that Lucretius' discussion of voluntary movement is an Atomist's commentary on this passage, or at least on the doctrine contained in it. His example—walking—is the same as Aristotle's. Both of them stress the mental picture which starts off the reaction: Lucretius speaks of the *imago*, Aristotle of φαντασία. Aristotle observes that the mental pictures may be caused either by thinking (i.e. imagination, in the usual modern sense of the word) or by sense perception. Lucretius, being committed to the theory of *simulacra*, says that the mind must already have been in contact with *simulacra* of walking—which is true for him whether it is a case of imagination or sense perception. The mental picture stimulates desire, says Aristotle. This corresponds to Lucretius' statement: "The mind moves itself so as to want to go." This is the sentence in which the editors have most plausibly sought for the "spontaneous movement of the mind which constitutes free choice." The close correspondence of Lucretius' account with Aristotle's, however, makes this much less plausible.

The rest of this passage of Lucretius is closely related to Aristotle's *De Motu Animalium* 10. Lucretius describes how the mind operates on the limbs through the "force of the *anima* dispersed through the limbs." This force is the Atomists' version of the Aristotelian *pneuma*, which is introduced and explained in the chapter

---

[f] τούτων δὲ συμβαινόντων τὸν τρόπον τοῦτον, καὶ ἔτι τοῦ παθητικοῦ καὶ ποιητικοῦ τοιαύτην ἐχόντων τὴν φύσιν οἵαν πολλαχοῦ εἰρήκαμεν, ὁπόταν συμβῇ ὥστ' εἶναι τὸ μὲν ποιητικὸν τὸ δὲ παθητικόν, καὶ μηδὲν ἀπολίπῃ αὐτῶν ἑκάτερον τῶν ἐν τῷ λόγῳ, εὐθὺς τὸ μὲν ποιεῖ τὸ δὲ πάσχει. διὰ τοῦτο δ' ἅμα ὡς εἰπεῖν νοεῖ ὅτι πορευτέον καὶ πορεύεται, ἂν μή τι ἐμποδίζῃ ἕτερον. τὰ μὲν γὰρ ὀργανικὰ μέρη παρασκευάζει ἐπιτηδείως τὰ πάθη, ἡ δ' ὄρεξις τὰ πάθη, τὴν δ' ὄρεξιν ἡ φαντασία· αὕτη δὲ γίνεται ἢ διὰ νοήσεως ἢ δι' αἰσθήσεως. ἅμα δὲ καὶ ταχὺ διὰ τὸ ⟨τὸ⟩ ποιητικὸν καὶ παθητικὸν τῶν πρὸς ἄλληλα εἶναι τὴν φύσιν. (*Ibid.* 702 a 10-21.)

Psychology of Action, Epicurean and Aristotelian

just mentioned. There is no need to go into this more fully now; but one further point of similarity should be briefly mentioned. Aristotle stresses the part played in the physiology of movement by expansion and contraction. This concept had to be modified by the Atomists, since matter cannot in their theory precisely expand, but can only become more dispersed, with larger interstices between the atoms. So Lucretius says the body becomes less dense when the *anima* operates on it (he does not say why), and admits particles of air. And he uses this thought, with some cunning, to explain another of Aristotle's points—how such tiny movements in the parts where motion originates can produce large movements in the heavy limbs. The air, says Lucretius, gets inside and works as it does on the sail of a boat.

Now in the whole section of *De Motu Animalium* devoted to voluntary movement Aristotle never states that there must be some "free" movement of the mind between stimulus and response; nor has anyone, so far as I know, tried to find room for one in his theory. He does not say that at the time when the external object stimulated the man's desire and provoked a movement, the man "could have chosen otherwise," but as a matter of fact chose *this* course. He arouses an expectation in the modern reader, at one point, that he is about to discuss this, when he says at the beginning of chapter 7: "How is it that when one thinks, one sometimes acts and sometimes does not?" (This comes immediately after he has said that thinking—or, more precisely, the mental picture caused by imagination or sense perception—is the cause of motion.) But the reader's expectation is disappointed. Aristotle's point is simply that *some* thinking is concerned with reaching theoretical conclusions only, and this kind of thinking does not produce movement.

The section of *De Motu Animalium* which I have just outlined may be compared with the discussion of *akrasia* in the *Nicomachean Ethics*. In dealing with this topic, if nowhere else, we might expect to find a discussion of "will." For Aristotle attributed to Socrates the doctrine that there is no such thing as *akrasia*, on the ground that "no one acts contrary to what is best, supposing that that is what he is doing, but ⟨only⟩ through ignorance."[5] Aristotle found this doctrine contrary to the facts. How could he refute Socrates, we may wonder, without saying that *akrasia* is not a matter of a failure in knowledge, but of a failure of *will*?

But Aristotle does refute him without saying this. The relevant chapters of *Nicomachean Ethics* are difficult, and much discussed,[6] but fortunately we can deal with them briefly here. Aristotle's analysis depends on the distinction between *proairesis* (rational choice) and *epithymia* (appetite) or *thymos* (anger or passion). The actions of the incontinent man do not result from his choice; but they do result from his appetites or passions, and we have already learned[7] that such actions are to be classed as voluntary rather than involuntary. Hence we must not after all expect to find any important contribution to the question of what makes actions voluntary in this context.

Aristotle's solution depends, not on the concept of *will*, but on the concept of *knowing*. He finds that the incontinent man acts in one sense knowingly and in another sense unknowingly. His position is after all not very far from that of Socrates. His analysis of the psychological processes which produce actions is perfectly consistent with the analysis given in *De Motu Animalium*. Again he stresses that given the premises of the practical syllogism, the conclusion, which is an action, follows "immediately" and "necessarily." [8]

Even in Aristotle's treatment of *akrasia*, then, we find the same picture of the voluntary as in the earlier book of the *Nicomachean Ethics*: the criterion of the voluntary act is not that it is "spontaneous" or "freely chosen" or that "he could have chosen otherwise," but that the source of the action cannot be traced back to something outside the agent. The criterion is still a negative one.

It has been maintained, however, that a more positive criterion can be found in Aristotle in the operations of the *mind*, and it may be useful to look briefly at some texts which appear to confirm this.

It may be suggested that a positive criterion is indicated in the last chapter of *De Motu Animalium*. Aristotle begins it by remarking that he has now discussed the voluntary movement of animals, and will turn to involuntary or non-voluntary movements (this last distinction is explained in *Nicomachean Ethics* Γ 1, and depends on whether or not the action in question is regretted afterwards—though this criterion cannot perhaps be applied very literally here)

Psychology of Action, Epicurean and Aristotelian

> I mean by "involuntary" such movements as that of the heart and the penis (which often move when some mental image is present *but no command is given by the mind*); and by "nonvoluntary" such as sleeping and waking and breathing and so on. Strictly speaking, neither imagination nor desire is master of any of these movements. The fact is rather that animals must *necessarily* undergo physical change, and when the tissues change some parts swell and some contract, and so they move immediately and undergo the changes which are naturally in sequence one with another (the causes of these motions are heating and cooling, either external or internal and natural). Hence even those movements of the parts mentioned above which are contrary to reason occur when there is a change. For thinking and imagination, as has been said before, bring with them the things which produce feelings, in that they bring with them the *forms* of these things.[g]

There is certainly a hint here that an involuntary movement is one which is not "commanded by the mind," and hence that a voluntary movement is one which *is* commanded. Does Aristotle then envisage another more positive criterion of the voluntary? The same idea is repeated in *De Anima* Γ 9.

> But what causes movement is not the reasoning faculty or what is called "mind." For the speculative mind does not think of what is practical and says nothing about what is to be avoided or pursued, and movement is always a matter of avoiding or pursuing something. Even when the mind *does* think of a practical object, it does not at once give orders to avoid or pursue. For instance, it often thinks of something that provokes fear or pleasure, but does not give the command to be afraid—though the heart moves, or if it is a case of pleasure, some other part.[h]

---

[g] λέγω δ' ἀκουσίους μὲν οἷον τὴν τῆς καρδίας τε καὶ τὴν τοῦ αἰδοίου (πολλάκις γὰρ φανέντος τινός, οὐ μέντοι κελεύσαντος τοῦ νοῦ κινοῦνται), οὐχ ἑκουσίους δ' οἷον ὕπνον καὶ ἐγρήγορσιν καὶ ἀναπνοήν, καὶ ὅσαι ἄλλαι τοιαῦταί εἰσιν. οὐθενὸς γὰρ τούτων κυρία ἁπλῶς ἐστὶν οὔθ' ἡ φαντασία οὔθ' ἡ ὄρεξις, ἀλλ' ἐπειδὴ ἀνάγκη ἀλλοιοῦσθαι τὰ ζῷα φυσικὴν ἀλλοίωσιν, ἀλλοιουμένων δὲ τῶν μορίων τὰ μὲν αὔξεσθαι τὰ δὲ φθίνειν, ὥστ' ἤδη κινεῖσθαι καὶ μεταβάλλειν τὰς πεφυκυίας ἔχεσθαι μεταβολὰς ἀλλήλων (αἴτιαι δὲ τῶν κινήσεων θερμότητές τε καὶ ψύξεις, αἵ τε θύραθεν καὶ αἱ ἐντὸς ὑπάρχουσαι φυσικαί), καὶ αἱ παρὰ τὸν λόγον δὴ γινόμεναι κινήσεις τῶν ῥηθέντων μορίων ἀλλοιώσεως συμπεσούσης γίνονται. ἡ γὰρ νόησις καὶ ἡ φαντασία, ὥσπερ εἴρηται πρότερον, τὰ ποιητικὰ τῶν παθημάτων προσφέρουσιν· τὰ γὰρ εἴδη τῶν ποιητικῶν προσφέρουσιν. (Ibid. 703 b 5–20.)

[h] ἀλλὰ μὴν οὐδὲ τὸ λογιστικὸν καὶ ὁ καλούμενος νοῦς ἐστιν ὁ κινῶν· ὁ μὲν γὰρ θεωρητικὸς οὐθὲν θεωρεῖ πρακτόν, οὐδὲ λέγει περὶ φευκτοῦ καὶ διωκτοῦ οὐθέν, ἀεὶ δὲ ἡ κίνησις ἢ φεύγοντος ἢ διώκοντός τί ἐστιν. ἀλλ' οὐδ' ὅταν θεωρῇ τι τοιοῦτον, ἤδη κελεύει φεύγειν ἢ διώκειν, οἷον πολλάκις διανοεῖται φοβερόν τι ἢ ἡδύ, οὐ κελεύει δὲ

Aristotle and Epicurus on Voluntary Action

The involuntary leap of the heart in the presence of some terrifying object (real or imagined), and the involuntary movement of the penis in the presence of an erotic object, are contrasted with voluntary reactions to these stimuli. Both the brave man's and the coward's heart beat faster when the enemy's tanks begin to move forward, but only the coward deserts his post on the gun. Why? The heartbeat is apparently caused by a natural sequence of changes: the chill of fear is an inevitable result of seeing the enemy's tanks, and the chill causes some physical part to contract, and this causes the heart to thump. But how does this differ from Aristotle's account of the coward's running away, as we can infer it from the discussion of *voluntary* movement in *De Motu Animalium*? We find there the same sort of talk about heating and cooling, expansion and contraction, caused by the mental image of an object seen as terrifying.

I am not sure that Aristotle has worked out a clear and consistent solution of this problem; but there seems to be a hint in the passage just quoted from *De Anima*. The mind, he says, "often thinks of something that provokes fear or pleasure, but does not give the command *to be afraid*—though the heart moves." That is to say, the terrifying mental image necessarily produces a primary reaction—the chill of fear which makes the heart jump; but the secondary reaction, "being afraid," depends on the "command" given by the mind. To some extent this outline can be filled in from other sources. The feelings which cause physical heating and cooling are ultimately reducible to pleasure and pain (*De Motu Animalium* 701 b 34ff.). But these feelings are a matter of *training* (*Nicomachean Ethics* B 3):

> For a sign of what our dispositions really are we must look to the pleasure or pain which accompanies our actions. For the man who abstains from physical pleasures and takes pleasure in his abstinence itself is a temperate man, and the one who feels pain about it is an intemperate man; the one who stands fast in the face of danger and feels pleasure or at any rate no pain in doing so is a brave man, and the one who feels pain is a coward. For moral virtue is a matter of pleasures and pains; it is for the sake of pleasure that we do what is bad, and because of pain we fail to

φοβεῖσθαι, ἡ δὲ καρδία κινεῖται, ἂν δ' ἡδύ, ἕτερόν τι μόριον. (*De Anima* Γ 9, 432 b 26–433 a 1.)

Psychology of Action, Epicurean and Aristotelian

do what is good. Hence we must be brought up from youth, as Plato says, to feel pleasure and pain about the right objects; that is right education.[1]

We may take it, then, as Aristotle's doctrine, that moral training is not merely a matter of practice in *doing* the right things, but also involves, as an essential and perhaps even the most important ingredient, having the right feelings about the action. Thus the brave man cannot avoid the primary chill of fear at the sight of danger; but *because of his training* he has no further painful feeling. By definition, the brave man is one who has a fixed disposition to stand fast in the face of danger. His mind is trained, by practice, in checking the primary reaction and so checking the spread of painful feelings; his mind does not "give the command to be afraid."

It will be seen that this "command" of the mind is still consistent with the account of voluntary action I have given above. In Aristotle's theory the mind gives its commands *according to its disposition*. It is nowhere implied, so far as I have discovered, that its commands are "spontaneous" and "free," in the sense of "uncaused" or "unpredictable"—or at any rate this is true once the mind has acquired fixed dispositions. The actions it commands are voluntary, because dispositions are voluntary, in the sense already explained.[9]

The same point may be made more directly by referring to Aristotle's definition of moral virtue[10] as a disposition to *choose* in a certain way, rather than a disposition to *act* in a certain way. It may be a typical characteristic of a voluntary action that it should proceed from a "command of the mind"; usually this command will be classifiable as a *choice* (προαίρεσις), in Aristotle's use of the term, though this need not always be so.[11] But it is not part of Aristotle's criterion of a voluntary action that this choice (or whatever else it may be) is "spontaneous," if by "spontaneous" we mean uncaused by previous events. Choice is determined by disposition;

---

[1] Σημεῖον δὲ δεῖ ποιεῖσθαι τῶν ἕξεων τὴν ἐπιγινομένην ἡδονὴν ἢ λύπην τοῖς ἔργοις· ὁ μὲν γὰρ ἀπεχόμενος τῶν σωματικῶν ἡδονῶν καὶ αὐτῷ τούτῳ χαίρων σώφρων, ὁ δ' ἀχθόμενος ἀκόλαστος, καὶ ὁ μὲν ὑπομένων τὰ δεινὰ καὶ χαίρων ἢ μὴ λυπούμενός γε ἀνδρεῖος, ὁ δὲ λυπούμενος δειλός. περὶ ἡδονὰς γὰρ καὶ λύπας ἐστὶν ἡ ἠθικὴ ἀρετή· διὰ μὲν γὰρ τὴν ἡδονὴν τὰ φαῦλα πράττομεν, διὰ δὲ τὴν λύπην τῶν καλῶν ἀπεχόμεθα. διὸ δεῖ ἦχθαί πως εὐθὺς ἐκ νέων, ὡς ὁ Πλάτων φησίν, ὥστε χαίρειν τε καὶ λυπεῖσθαι οἷς δεῖ· ἡ γὰρ ὀρθὴ παιδεία αὕτη ἐστίν. (Nicomachean Ethics B 3, 1104 b 3-13.)

Aristotle and Epicurus on Voluntary Action

once the disposition is fixed, a stimulus of a certain type will produce a *characteristic* reaction, not a random one.[12]

Before leaving Aristotle's ideas on the Voluntary, we must look at a passage of the *Ethics* which may seem at first sight to be somewhat inconsistent with the rest. This is part of his discussion of Justice. An act of injustice, he says first, must be voluntary; and he offers a definition of the voluntary which accords well enough with the definition of Book Γ.[13] But later there comes this curious argument:

> People think that it is in their power to act unjustly, and therefore that it is easy to be a just man. But it isn't. It *is* easy, and in their power, to go to bed with their neighbor's wife or to strike the man next door or to pass money across the table. But to do these things *in a certain manner* is neither easy nor in their power.... And they think the just man is none the less able to act unjustly, because the just man is equally or even more able than others to commit acts of this kind—I mean, go to bed with his neighbor's wife, or strike someone. The brave man, too, can throw away his shield and turn and run in any direction. But being a coward and being unjust are not a matter of doing these things, except incidentally, but of doing them *in a certain manner*.[j]

This is of course an application of Aristotle's doctrine that virtue is not defined merely by performing acts of a given kind, but by performing them in a certain way, or more precisely by performing them from a certain state of mind.[14] A just man is not merely one who performs a number of actions of the kind we recognize as just, but one who performs these actions in the way a just man performs them. To that extent this passage is perfectly consistent with the rest. What may seem inconsistent is the suggestion that anyone can perfectly easily commit an *act* of injustice. This seems to imply that *acts* are detached from dispositions, in such a way that everyone—

---

[j] Οἱ δ' ἄνθρωποι ἐφ' ἑαυτοῖς οἴονται εἶναι τὸ ἀδικεῖν· διὸ καὶ τὸ δίκαιον εἶναι ῥᾴδιον. τὸ δ' οὐκ ἔστιν· συγγενέσθαι μὲν γὰρ τῇ τοῦ γείτονος καὶ πατάξαι τὸν πλησίον καὶ δοῦναι τῇ χειρὶ τὸ ἀργύριον ῥᾴδιον καὶ ἐπ' αὐτοῖς, ἀλλὰ τὸ ὡδὶ ἔχοντας ταῦτα ποιεῖν οὔτε ῥᾴδιον οὔτ' ἐπ' αὐτοῖς....
(17) δι' αὐτὸ δὲ τοῦτο καὶ τοῦ δικαίου οἴονται εἶναι οὐδὲν ἧττον τὸ ἀδικεῖν, ὅτι οὐχ ἧττον ὁ δίκαιος ἀλλὰ καὶ μᾶλλον δύναιτ' ἂν ἕκαστον πρᾶξαι τούτων· καὶ γὰρ συγγενέσθαι γυναικὶ καὶ πατάξαι· καὶ ὁ ἀνδρεῖος τὴν ἀσπίδα ἀφεῖναι καὶ στραφεὶς ἐφ' ὁποτεραοῦν τρέχειν. ἀλλὰ τὸ δειλαίνειν καὶ ἀδικεῖν οὐ τὸ ταῦτα ποιεῖν ἐστί, πλὴν κατὰ συμβεβηκός, ἀλλὰ τὸ ὡδὶ ἔχοντα ταῦτα ποιεῖν. (*Nicomachean Ethics* E 9, 1137 a 4-9; 17-23.)

Psychology of Action, Epicurean and Aristotelian

whether his disposition is just, unjust or neither—may at any time commit an injustice. But I think we need not trouble seriously about this. Aristotle rejects the suggestion that the just man will also excel at injustice, or the brave man at running away. He says firmly that dispositions are *not* productive of opposites.[15]

What we find in Aristotle, then, is first an insistence that there is a real distinction between voluntary and involuntary actions, such that moral categories are relevant to the former but not to the latter; and secondly a theory of the psychology of action which locates this distinction not in the individual actions of the adult but in the way in which his habits of behavior are formed. It has been my purpose in this chapter to stress the latter point: we do not find in Aristotle the "free volitions" dear to later ethical philosophers.[16]

Notes to Chapter 4

1. 4.962ff., particularly 976-977. It may be objected that this is about dreams, not about voluntary action. But we have already seen that the whole idea of "focusing" was introduced to explain dreams and visions. It is hardly likely that the same process constitutes the essential *differentia* of voluntary action.
2. The similarity was observed by Brieger, briefly discussed by Giussani, and wholly ignored by Bailey.
3. See Introduction, p. 162f.
4. *De Motu Animalium* 6.
5. 1145 b 26.
6. See most recently Gauthier and Jolif (1959), II, 579-654, and Walsh (1963).
7. *Nicomachean Ethics* Γ 1, 1111 a 24-b 3. Cf. *Eudemian Ethics* 1224 b 26-36, where Aristotle remarks that the *parts* of the soul in *akrasia* may be said to act by compulsion, and hence involuntarily, but as a whole the soul acts voluntarily.
8. εὐθύς 1147 a 28, ἀνάγκη . . . πράττειν a 30.
9. See also *Eudemian Ethics* B 7, 1223 a 23-28, 1224 a 7. The relation between Aristotle's two *Ethics* on this problem is particularly interesting, but a thorough examination of it would take too long now. My own view is that the treatment in the *Eudemian Ethics* is consistent with its being intermediate between Plato's theory and that of the *Nicomachean Ethics*, and that *Nicomachean Ethics* (including the controversial books E-H), rather than *Eudemian Ethics*, is likely to have influenced Epicurus.

   On the important issue now being discussed—that of a negative or positive criterion for distinguishing a voluntary action—*Eudemian Ethics* seems to be more positive than *Nicomachean Ethics* in concluding that "the voluntary is a matter of acting with some kind of thought" (διανοούμενόν πως πράττειν, 1224 a 7). For a discussion of this, see Adkins (1960), ch. 15.

Aristotle and Epicurus on Voluntary Action

10. 1106 b 36 f.
11. Cf. 1135 b 8-11.
12. I have said little about the rôle of mind in Aristotle's psychology of action, and this may give the false impression that I intend to attribute a sort of behaviorism to him. The rôle of mind is important and complex, and not easily summarized (see especially *De Anima* Γ 7-11). Mind is of course involved in knowing the major premise of the practical syllogism, and also in appreciating the particular circumstances within which any choice is made.

    My aim in this chapter is not to deny the rôle of mind in Aristotle's psychology of action, but rather to show that his theory of responsibility does not involve any "free" or "uncaused" motion of the mind.
13. *Nicomachean Ethics* E 8, 1135 a 23 ff.
14. *Ibid.* B 4, 1105 b 2-18.
15. *Nicomachean Ethics* E 1, 1129 a 11-16. I may have overstated the degree to which a fixed disposition of the mind *determines* a man's actions in Aristotle's theory. He allowed that a just man could (in some sense of "could") commit an unjust act. But this does not weaken the force of my main contention, that the "freedom" of an action, for Aristotle, does not depend on his being able to choose otherwise at the time of the action. The act might still be liable to praise or blame, even though his character were so rigidly fixed that he could not possibly in the circumstances choose otherwise. Dispositions (ἕξεις) obviously vary in the degree of their fixity. Man's responsibility for his actions depends on the claim that his dispositions are created *by himself*, not on the degree to which his dispositions are now unfixed.
16. If anyone still doubts this, let him read the spirited chapter 18 "Angebliche Willensfreiheit" in Loening's *Die Zurechnungslehre des Aristoteles*, and D. J. Allan's quieter but equally compelling article "The Practical Syllogism" in *Autour d'Aristote*.

CHAPTER 5

THE WEIGHT AND THE SWERVE OF ATOMS

ARISTOTLE, as we have seen, defined the Voluntary as "that of which the source is in the agent himself, provided that he knows the particular circumstances in which his action takes place." We have seen that the main target of his criticism was the Socratic theory that virtue is knowledge, and its corollary that vice is a kind of ignorance, but that he also examined two theories which would make all vice involuntary, not because of ignorance, but because the source can be traced back beyond the agent himself. One of these theories was that external objects are to blame for our bad actions since they exercise compulsion on us; and the answer to this was that our own weakness is to blame. The other theory is that our dispositions are given—by nature, or somehow else—and so they are out of our hands and we are not responsible for them. The answer to this was that our dispositions cannot be traced back to sources outside ourselves; they are the product of our own actions. We have seen already that the content of these two theories which Aristotle refutes bears a strong and significant resemblance to the two kinds of necessity which Lucretius is out to refute in Book 2, lines 288-293, and to the two concepts contrasted with "having the cause in ourselves" in a fragment of Epicurus' *On Nature*.

We must now return to the Epicurean theory, and try to work it out in detail.

"Weight prevents all things coming about through blows, as if by external force" (Lucretius 2.288-289). I have argued[*1] that this must be about the mind, and not about atoms and the world at large (provided that *mens* is the right reading in line 289). In chapter 2 I have argued that the "blows" must be the impact of *simulacra*

* Please see end of chapter for numbered references.

227

upon the *psyche* atoms. The question remains: how can *weight* save the mind from being forced by the blows of the *simulacra*?

If I am right about the close relationship between the theories of Epicurus and Aristotle, it seems reasonable to look first at Aristotle's solution of the problem of external force. His view was that external objects stimulate *characteristic* responses in us; what we do as moral agents depends not only on the nature of the stimulus but also on our own trained disposition.

Could this have been Epicurus' solution too? I think it was. Unfortunately the texts leave us in the dark on this point, and we have to guess our way, with only a glimmer of indirect light to guide us.

We have already seen that the Epicureans were certainly interested in the effect of *learning* on the atomic soul, and I have argued that its effect can only have been to rearrange the stock of atoms into new patterns.[2] Expressed in epistemological terms, the results of learning are general notions which can be used as προλήψεις; the corresponding physical facts can only be durable patterns of motion among the atoms of the *psyche*. This process clearly has to do not only with acquiring information, but also with acquiring knowledge of how to behave. Indeed, it is in this connection that it is mentioned by Lucretius. The same point emerges clearly from the introductory paragraphs of Epicurus' two letters (to Herodotus and to Menoeceus) which summarize the main principles of a branch of philosophy. By going over and over the main principles the Epicurean pupil should fix them in his memory so that they are available to help him in the business of living; by studying natural philosophy he will learn peace of mind, and by studying the principles of ethics he will learn how to discipline his desires. The extant works of Epicurus do not seem to contain any special vocabulary corresponding to the Aristotelian διάθεσις or ἕξις.[3] But this does not mean that Epicurus did not believe in the existence of durable characteristics; the well-trained Epicurean certainly has a characteristic attitude, for instance, towards thunder and lightning, which others believe to be an expression of the gods' anger. Expressed in physical terms, such durable characteristics can only be patterns of motion among the *psyche* atoms. They are certainly properties of the *psyche*,

The Weight and the Swerve of Atoms

which consists of nothing but atoms; the atoms are all of four definite kinds and cannot change; so changes in the *psyche* can only be rearrangements of the component atoms.

It is possible to find a little more evidence on the movement of atoms in the *psyche*. First, there is a point about their movement in compounds in general. Lucretius concludes a description of atoms in compounds with the following remark:

> Besides these, many atoms wander through the great void;
> they have been rejected by the compounds and have nowhere
> been able to be received and to link their motion in association.[a]

On the evidence of the last phrase, Bailey built a theory that some compounds in the Epicurean system were held together by a sort of harmony of motion (this would be a third form of grouping: other forms are simple interlocking of atoms, and the retention of more or less loose atoms inside a skin of interlocking atoms).[4] "It is just this harmony of motion," Bailey wrote, "which constitutes the unity of the 'thing' and distinguishes it from external things and independent atoms." It may be that this is too much to build upon a single phrase, but at least it is proved that a "pattern of motion" is a concept of some significance in Epicurean theory. Then we have some more direct evidence about patterns of motion among *psyche* atoms. Lucretius argues that the *psyche* is a living thing only when it is confined within the body:

> No doubt because the soul atoms, through veins and flesh
>   intermingled,
> through sinews and bones too, are contained within the
>   whole body
> and cannot over great distances
> freely leap apart, for this reason they move, restrained,
> with sense-giving movements, which outside the body
>   among the airy breezes   570
> they cannot perform after death when they are ejected,
> because they are not contained in the way they were before.
> For *air* will be a body and a living thing, if the soul

> [a] multaque praeterea magnum per inane vagantur,
> conciliis rerum quae sunt reiecta nec usquam
> consociare etiam motus potuere recepta.
>   (2.109–111)

Aristotle and Epicurus on Voluntary Action

can hold itself together and confine itself to those movements which formerly it made in the sinews and in the body itself.[b]

It does not seem to be merely the *dispersal* of *psyche* atoms which Lucretius has in mind here. He does not say that *psyche* atoms will be so few and far between that their presence is insignificant. His point is that the work of the *psyche* is a matter of restrained and ordered movements; it depends on the correct interactions between the *psyche* atoms themselves and between *psyche* atoms and body atoms.

We have to consider the interaction between the atoms of the *psyche* and the atoms of the *simulacra* which impinge upon it in sense perception and imagination. We cannot expect to find in Epicurus a sophisticated theory of dynamics, particularly at this impossibly difficult point of his system. But it is reasonable to say that he cannot have believed that every collision between the *psyche* atoms and the atoms of the *simulacra* produced a result on the *psyche* atoms that was wholly determined by the entering atoms. The result must partly have been determined by the state of the *psyche* atoms themselves at the time of the collision. To put it in another way, it is reasonable to suppose that the *psyche* atoms offered some resistance to the colliding atoms.

The reason why they offered resistance is simply that they had *weight*. In saying this, I am not attributing to Epicurus an anachronistic theory of inertia: it is a matter of pure common sense, and one which cannot have escaped his observation, that heavier objects are harder to budge than lighter ones. Fortunately it is not necessary to rely wholly on this *a priori* argument, since we have confirmation in Epicurus' *Letter to Herodotus* that the weight of an atom may

>   [b] nimirum quia per venas et viscera mixtim,
>   per nervos atque ossa, tenentur corpore ab omni
>   nec magnis intervallis primordia possunt
>   libera dissultare, ideo conclusa moventur
>   sensiferos motus quos extra corpus in auras   570
>   aeris haud possunt post mortem eiecta moveri
>   propterea quia non simili ratione tenentur.
>   corpus enim atque animans erit aer, si cohibere
>   sese anima atque in eos poterit concludere motus
>   quos ante in nervis et in ipso corpore agebat.
>   (3.566–575)

The Weight and the Swerve of Atoms

counteract the force of a blow from another atom:

> (No atomic motion is faster than another), neither motion upward or sideways due to collisions, nor motion downward due to their own weight. For as long as each of them holds out, so long will it have a course as quick as thought, until something counteracts it, either from outside or from its own weight (working) against the force of that which struck it.[c]

The suggestion here is that the weight of an atom reasserts itself, and causes downward motion again, some time after a collision has knocked the atom upward or sideways. This is a suggestion that seems to fit the motion of free atoms, rather than those joined together in a compound such as the *psyche*. Nevertheless, the passage permits us to say that in computing the result of a collision between two atoms (if it were possible to do so), the weight of the atoms would enter into the calculation. This is confirmed by the testimony of Simplicius,[5] who explains how some atoms, in Epicurean theory, move upward and therefore have the appearance of being weightless; it is because some atoms are heavier than others, and the lighter ones are squeezed out and forced upward by the heavier ones as they settle down.

It is certainly reasonable, then, to conclude that the weight of an Epicurean atom did indeed "prevent all things coming about through blows," in the sense that the result of a blow was determined not only by the force of the striking atom but also by the weight of the one that was struck. There is no reason why *psyche* atoms should be exempt from this principle; they were admittedly said to be particularly small, smooth, and mobile, but that is not to say that they had *no* weight. Their weight would prevent them from being knocked into totally new and unrecognizable patterns by the atoms of entering *simulacra*; it would ensure some continuity of behavior in the *psyche*.

The second type of necessity or force mentioned by Lucretius may now be considered.

          ... but that the mind itself [6]

---

[c] οὔθ' ἡ ἄνω οὔθ' ἡ εἰς τὸ πλάγιον διὰ τῶν κρούσεων φορά, οὔθ' ἡ κάτω διὰ τῶν ἰδίων βαρῶν. ἐφ' ὁπόσον γὰρ ἂν κατίσχῃ ἑκάτερον, ἐπὶ τοσοῦτον ἅμα νοήματι τὴν φορὰν σχήσει, ἕως ἀντικόψῃ ἢ ἔξωθεν ἢ ἐκ τοῦ ἰδίου βάρους πρὸς τὴν τοῦ πλήξαντος δύναμιν. (*Letter to Herodotus* §61.)

Aristotle and Epicurus on Voluntary Action

has no internal necessity in performing all its acts
and is not overpowered and forced, as it were, to suffer and
                                                                         endure,
that is the work of a tiny swerve of atoms
at no fixed place and at no fixed time.[d]

It was argued in chapter 2 that this "internal necessity" is certainly to be identified with the necessity imposed by the original constitution of the *psyche*. This is what we should expect Epicurus to deal with, if he had studied Aristotle; it is what we find mentioned at the right moment in his *On Nature*; and it is singled out for emphasis in another passage of Lucretius.[7]

If we now put together the introduction to Lucretius' passage on *voluntas* and Aristotle's theory of the voluntary, we can see how the swerve of atoms was supposed to do its work. Aristotle's criterion of the voluntary was a *negative* one: the source of the voluntary action is in the agent himself, in the sense that it cannot be traced back beyond or outside the agent himself. Lucretius says that *voluntas* must be saved from a succession of causes which can be traced back to infinity. All he needs to satisfy the Aristotelian criterion is *a break in the succession of causes*, so that the source of an action cannot be traced back to something occurring before the birth of the agent.[8] A single swerve of a single atom in the individual's *psyche* would be enough for this purpose, if all actions are to be referred to the *whole* of the *psyche*. But there is no evidence about the number of swerves. One would be enough, and there must not be so many that the *psyche* exhibits no order at all; between these limits any number would satisfy the requirements of the theory.

The swerve, then, plays a purely negative part in Epicurean psychology. It saves *voluntas* from necessity, as Lucretius says it does, but it does not feature in every act of *voluntas*. There is no need to scrutinize the psychology of a voluntary action to find an uncaused or spontaneous element in it. The peculiar vulnerability

    [d]   . . . se ne mens ipsa necessum
        intestinum habeat cunctis in rebus agendis
        et devicta quasi cogatur ferre patique,
        id facit exiguum clinamen principiorum
        nec regione loci certa nec tempore certo.
                                    (2.289–293)

The Weight and the Swerve of Atoms

of Epicurean freedom—that it seemed to fit random actions, rather than deliberate and purposive ones—is a myth, if this explanation is correct.

We can now understand why the swerve gets no mention in Lucretius' account of voluntary action. It gets no mention because it plays no direct part in it. The theory of the swerve asserts merely that our actions are *not* caused conjointly by the environment and our parentage. There was no need for Lucretius to mention this in his account of the psychology of action, any more than there was for Aristotle to insist on his negative criterion of the voluntary in *De Motu Animalium*.

It may be objected that a swerve in the *psyche* must have been supposed to produce *some* observable effect. But not even this is true. We have already glanced at Lucretius' doctrine that the mind has before it innumerable *simulacra* which never reach the level of consciousness, because the time interval during which they are present is imperceptibly small.[9] But if the impact of those complicated atomic configurations which constitute *simulacra* could have no observable effect, it is a safe inference that the minute swerve of a single atom would be undetectable. So we can, after all, make use of the Epicurean concept of the *concilium* in our explanation. I argued previously[10] against Bailey's use of it in saying that "what in the individual atom is a matter of chance, in the conscious complex of the *animus* is 'conscious chance.'" It is impossible to see how the random motion of an individual atom can by itself account for the end-directed motions of the complex of which it is a part. It is perfectly reasonable, however, that the random motion of a single atom should be *concealed* by the fact that it is just one element in a complex.

THE Epicurean psychology of action, if I am right, was in outline as follows.[11]

Each person is born with a *psyche* of a particular character, determined by the proportions of atoms of the four different kinds which constitute a *psyche*. From the beginning of life, reactions occur between the *psyche* and the external world, through the medium of atomic *eidola* which flow from all objects and may reach the *psyche* through the sense organs and the mind. From the beginning, the child experiences feelings of pleasure and pain; in atomic terms, pain is a disturbance of the motions of the *psyche* atoms caused by a lack of something, and pleasure is either the restoration of the undisturbed motions which constitute tranquillity, or else the state of tranquillity itself. The child learns to associate external objects with one or other of these feelings. A feeling of something lacking constitutes a motive to make good the lack, and so creates an impulse towards an object in the external world which the child has learned will supply the deficiency.

A person's feelings, and therefore his motives and his behavior, are to some extent determined by his genetic inheritance of a *psyche* of such and such a constitution. But the motions of the *psyche* (and it is in its motions that all its character and action consists) are not determined *ab initio*, because a discontinuity is brought about by the atomic swerve. The swerve of an atom or atoms in the *psyche* means that the inherited motions are disturbed, and this allows new patterns of motion to be established which cannot be explained by the initial constitution of the *psyche*.

There is both continuity and discontinuity. The character of the person is to some extent still determined by the initial constitution of his *psyche*, because the proportions of atoms of different types in it remain the same. But to a much greater extent his character is adaptable, because the motions of the atoms are not determined and can be changed by learning.

A person learns by experience. He learns what desires must be satisfied, and what objects satisfy them, simply by constant repetition of the experience of desire and satisfaction. He can learn by individual trial and error, or by precept and example from others. If he is indoctrinated in the Epicurean philosophy, he learns to distinguish desires which arise from nature and *must* be satisfied from those which arise from nature but need not be satisfied and from those which do not arise from nature and are best eliminated. He learns that the limit of pleasure is the absence of pain, and so ceases to feel pain through desire for some *extra* pleasure. His feelings become disciplined, so that an improper object—one that brings more pain than pleasure in the long run—no longer arouses desire in him. He learns not so much to reject some of the things he desires as to cease to desire the things he ought to reject.

The wise Epicurean is not to be pictured as asserting himself by repeated "acts of volition" against the temptations of the world, but as having learned not to be tempted. His "freedom" does not consist in being presented with possible alternatives, and in choosing one when he might have chosen the other. It consists rather in the fact that his *psyche* is the product of his own actions and is not unalterably shaped by some "destiny" from the time before his birth.

The weakness of this theory of "freedom," both in its Epicurean and in its Aristotelian form, is to be found chiefly in its refusal to consider the processes of character formation.[12] When Aristotle says that children should be brought up from the beginning to feel pleasure and pain in the right objects, he obviously does not consider such education to be equivalent to compulsion.[13] He stresses that educators and lawgivers use punishments and other incentives to make people behave in the right way, and at the same time insists that the acts which create virtuous dispositions are not to be referred to causes outside ourselves.[14] It is curious that he does not see this as a problem, since it was clearly raised by Gorgias in his *Praise of Helen*, almost a century before, when he offered as one of his excuses for Helen's behavior the possibility that she was persuaded by argument.[15] It might well have arisen, too, from a consideration of Democritus' ethical opinions.[16] Part of the explanation is probably that persuasion was commonly seen as an antithesis to compulsion.[17] But Aristotle should have seen the need to reestablish this antithesis, since he had to some extent broken it down himself in talking of a class of actions which were a mixture of the voluntary and the involuntary.[18]

If Aristotle had seriously examined the reasons why he took the results of education to be "in our own power," he would have been compelled to specify more exactly what he meant by saying "the source is in us." He might then have been led to say that the criterion of morality (that is to say, the criterion that determines whether an action is liable to moral appraisal or not) is to be found precisely

Aristotle and Epicurus on Voluntary Action

in our ability to be influenced by persuasion as opposed to force. If he had stressed this, then I think Epicurus might after all have thought the swerve unnecessary (unnecessary, that is to say, in his psychology; it was still needed in his cosmology). For in his theory, the effects of persuasion would be similarly explained whether the swerve were there or not. Persuasion is by words, and words, in the crude atomism of the time, do their work by collisions, through the medium of the sense organs. The swerve is not needed for them to have this effect. I leave it to others to decide whether the Epicurean theory, without the swerve, would have been "determinist" as opposed to "libertarian," because I do not yet see how to define this particular antithesis. But if it would be determinist, I think it would be a sort of determinism that is compatible with morality.

Notes to Chapter 5

1. See chapter 1, pp. 180ff.
2. See chapter 3, p. 197.
3. Diogenes Laertius, in a summary of Epicurean doctrine, speaks of the "wise man" as being unable to change his διάθεσις (10.117); but one cannot be sure that the vocabulary is Epicurean. The word διάθεσις occurs two or three times in the fragments of the book of Epicurus' *On Nature* which deals with voluntary action— once in connection with the motion of the *psyche* (31.24.8 Arrighetti: μέχρι μὴν τοῦ ψυχὴν γενέσθαι ἢ καὶ τοσαυτηνὶ διάθεσιν καὶ κίνησιν ἔχουσαν ψυχήν).
4. See Bailey (1928), pp. 330-350.
5. Simplicius *De Caelo* 569, 5-9 = Usener fr. 276.
6. For this reading, see chapter 1, p. 179ff.
7. See pp. 194 and 198.
8. There is a close resemblance between Lucretius' passage on the need for a break in the succession of causes (2.251-260), and Aristotle's *Metaphysics* E 3, especially 1027 a 29-31: "Evidently there exist principles and causes which are subject to generation and destruction without going through any *process* of generation or destruction; otherwise everything will be of necessity." The Epicurean swerve is just such a principle.
9. See chapter 4, p. 211.
10. Introduction, p. 164.
11. I am much indebted to Diano's articles in *Giornale Critico di Filosofia Italiana* for those parts of this summary which I have not discussed before.
12. Reginald Jackson made this point about Aristotle's theory some years ago (1942, p. 349): "We are directly responsible not for what we at a given time do but only for having at an earlier time made ourselves such as to do it. But the limited

concession plainly implies an unlimited concession. The agent's earlier conduct must in turn depend on the kind of man he then was. Unless we are *directly* responsible for something, we are not *even indirectly* responsible for anything. But of direct responsibility Aristotle has despaired."

Similarly Gauthier and Jolif (1959), in their note on 1114 b 1-3, observe that if the young man, before his character is formed, could be said to choose the end he will pursue by "un souhait libre," Aristotle's theory would be firmly based. But in fact it is education which determines a young man's ethical ends, and education was not only rational exhortation (which respects liberty) but also the constraint of law.

13. *Nicomachean Ethics* B 3, 1104 b 11-13.
14. *Ibid.* Γ 5, 1113 b 17-26.
15. DK 82 B 11, §§8 and 12.
16. Particularly DK 68 B 181, where persuasion is said to be better than law and necessity as an educative influence.
17. See the article on Peitho in Pauly-Wissowa *Realenkyklopedie*, by Voigt, especially column 211.
18. *Nicomachean Ethics* Γ 1, 1110 a 11.

BIBLIOGRAPHY

The following abbreviations are used:

DK = Diels, H., and Kranz, W. (1951), *Fragmente der Vorsokratiker*, 3 vols., 6th edn., Berlin, Weidmann.

KR = Kirk, G. S., and Raven, J. E. (1957), *The Presocratic Philosophers*, Cambridge University Press.

LSJ = Liddell, H. S., and Scott, R., *A Greek-English Lexicon*, New Revised Edition by Sir H. S. Jones, Oxford, Clarendon Press, 1948.

SVF = von Arnim, H. (1921–24), *Stoicorum Veterum Fragmenta*, 4 vols. Leipzig, Teubner.

U = Usener, H. (1887), *Epicurea*, Leipzig, Teubner.

ANCIENT AUTHORS, WITH EDITIONS CITED

AËTIUS:
Diels, H. (1929), *Doxographi Graeci*, Berlin, De Gruyter.

ALEXANDER, *De Sensu*:
P. Wendland (1901), *Commentaria in Aristotelem Graeca*, Vol. 3, Part 1, Berlin.

ALEXANDER (AND PSEUDO-ALEXANDER), *In Metaphysica*:
M. Hayduck (1891), *Commentaria in Aristotelem Graeca*, Vol. I, Berlin.

ANAXAGORAS:
DK, Vol. 2.

ARCHIMEDES:
Heiberg, J. L. (1910–15), Leipzig, Teubner.

ARISTOTLE, *De Anima*:
Hicks, R. D. (1907), Cambridge University Press.

ARISTOTLE, *De Caelo*:
Guthrie, W. K. C. (1939), *Aristotle: On the Heavens*, London, Heinemann, Loeb Classical Library.

Bibliography

ARISTOTLE, *Eudemian Ethics*:
Rackham, H. (1935), London, Heinemann, Loeb Classical Library.

ARISTOTLE, *De Generatione et Corruptione*:
Joachim, H. H. (1922), *Aristotle: On Coming-to-be and Passing-away*, Oxford, Clarendon Press.

ARISTOTLE, *Metaphysics*:
Ross, W. D. (1924), Oxford, Clarendon Press.

ARISTOTLE, *De Motu Animalium*:
Forster, E. S. (1937), *Movement of Animals*, London, Heinemann, Loeb Classical Library.

ARISTOTLE, *Nicomachean Ethics*:
Bywater, I. (1894), Oxford, Clarendon Press.

ARISTOTLE, *Physics*:
Ross, W. D. (1936), Oxford, Clarendon Press.

(PSEUDO-ARISTOTLE) *On Indivisible Lines*:
text, Bekker, I. (1831), *Aristotelis Opera*, Vol. 1, Berlin, Prussian Academy;
translation, Joachim H. H. (1908), in *The Works of Aristotle translated into English* (ed. W. D. Ross), Vol. 6, Oxford, Clarendon Press.

ARRIAN, *Epicteti Dissertationes*:
Schenkl, H. (1916), Leipzig, Teubner.

DEMOCRITUS:
DK, Vol. 2.

DIOGENES LAERTIUS:
Long, H. S. (1964), Oxford, Clarendon Press.

DIOGENES OF OENOANDA:
William, J. (1907), Leipzig, Teubner.

EMPEDOCLES:
DK, Vol. 1.

EPICURUS:
Arrighetti, Graziano (1960), *Epicuro: Opere*, Torino, Einaudi (text, Italian translation, and commentary). I have used this edition as standard. Others cited are:
Bignone, E. (1920), *Epicuro*, Bari, Laterza (Italian translation with notes).

Ancient Authors

Bailey, C. (1926), *Epicurus*, Oxford, Clarendon Press (text, English translation, and commentary).

Brieger, A. (1882), *Epikurs Brief an Herodot*, Halle, Program des Stadt-Gymnasiums (German translation and commentary).

Cobet, C. C. (1850), *Diogenes Laertius*, Paris, Didot (text and Latin translation).

Gassendi, P. (1649), *Animadversiones in decimum librum Diogenis Laertii*, Lyons, G. Barbier.

Hicks, R. D. (1925), *Diogenes Laertius*, Vol. 2, London and New York, Loeb Classical Library (text and English translation).

Long, H. S. (1964), *Diogenes Laertius*, Vol. 2, Oxford, Clarendon Press (text only).

Meibom, M. (1692–93), *Diogenes Laertius*, Amsterdam.

von der Muehll, P. (1922), *Epicuri Epistolae Tres et Ratae Sententiae*, Leipzig, Teubner (text only).

Schneider, I. G. (1813), *Epicuri Physica et Meteorologica*, Leipzig.

Usener, H. (1887), *Epicurea*, Leipzig, Teubner (text only).

EUSEBIUS, *Praeparatio Evangelica*:

Mras, K. (1954–56), Berlin, Akademie.

GORGIAS:

DK, Vol. 2.

LEUCIPPUS:

DK, Vol. 2.

LUCRETIUS, *De Rerum Natura*:

Bailey, C. (1922), 2nd edn., Oxford, Clarendon Press. I have cited texts from this edition. Other editions mentioned are:

Bailey, C. (1947), Oxford, Clarendon Press (text, English translation, and commentary).

Brieger, A. (1894), Leipzig, Teubner (text only).

Diels, H. (1923), Berlin, Weidmann (text only).

Ernout, A., and Robin, L. (1925), *Lucrèce, Commentaire*, Paris, Les Belles Lettres (commentary only).

Giussani, C. (1896), Turin, Loescher (text and Italian commentary).

Lachmann, C. (1853), 2nd edition, Berlin (text).

Lambinus, A. D. (1565), Paris (text).

Martin, J. (1953), 2nd edn., Leipzig, Teubner (text only).

Bibliography

Munro, H. A. J. (1873), 3rd edition, Cambridge University Press (text and English commentary).

MELISSUS:
DK, Vol. 1.

PARMENIDES:
DK, Vol. 1.

PHILODEMUS, *Volumina Rhetorica*:
Sudhaus, S. (1892–96), Leipzig, Teubner.

PHILOPONUS, *In De Generatione et Corruptione*:
Vitelli, M. (1897), *Commentaria in Aristotelem Graeca*, Vol. 14, Part 2, Berlin.

PLATO:
Burnet, J. (1901–06), Oxford, Clarendon Press.

PLUTARCH, *De Communibus Notitiis contra Stoicos* and *Adversus Coloten*:
Pohlenz, M. (1952), *Plutarchi Moralia*, Vol. 6, Fasc. 2, Leipzig, Teubner.

PROCLUS, *In Euclidem Commentaria*:
Friedlein, G. (1873), Leipzig, Teubner.

SEXTUS EMPIRICUS:
Bury, R. G. (1933–49), 4 vols., London, Heinemann, Loeb Classical Library.

SIMPLICIUS, *In Physica*:
Diels, H. (1895), *Commentaria in Aristotelem Graeca*, Vols. 9–10, Berlin.

SIMPLICIUS, *In De Caelo*:
Heiberg, I. L. (1894), *ibid.*, Vol. 7.

STOBAEUS, *Eclogae*:
Wachsmuth, C., and Hense, O. (1884–1923), 5 vols., Berlin, Weidmann.

THEMISTIUS, *In Physica*:
Schenkl, H. (1900), *Commentaria in Aristotelem Graeca*, Vol. 5, Part 2, Berlin.

THEOPHRASTUS, *Metaphysics*:
Ross, W. D., and Fobes, F. H. (1929), Oxford, Clarendon Press.

ZENO:
DK, Vol. 1.

MODERN WORKS: STUDY I

Ahlvers, Arthur (1952), *Zahl und Klang bei Platon*, Bern, Paul Haupt.

Alfieri, V. E. (1953), *Atomos Idea*, Firenze, Le Monnier.

Arnim, H. von (1907), "Epikurs Lehre vom Minimum," *Almanach der Wiener Akademie der Wissenschaften*, 1907, p. 385.

Atanassievitch, Xenia (n.d.–c. 1926), *L'Atomisme d'Épicure*, Paris, Presses Universitaires de France.

Bailey, C. (1928), *The Greek Atomists and Epicurus*, Oxford University Press.

Basson, A. H. (1958), *David Hume*, London, Pelican Books.

Becker, Oskar (1956), "Über den κυριεύων λόγος des Diodoros Kronos," *Rheinisches Museum für Philologie* 99, pp. 289-304.

——— (1957), *Das mathematische Denken der Antike*, Göttingen, Vandenhoeck und Ruprecht.

Block, Kurt (1959), "Anaxagoras und die Atomistik," *Classica et Mediaevalia* 20, pp. 1-13.

Booth, N. B. (1957a), "Were Zeno's Arguments a Reply to Attacks upon Parmenides?" *Phronesis* 2, pp. 1-9.

——— (1957b), "Were Zeno's Arguments Directed against the Pythagoreans?" *Phronesis* 2, pp. 90-103.

——— (1957c), "Zeno's Paradoxes," *Journal of Hellenic Studies* 77, pp. 187-201.

——— (1958), "Did Melissus Believe in Incorporeal Being?" *American Journal of Philology* 79, pp. 61-65.

Boyer, C. B. (1959), *The History of the Calculus and its Conceptual Development*, New York, Dover.

Broad, C. D. (1961), "Hume's Doctrine of Space," *Proceedings of the British Academy* 47, pp. 161-176.

Burnet, John (1930), *Early Greek Philosophy*, 4th edn., London, A. & C. Black.

Cherniss, Harold (1935), *Aristotle's Criticism of Presocratic Philosophy*, Baltimore, Johns Hopkins Press.

——— (1944), *Aristotle's Criticism of Plato and the Academy*, I, Baltimore, Johns Hopkins Press.

Bibliography

Cherniss, Harold (1950), review of J. E. Raven, *Pythagoreans and Eleatics*, in *Philosophical Review* 59, pp. 375-377.

——— (1951), "Plato as Mathematician," *Review of Metaphysics* 4, pp. 395-425.

Cornford, F. M. (1922-23), "Mysticism and Science in the Pythagorean Tradition," *Classical Quarterly* 16, pp. 137-150, and 17, pp. 1-12.

——— (1937), *Plato's Cosmology*, London, Routledge and Kegan Paul.

——— (1939), *Plato and Parmenides*, London, Routledge and Kegan Paul.

Denniston, J. D. (1954), *Greek Particles*, 2nd edn., Oxford, Clarendon Press.

Fränkel, Hermann (1955), *Wege und Formen frühgriechischen Denkens*, München, C. H. Beck.

Fritz, K. von (1945), "The Discovery of Incommensurability by Hippasus of Metapontum," *Annals of Mathematics* 46, pp. 242-264.

Giussani, C. (1896), *Studi lucreziani* (Vol. I of edition of *Lucretius*), Turin, Loescher.

Gomperz, H. (1932), "ΑΣΩΜΑΤΟΣ," *Hermes* 67, pp. 155-167.

Guthrie, W. K. C. (1962), *A History of Greek Philosophy*: Vol. I: *The Earlier Presocratics and the Pythagoreans*, Cambridge, Cambridge University Press. Vol. II: *The Presocratic Tradition from Parmenides to Democritus* was published in 1965, after this book went to press.

Hammer-Jensen, I. (1910), "Demokrit und Platon," *Archiv für Geschichte der Philosophie* 23, pp. 92-105 and 211-229.

Heath, T. L. (n.d.), *Archimedes*, New York, Dover.

——— (1912), *The Method of Archimedes*; this is included as a supplement to *Archimedes*, Dover, n.d.

——— (1921), *A History of Greek Mathematics*, Oxford, Clarendon Press.

Heidel, W. A. (1940), "The Pythagoreans and Greek Mathematics," *American Journal of Philology* 61, pp. 1-33.

Heinze, R. (1892), *Xenokrates*, Leipzig, Teubner.

Heller, Siegfried (1958), "Die Entdeckung der stetigen Teilung durch die Pythagoreer," *Abhandlungen der Deutschen Akademie der Wissenschaften zu Berlin (Kl. Math. Physik Tech.)* 1958, No. 6.

Hume, David (1886), *Treatise of Human Nature* (ed. T. H. Green and T. H. Grose), London, Longmans.

Junge, Gustav (1958), "Von Hippasos bis Philolaos; das Irrationale und die geometrischen Grundbegriffe," *Classica et Mediaevalia* 19, pp. 41-72.

Kirk, G. S., and Raven, J. S. (1957), *The Presocratic Philosophers*, Cambridge University Press.

Kirk, G. S., and Stokes, M. C. (1960), "Parmenides' Refutation of Motion," *Phronesis* 5, pp. 1-4.

Kullmann, Wolfgang (1958), "Zenon und die Lehre des Parmenides," *Hermes* 86, pp. 157-172.

Lee, H. D. P. (1936), *Zeno of Elea*, Cambridge Classical Studies, Cambridge University Press.

Luria, S. (1933), "Die Infinitesimallehre der antiken Atomisten," *Quellen und Studien zur Geschichte der Mathematik* B 2, pp. 106-185.

Mau, Jürgen (1952/53), "Studien zur erkenntnistheoretischen Grundlage der Atomlehre im Altertum," *Wissenschaftliche Zeitschrift der Humboldt-Universität zu Berlin* 2 (Heft 3), pp. 1-20.

——— (1954), *Zum Problem des Infinitesimalen bei den antiken Atomisten*, Berlin, Akademie-Verlag.

——— (1955), "Über die Zuweisung zweier Epikur-Fragmente," *Philologus* 99, pp. 93-111.

McDiarmid, J. B. (1960), "Theophrastus *De Sensibus* 61-62," *Classical Philology* 55, pp. 28-30.

Melsen, A. G. van (1960), *From Atomos to Atom*, New York, Harper.

Michel, P.-H. (1950), *De Pythagore à Euclide*, Paris, Les Belles Lettres.

Milhaud, Gaston (1934), *Les Philosophes géomètres de la Grèce*, Paris, Vrin.

Nicol, A. T. (1936), "Indivisible Lines," *Classical Quarterly* 30, pp. 120-126.

Owen, G. E. L. (1957-58), "Zeno and the Mathematicians," *Proceedings of the Aristotelian Society* 58, pp. 199-222.

——— (1960), "Eleatic Questions," *Classical Quarterly* 10, pp. 84-102.

Bibliography

Philippson, R. (1929), "Democritea," *Hermes* 64, pp. 167-183.
Pines, Salomon (1936), *Beiträge zur islamischen Atomenlehre*, Berlin.
Raven, J. E. (1948), *Pythagoreans and Eleatics*, Cambridge Classical Studies, Cambridge University Press.
—— (1951), "Polyclitus and Pythagoreanism," *Classical Quarterly* 45, pp. 147-152.
—— (1954), "The Basis of Anaxagoras' Cosmology," *Classical Quarterly* 4, pp. 124-137.
—— (1957) see Kirk and Raven (1957).
Sambursky, S. (1959), *Physics of the Stoics*, London, Routledge and Kegan Paul.
Schramm, Matthias (1957), "Zur Schrift über die unteilbaren Linien aus dem Corpus Aristotelicum," *Classica et Mediaevalia* 18, pp. 36-58.
Solmsen, Friedrich (1960), *Aristotle's System of the Physical World*, Ithaca, Cornell University Press.
Tannéry, Paul (1887), *Pour l'histoire de la science hellène*, Paris, Gauthier-Villars.
Taylor, A. E. (1928), *A Commentary on Plato's Timaeus*, Oxford, Clarendon Press.
Verdenius, W. J., and Waszink, J. H. (1946), *Aristotle: Coming-to-be and Passing-away; Some Comments*, Philosophia Antiqua Vol. I, Leiden.
Vlastos, Gregory (1953), review of J. E. Raven, *Pythagoreans and Eleatics*, in *Gnomon* 25, pp. 29-35.
—— (1959a), review of Kirk and Raven, *The Presocratic Philosophers* in *Philosophical Review* 69, p. 531-535.
—— (1959b), review of Hermann Fränkel, *Wege und Formen . . .*, in *Gnomon* 31, pp. 193-204.
—— (1961), "Zeno," in W. Kaufmann, *Philosophic Classics, Thales to St. Thomas*, Englewood Cliffs, N.J., Prentice Hall, pp. 27-45.
—— (1965), "Minimal Parts in Epicurean Atomism," *Isis* 56, pp. 121-147; published after this book went to press.
Vogt, H. (1909-10), "Die Entdeckungsgeschichte des Irrationalen nach Platon und anderen Quellen des 4. Jahrhunderts," *Bibliotheca Mathematica* (Series 3), 10, pp. 97-155.
Waerden, B. L. van der (1940), "Zenon und die Grundlagenkrise

der griechischen Mathematik," *Mathematische Annalen* 117, pp. 141-161.
Wieland, W. (1962), *Die aristotelische Physik*, Göttingen, Vandenhoeck und Ruprecht.
Zeller, E. (1920-23), *Die Philosophie der Griechen* Part I, 6th-7th edn., 2 vols., Leipzig.
―――― (1921-22), *idem* Part II, 4th-5th edn., 2 vols., Leipzig.
―――― (1923), *idem* Part III, 5th edn., Leipzig.

MODERN WORKS: STUDY II

Adkins, Arthur W. H. (1960), *Merit and Responsibility*, Oxford, Clarendon Press.
Allan, D. J. (1955), "The Practical Syllogism," in *Autour d'Aristote* (Festschrift for A. Mansion), Louvain, Publications Universitaires de Louvain.
Amand, Dom David (1945), *Fatalisme et liberté dans l'antiquité grecque*, Louvain, Bibliothèque de l'Université.
Austin, J. L. (1956-57), "A Plea for Excuses," *Proceedings of the Aristotelian Society* 57, pp. 1-29.
Bailey, Cyril (1928), *The Greek Atomists and Epicurus*, Oxford, Clarendon Press.
Bignone, Ettore (1936), *L' Aristotele perduto e la formazione filosofica di Epicuro*, Firenze, La Nuova Italia.
―――― (1940), "La dottrina epicurea del 'clinamen,' sua formazione e la sua cronologia, in rapporto con la polemica con le scuole avversarie; nuove luci sulla storia dell' atomismo greco," *Atene e Roma* 1940, pp. 157-198.
Brieger, A. (1888), "De atomorum Epicurearum motu principali," in *Philosophische Abhandlungen* (Martin Hertz zum siebzigsten Geburtstag), Berlin.
Calogero, G. (1938), *L' Ippia Minore*, Firenze, Sansoni.
Croissant, Jeanne (1942), review of Maurice Solovine, *Épicure: Doctrines et maximes*, in *L'Antiquité Classique* 11, pp. 161-163.
De Lacy, P. H. (1948), "Lucretius and the History of Epicureanism," *Transactions of the American Philological Association* 79, pp. 12-23.

Bibliography

Diano, C. (1939-42), "La psicologia d' Epicuro e la teoria delle passioni," *Giornale Critico della Filosofia Italiana*, 1939, pp. 105-145; 1940, pp. 151-165; 1941, pp. 5-34; 1942, pp. 5-49 and 121-150.

———— (1946), *Epicuri Ethica*, Firenze, Sansoni.

Drabkin, Israel E. (1938), "Notes on Epicurean Kinetics," *Transactions of the American Philological Association* 69, pp. 364-374.

Fouillée, A. (1872), *Platonis Hippias Minor*, Paris.

Gauthier, R. A. (1958), *La Morale d'Aristote*, Paris, Presses Universitaires de France.

Gauthier, R. A., and Jolif, J. Y. (1959), *Aristote: L'Éthique à Nicomaque*, Louvain, Publications Universitaires, and Paris, Béatrice Nauwelaerts.

Gomperz, T. (1876), "Neue Bruchstücke Epikurs insbesondere über die Willensfrage," *Sitzungsberichte der Kaiserlichen Akademie der Wissenschaften zu Wien* 83, pp. 87-98.

———— (1879), "Die Überreste eines Buches von Epikur Περὶ Φύσεως," *Wiener Studien*, 1, pp. 27-31.

Hamburger, Max (1951), *Morals and Law: The Growth of Aristotle's Legal Theory*, New Haven, Yale University Press.

Jackson, Reginald (1942), "Rationalism and Intellectualism in the Ethics of Aristotle," *Mind* 51, pp. 343-360.

Jolif, J. Y., see Gauthier.

Loening, Richard (1903), *Geschichte der strafrechtlichen Zurechnungslehre*, Vol. 1, *Die Zurechnungslehre des Aristoteles*, Jena, Verlag Gustav Fischer.

Mau, Jürgen (1955), "Über die Zuweisung zweier Epikur-Fragmente," *Philologus* 99, pp. 93-111.

Merlan, Philip (1941), review of Bignone, *L' Aristotele perduto* . . ., in *Gnomon*, 17, pp. 32-41.

———— (1960), *Studies in Epicurus and Aristotle*, Wiesbaden, Otto Harrassowitz.

Müller, G. (1959), *Die Darstellung der Kinetik bei Lukrez*, Berlin, Akademie Verlag.

Solmsen, Friedrich (1951), "Epicurus and Cosmological Heresies," *American Journal of Philology* 72, pp. 1-23.

Walsh, J. J. (1963), *Aristotle's Conception of Moral Weakness*, New York, Columbia University Press.

Modern Works: Study II

Walzer, Richard (1929), *Magna Moralia und aristotelische Ethik*, Berlin, Weidmann.

Wittmann, M. (1921), "Aristoteles und die Willensfreiheit," *Philologische Wochenschrift* 34, pp. 5-30.

Wüst, E. (1958), "Von den Anfängen des Problems der Willensfreiheit," *Rheinisches Museum für Philologie* 101, pp. 75-91.

INDEX OF PASSAGES CITED

Aëtius
  1.3.18: 96 *n*31
  4.3.11: 196 *n*1
Alexander
In Metaphysica
  36.25-27: 39 *n*8, 98ʳ
  55.20*ff*.: 110 *n*3
  512.37: 53 *n*19
  827.9*ff*.: 45ᵉ
In De Sensu
  122.23: 132
  172.29: 132
Anaxagoras
  B 3: 37 *n*3
  B 6: 37 *n*4
Archimedes
  II, 436.23: 157 *n*7
Method: 153
Aristotle
Topics
  Z 4, 141 b 5: 110 *n*3
Physics
  A 3, 187 a 1-3: 81ᶜ
  Γ 2, 210 b 31-33: 157
  4, 204 a 3: 14
  5, 204 a 20*ff*.: 37 *n*6
  6, 206 a 16-b 3: 149
  6, 206 a 16-18: 107
  6, 206 b 7-12: 151ᵇ
  6, 207 a 1-2: 150 *n*2
  7, 207 b 14: *n*4
  Δ 6, 213 b 22: 53 *n*18
  E 3: 92
  Z 1, 231 a 24: 89 *n*18
  1, 231 b 3: 18
  1, 231 b 15-18: 117ᵍ
  1, 231 b 21-25: 117ʰ
  1, 231 b 25-232 a 17: 118ⁱ
  1, 232 a 18-22: 119 *n*6
  2: 89
  2, 232 b 20-233 a 12: 120ᵏ

Physics—contd.
  3.234 a 24*ff*.: 74 *n*24
  9: 82
  9, 239 b 9*ff*.: 69-77
  9, 239 b 19-22: 82
  9, 240 a 2: 73 *n*23
  9, 240 a 9*ff*.: 72ᵍ
  10, 240 b 8-241 a 6: 89 *n*19, 112ᵇ
  10, 240 b 26: 132 *n*4
  Θ 8, 263 b 3-9: 152ᶜ
De Caelo
  A 2, 269 a 2: 135 *n*7
  5, 271 b 9-11: 87ʰ
  Γ 4, 303 a 12: 97 *n*34
  4, 303 a 20-24: 87ᵍ, 90
  4, 303 a 29-b 3: 97ᑫ
  5, 304 a 10: 98 *n*36
  7, 306 a 26-b 2: 88ʲ
De Generatione et Corruptione
  A 2, 315 b 6: 83 *n*6
  2, 316 a 11-14: 84ᵈ
  2, 316 a 17-23: 93ⁿ
  2, 316 a 24-34: 84ᵉ
  2, 316 b 16-18: 87ᶠ
  2, 316 b 18-27: 90ᵏ
  2, 316 b 28-317 a 1: 91ˡ
  2, 316 b 33: 83 *n*6
  2, 317 a 1-9: 92ᵐ
  8, 324 b 32-325 a 12: 79ᵃ
  8, 325 a 8: 82
  8, 325 a 14: 59 *n*7
  8, 325 a 23-32: 81ᵇ
De Anima
  A 4, 409 a 10-16: 102 *n*22
  Γ 7-11: 226 *n*12
  9, 432 b 26-433 a 1: 222ʰ
Historia Animalium
  563 b 20: 19
De Motu Animalium
  6: 216 *n*4
  7: 219

Index of Passages Cited

De Motu Animalium—contd.
  7, 701 a 4-6: 216ᶜ
  7, 701 b 13-22: 217ᵈ
  8, 701 b 33–702 a 1: 217ᵉ 222
  8, 702 a 10-12: 218ᶠ
  10: 218ff.
  11, 703 b 5-20: 221ᵍ
Metaphysics
  A 4, 985 b 19: 98 n37
  5, 985 b 26: 51 n9
  5, 986 a 8: 53 n15
  5, 986 a 15: 44 n2
  8, 990 a 22: 51 n11
  9, 992 a 20ff.: 104ᵃ, 155 n11
  B 4, 1001 b 7: 66
  6, 1002 b 18: 10
  Δ 6, 1016 b 23-26: 48ᵈ
  E 3, 1027 a 29-31: 236 n8
  I 1, 1052 b 16-33: 19, 48ᵉ, 51
  Θ 8: 149
  M 4, 1078 b 21: 51 n9
  6, 1080 b 16-20: 49ᶠ
  8, 1083 b 8-19: 50ᵍ
  8, 1084 b 26: 103 n22
  N 2, 1089 a 2-6: 81
  3, 1091 a 15: 53 n17
  5, 1092 b 8-15: 44-45
  5, 1092 b 18: 46
Nicomachean Ethics
  A 3, 1095 a 2-11: 190 n3
  B 3, 1104 b 3-13: 223ⁱ, 235 n13
  4, 1105 b 2-18: 224 n14
  6, 1106 b 36f.: 223 n10
  Γ 1, 1109 b 30-34: 184ᵇ
  1, 1110 a 11: 235 n18
  1, 1110 b 9-15: 185ᵈ
  1, 1110 b 18ff.: 220
  1, 1111 a 23: 185ᶜ
  1, 1111 a 24–b 3: 220 n7
  5, 1113 b 14: 193
  5, 1113 b 17ff.: 188ᵍ, 235 n14
  5, 1113 b 30ff.: 189ʰ
  5, 1114 a 3: 189ⁱ, 193
  5, 1114 a 12ff.: 190ʲ
  5, 1114 a 31–b 25: 192ᵏ
  E 1, 1129 a 11-16: 225 n15
  8, 1135 a 23ff.: 224 n13

Nicomachean Ethics—contd.
  8, 1135 b 8-11: 223 n11
  9, 1137 a 4-9, 17-23: 224ʲ
  H 2, 1145 b 26: 219 n5
  3, 1147 a 28-30: 220 n8
  8, 1150 b 32-35: 191 n4
Eudemian Ethics
  B 7, 1223 a 23-28: 225 n9
  8, 1224 a 7: 225 n9
  8, 1224 b 26-36: 220 n7
On Democritus fr. 1: 96ᵖ
On the Pythagoreans: 53
[Aristotle]
On Indivisible Lines: 104-106
  968 a 2ff.: 37
  968 a 18ff.: 71ᶠ
Arrian
Epicteti Dissertationes
  2.19.1: 157 n1
Democritus
  B 11: 96, 100 n41
  B 155: 100ᵍ
  B 181: 235 n16
Diogenes Laertius
  2.111: 131
  2.115: 131
  5.21.100: 77
  7.149: 174 n5
  9.44: 96 n32
  10.31: 202
  10.117: 236 n3
Diogenes of Oenoanda
  33.2: 175
Empedocles
  B 27, 28, 29: 58 n4
Epicurus
Letter to Herodotus
  37-38: 7, 202, 204ᶠ, 228
  41-42: 8
  41: 7ᵃ, 103 n40
  42: 23-24
  42.2: 11
  43-44: 8
  45: 8
  46-53: 8
  46-47: 121, 125-127
  49-50: 201ᵈ

252

Index of Passages Cited

Letter to Herodotus—contd.
49: 186[e]
50–52: 207[g]
54: 8, 24
55: 24, 96 n30
56–59: 3, 7–27, 32, 154
56 (A): 8, 10–12
56 (B1): 8, 12–14, 138
56 (B2): 9, 12–14
57 (C1): 9, 14–16, 69, 151
59 (C2): 9, 16–17, 71 n17, 115[d], 136, 140, 143
58 (D1): 9, 17–22, 34
58 (D2): 9, 17–22, 138
58 (D3): 9, 17–22, 34, 115[f], 141
58–59 (E): 9, 22–24
59 (F): 9, 24–27, 125, 140
61–62: 121–125
61: 231[c]
63: 196[a], 202
64: 23
68: 202
72: 202
74: 26
75–76: 204
82: 202
Letter to Menoeceus: 228
124: 202
133: 184[a]
134: 175[d]
Principal Doctrines
37–38: 203[e]
On Nature
31.24.8: 236 n3
31.27: 187[f], 194, 227, 232
Euclid, scholium on Book 10: 88[1]
Eusebius
Praeparatio Evangelica
14.23: 95 n28, 131
Galen
De Elementis secundum Hippocratem
1.2: 94 n26
Gorgias
Praise of Helen: 235 n15
Lucretius
De Rerum Natura
1.333*ff*.: 28

De Rerum Natura—contd.
1.528–539: 103 n40
1.565–573: 28
1.578: 31
1.599–634: 30–35, 40–41
1.600: 29
1.609: 25
1.615–627: 20, 35–38
1.628–634: 38–40
1.645–646: 40
1.746–752: 28–30, 32, 115[e]
1.843*ff*.: 30
2.62–332: 169–173
2.80–82: 171[a]
2.83–88: 172[b]
2.109–111: 229[a]
2.251–260: 236 n8
2.251–293: 164, 169–183
2.288–293: 227*ff*., 232[d]
2.333*ff*.: 24, 200
2.476–499: 41–43, 129 n3
2.481–521: 96 n30
3.231*ff*.: 196
3.294–307: 197[b]
3.307–322: 198[c]
3.566–575: 230[b]
4.722–776: 207, 210–212
4.779–806: 214
4.802–817: 212[a]
4.825–961: 213
4.877–890: 214[b], 218*ff*.
4.962–1036: 213, 215 n1
5.1028–1090: 204
5.1030–1032: 208 n5
Melissus
B 3: 59[d]
B 4–5: 59[e]
B 6: 59[f]
B 7: 80 n2
B 8: 57 n1
B 8, 42–44: 58[c]
B 9–10: 60[g], 67 n4
Pappus
Commentary on Euclid X: 110 n1
Parmenides
B 4: 58[b], 86

253

Index of Passages Cited

Parmenides—contd.
  B 8, 4: 57 n2
  B 8, 22-25: 57^a, 68, 80
  B 8, 42-44: 58^c
Plato
  Euthydemus
    287 b: 134 n1
  Parmenides
    128 c: 63 n2
    137 c 4–d 3: 67 n4
  Republic
    546 c: 103 n42
  Timaeus: 108-110
Plutarch
  De Communibus Notitiis
    1079 a: 37 n2
    1079 e: 100^g
    1079 f: 37 n5
  Adversus Coloten
    1118 d: 196 n1
[Plutarch]
  Stromateis
    7: 175
Proclus
  Commentary on Euclid: 156
Servius
  Commentary on Aeneid
    3 376: 174 n6
Sextus Empiricus
  Outlines of Pyrrhonism
    3.32: 132
  Adversus Mathematicos
    1.1ff.: 156
    9.363: 132
    10.37-154: 132-135
    10. 97: 133^a
    10.101: 133^b
Simplicius
  In Physica
    82.1: 95 n27, 103 n39

In Physica—contd.
  87.6ff.: 60^g
  97.12ff.: 66 n3
  99.10ff.: 77 n3
  109.20: 58 n5
  109.29ff.: 59^d
  109.32ff.: 60^g
  110.2ff.: 59^e, 61 n12
  139.10-19: 64^{a-b}, 66^e
  141.2-8: 64^{c-d}
  142.10-15: 157 n5
  459.22-26: 69 n11, 157 n5
  462.3-5: 77 n11
  925.13ff.: 94^o, 99, 111^a
  926.20: 132
  934.23-25: 114 n1, 119^d
In De Caelo
  295.5ff.: 96^p
  557.16: 59^f
  569.5-9: 231 n5
  609.17: 103 n23
  613.12-16: 98 n35
  648.26: 103 n39
  649.2ff.: 103 n39
Stobaeus
  Eclogae I
    128.10: 132
    142.2: 36 n1
Themistius
  In Physica
    184.9: 114^c
  In De Caelo
    186.26: 103 n39
Theophrastus
  Metaphysics
    6 a 19: 45 n3
  De Sensibus
    61: 99 n38
Zeno
  B 1-2: 63-69, 80

INDEX OF PROPER NAMES

Adkins, A. W. H., 225
Ahlvers, A., 108
Alexander of Aphrodisias, 66, 81-82
Allan, D. J., 226
Anaxagoras, v, 30, 37, 76-77
Anaximander, 54
Archytas, 56
Arnim, H. von, 10, 16, 24
Arrighetti, G., 10, 16, 121-123, 209

Bailey, C., 10, 12, 16, 22-26, 31-40, 94-95, 103, 121, 130, 162-183, 199-200, 206-209, 210-215, 225, 229, 233, 236-237
Becker, O., 157
Berkeley, 156
Bignone, E., 10, 22-24, 164-167
Bonitz, H., 10
Booth, N. B., 61-62, 74, 78
Boyer, C. B., 153
Brieger, A., 14, 24, 40, 162, 225
Broad, C. D., 145-147
Burnet, J., 81, 86, 101-103
Burnyeat, M. F., vi

Cherniss, H., 61, 83, 101-103, 107-110
Chrysippus, 36-38, 100
Cicero, 174
Cobet, 17
Cornford, F. M., 54, 108-110

Democritus, v, 4, 44, 63, 69, 79-104, 112ff., 127-130, 132, 170-175, 181-182, 235
Denniston, J. D., 19, 195
Diano, C., 167-168, 183, 187, 236
Diels, H., 103
Diodorus Cronus, 131-135, 150

Empedocles, v, 28-29, 79, 88
Ernout, A., 15, 31-32
Eudemus, 66, 77

Eudoxus, 104-105, 155-156
Eurytus, 45-46, 47, 56

Fränkel, 63-64, 66, 68
Fritz, K. von, 55

Gassendi, P., 13, 16, 22, 130
Gauthier, R. A., 193, 195, 225, 237
Giussani, C., 10, 12-16, 22, 32, 34, 40, 121, 162-183, 199-200, 208, 210-215, 225
Golding, W., 137
Guthrie, W. K. C., 62, 103, 130

Hammer-Jensen, I., 92-93, 102
Heath, Sir Thomas, 86, 89, 102-103, 110
Heidel, W. A., 44, 56
Helen, 133, 235
Heller, S., 55
Heraclitus, 40
Hicks, R. D., 22-23
Hume, D., 20, 136-147

Jackson, R., 236
Joachim, H. H., 101-102, 110
Jolif, J. Y., 193, 195, 225, 237
Junge, G., 55-56

Kant, 158
Kirk, G. S., 56, 61-62, 77-78, 86, 101-103
Kranz, W., 103

Lacey, A. R., vi
Lachmann, C., 174, 179, 213
Lambinus, 174, 179
Lee, H. D. P., 63, 73-74
Leucippus, v, 44, 63, 69, 79-103, 112, 127-130
Loening, R., 226
Long, H. S., 209
Luria, S., 3, 84, 97-99, 101-103

255

Index of Proper Names

Malezieu, 140
Martin, J., 179
Mathewson, I. R. D., vi
Mau, J., 3, 7, 10, 12, 16-19, 22-23, 77, 83, 97, 101-103, 121, 123, 127, 130, 168
McDiarmid, J. B., 103
Meibom, M., 13, 130
Melissus, 58ff., 67, 80, 86, 127-128, 132
Merlan, P., 167
Muehll, P. von der, 16, 121, 130
Munro, H. A. J., 29, 32-33

Nausiphanes, 175

Owen, G. E. L., vi, 44, 56, 59, 61-62, 64, 67, 76-78

Page, D. L., 12
Parmenides, 3, 58ff., 72, 80, 82, 127-128, 132
Philodemus, 175
Philolaus, 47
Philoponus, 87
Plato, v, 63, 70, 81, 88, 104-110, 155-156
Plutarch, 27, 61
Porphyry, 81
Ptolemy, 27
Ptolemy Soter, 131
Pythagoreans, 44ff., 76, 98, 103

Raven, J. E., 46-47, 50, 53-54, 56, 60-62, 71-72, 77-78, 102-103
Ross, Sir David, 56, 74, 78, 101-103, 104, 128, 129, 157-158

Sambursky, S., 37
Schneider, I. G., 14, 16-17
Simplicius, 88
Skutsch, O., vi
Socrates, 193-194, 219-220
Solmsen, F., 68, 77, 167
Speusippus, 52-53
Stilpo, 131
Stoics, v, 36-38, 174-175
Stokes, M. C., 101
Susemihl, 40

Tannéry, 47, 56
Taylor, A. E., 108-110
Theaetetus, 104-105
Theophrastus, 99

Usener, H., 13-14, 16, 22-24, 27, 130, 209

Verdenius, W. J., 102
Vlastos, G., vi, 21-22, 42-44, 47, 52, 56, 60, 62-64, 67, 69, 77-78, 102-103
Voigt, 237

Waerden, B. L. van der, 52
Walsh, J. J., 225
Waszink, J. H., 102
Webster, T. B. L., vi
Wieland, W., 150-154, 157

Xenocrates, 37, 81, 102, 104-110

Zeller, E., 61, 131, 134-135
Zeno of Elea, 14, 56, 58, 63-68, 105, 127-130, 147, 155-156

GPSR Authorized Representative: Easy Access System Europe - Mustamäe tee
50, 10621 Tallinn, Estonia, gpsr.requests@easproject.com

www.ingramcontent.com/pod-product-compliance
Lightning Source LLC
Chambersburg PA
CBHW050324020526
44117CB00031B/1744